THE UNFINISHED TASK

COMPILED BY JOHN E. KYLE

Regal Books

A Division of GL Publications
Ventura, California, U.S.A.

The translation of all Regal books is under the direction of GLINT. GLINT provides technical help for the adaptation, translation and publishing of books for millions of people worldwide. For information regarding translation contact: GLINT, P.O. Box 6688, Ventura, California 93006.

Published by Regal Books
A Division of GL Publications
Ventura, California 93006
Printed in U.S.A.

Library of Congress Cataloging in Publication data.
Main entry under title:

The unfinished task.

Proceedings of Haystack '81, held Aug. 1981 at Williams College; organized by the Inter-Varsity Christian Fellowship.
Includes bibliographies.
1. Missions—Congresses. I. Kyle, John E., 1926- . II. Inter-Varsity Christian Fellowship.
BV2390.U54   1984   266   84-11727
ISBN 0-8307-0983-5

Contents

Foreword   4
   Ralph D. Winter

List of Contributors   5

Introduction   9

1. Haystack Harvest   11
   J. Christy Wilson

2. Go Stand in the Middle   21
   David Bryant

3. John the Baptizer and Obedience   39
   Gordon MacDonald

4. World Missions in the Past: 49
   What Can We Learn
   J. Christy Wilson

5. Missions Today—   63
   A Look at the Future
   Ralph D. Winter

6. The Church and World Missions   87
   Paul McKaughan

7. Reflections on the Death   103
   of Five Missionaries
   Elisabeth Elliot

8. The Missionary's Personal   119
   Walk with Christ
   Robert B. Munger

9. First Year on the Field as a Missionary   131
   Warren W. Webster

10. Becoming a Frontier Missionary   155
   Elizabeth Cridland

11. Give and Go: How to Multiply Yourself   173
   Before Proceeding Overseas
   David Bryant

12. The History and Future of   192
   Interdenominational Missions
   Peter Stam

13. The Importance of Working as a Team   215
   Robert B. Munger

14. Pacesetters: Students in Prayer for Spiritual   235
   Awakening and World Evangelism
   David Bryant

15. The Unfinished Task   261
   Warren W. Webster

16. Prayer for the Nations   277
   Ralph D. Winter

FOREWORD
Ralph D. Winter

Instant condescension and ridicule greet many a student today who betrays an interest in missions. But physical attack?

The "haystack" prayer meeting back in 1806 tips us off to the fact that those students had to take refuge first in the forest and then under a mushroom-carved haystack if they were to pray where other students could not harass or interrupt.

In the chaotic years following the Declaration of Independence, out of a cauldron of both vital hope and poisonous license spilled an angry American spirit which declared independence from God as well as the King of England. This ungodly spirit invaded the colleges, and students began calling themselves by the names of atheistic French revolutionaries.

When Timothy Dwight, a grandson of Jonathan Edwards, became president of Yale, no student would admit to being a Christian. But, by 1806, the year of the haystack prayer meeting, the small scattering of colleges (virtually all were the result of the Great Awakening) began to be confronted by and they reacted against what later became a vast spiritual renewal.

Unfortunately, these five students were unable to count on that later work of grace: Christianity on their campus was deemed a return into medieval superstition, rather than the greatest revolution of all time.

I welcome publication of this profoundly meaningful book. My prayer is that its 15 vital chapters will last students an entire semester—a chapter a week read in the holy, quiet moment carefully set aside—to study, mark, and inwardly digest.

LIST OF CONTRIBUTORS
Haystack '81

DAVID BRYANT has been the Inter-Varsity Missions specialist since 1976. He is the author of *In the Gap* and introduced the concept of Christians becoming "World Christians" on campuses throughout the U.S.A. David serves on the National Prayer Committee and has been a pastor of a church in Kent, Ohio. He is married to Robyne and they have two children from India, Adam and Bethany. They reside in Madison, Wisconsin.

ELIZABETH CRIDLAND is the representative for Africa Inland Mission for the Mid-Atlantic states. She served over forty years in Africa with both the Africa Inland Mission and Sudan Interior Mission, responsible for many churches being planted in Africa. She helped start the Bible Alliance Mission on her return to the U.S.A. when most people would have retired. She is a gifted speaker well loved by students of this generation. She and her colleague of over forty years, Mary Beam, make their home in Greenville, South Carolina.

ELISABETH ELLIOT was a missionary to Ecuador with her husband Jim when he and four other missionaries were killed by the Auca Indians. She and her daughter Valarie eventually lived with the Auca Indians who killed Jim Elliot and his colleagues. She is a well-known speaker and author of many books on missions and other subjects. She and her husband Lars make their home in Massachusetts. Her daughter Valarie is married to a Presbyterian minister and lives in Mississippi.

JOHN E. KYLE is the Director of Missions for Inter-Varsity in the United States. His work involves presenting world missions to over 30,000 Christian students located on 850 college campuses. He also serves as the director of the Urbana World Mission Conventions.

GORDON MacDONALD has been the pastor of Grace Chapel in Lexington, Massachusetts since 1972. He has traveled in Africa, Asia, Europe and Latin America. He is an adjunct professor at Gordon-Conwell Theological Seminary. He serves as the Chairman of the Board of World Vision International and has written several books. He and his wife Gail have two children, Mark and Kristen.

PAUL McKAUGHAN is the Coordinator of Mission to the World of the Presbyterian Church in America. He served with the Billy Graham Evangelistic Association in Brazil and also O.C. Ministries for several terms. He was the Associate Director of the Billy Graham Crusade in Rio De Janiero in the mid 1970s. He is a young missions executive with keen managerial abilities and has placed 300 missionaries on the foreign fields of the world in seven years. Joanne and their three children, Don, Doug and Debbie, make their home in Decatur, Georgia.

ROBERT B. MUNGER is the associate pastor of the First Presbyterian Church of Menlo Park, California, and pastor emeritus of the First Presbyterian Church of Berkeley, California. He has served as pastor of the South Hollywood Presbyterian Church of Hollywood, California and the University Presbyterian Church of Seattle, Washington. He has also served as a professor at Fuller Theological Seminary. He makes his home in Menlo Park, California with his wife Edith. They have two daughters, Monica and Marilyn.

PETER STAM is the U.S. Director of the Africa Inland Mission responsible for the ministry of over 700 missionaries laboring in ten nations of Africa. He was a missionary to Zaire for many years and was one of the early leaders of the Student Foreign Missions Fellowship as a young man before going to Africa. He is an outstanding leader in the Interdenominational Foreign Mission Association. He and his wife Mary Lou make their home in Pearl River, New York and have four children, Sharon, Bruce, Marilyn and Blair.

WARREN W. WEBSTER is the Executive Director of the Conservative Baptist Foreign Mission Society having served for many years as a missionary in Pakistan. He is responsible for over 800 missionaries working in over twenty nations. He is an outstanding speaker in great demand, an author, and recently president of Evangelical Foreign Missions Association. He and his wife Shirley live in Wheaton, Illinois and have two children, Deborah and Cindy.

J. CHRISTY WILSON was a missionary to Afghanistan for 22 years. He eventually pastored an English speaking church in Kabul, Afghanistan which was allowed to be constructed due to a visit by President Eisenhower and his request to the king. Wilson is a graduate of Princeton Theological Seminary and presently serves as the professor of missions at Gordon-Conwell Theological Seminary. He and his wife Betty have three children, Nancy, Chris, and Martin.

RALPH D. WINTER is the founder and director of the U.S. Center for World Mission in Pasadena, California. He served in Guatemala as a missionary for several years with the Presbyterian Church in the United States of America's Board of Foreign Missions. He also was professor of history and missions at the School of World Mission of Fuller Theological Seminary for several years. He has been largely responsible for the missions strategy directed toward outreach to the "Unreached Peoples." He and his wife Roberta have four children, Patricia, Linda, Becky and Beth.

INTRODUCTION
John E. Kyle

In August 1806, five young fellows from Williams College in Williamstown, Massachusetts were enjoying Christian fellowship outdoors when they were forced to find shelter from a rainstorm under a haystack. While gathered together there, they began to pray concerning the need for missionaries around the world. They put their prayers into action by asking their denomination to create the first missionary sending agency in North America. The Haystack Prayer Meeting gave the initial impulse to the foreign missionary movement of the churches of the United States.

That historical event called for a celebration named Haystack '81 which commemorated the one hundred and seventy-fifth anniversary of the Haystack Prayer Meeting. It was Inter-Varsity Christian Fellowship's privilege to organize that conference which was held for four marvelous days in August 1981 at Williams College.

I was privileged to invite ten of God's wonderfully gifted missionary speakers to address the conference.

For delegates, we especially invited those young adults who believed God was leading them to the overseas mission fields of the world. We asked the speakers to bring messages that would prepare these people for mission service.

A keen atmosphere of prayer prevailed as the conference began. Instead of bringing the messages I had prepared, I was led to set aside blocks of time for group prayer. The speakers brilliantly presented the burdens of their hearts, and the delegates immediately requested cassette copies of each of their messages. Later I had those tapes transcribed into written form for larger audiences, and now they are contained in this book so graciously published by Regal Books.

One of the delegates from Haystack '81 is in Mexico helping a group of Mexican Christians to begin a Christian radio station and form an overseas mission sending agency. Many others have also found their way to overseas service.

May this book encourage and speed many Christians onward to the mission fields where over 2.7 billion people await word of the gospel of Jesus Christ.

John E. Kyle

1

HAYSTACK HARVEST
J. Christy Wilson

In Afghanistan, where they have all kinds of dry river beds, there is a saying that where water has flowed once it can flow again. When there is a cloudburst in that country, or when the snows melt from the mountaintops, those stream beds fill with torrents of life-giving water.

Our Lord Jesus Christ said, "Whoever believes in me, as the Scripture has said, streams of living water will flow from within him" (John 7:38). He really knew His Bible. From where was He quoting? He was referring to Isaiah 58:10-11, where we read: "If you . . . satisfy the needs of the oppressed, . . . the Lord will guide you always; . . . you will be like . . . a spring whose waters never fail."

The greatest need our world has today, is for this living water to flow in rivers, to reach all the unreached for Jesus Christ. At the Haystack Monument at Williams College, Williamstown, Massachusetts, we see the fountainhead of the missionary movement in North America. As the words carved in stone on it state, this is

"THE BIRTHPLACE OF AMERICAN FOREIGN MIS-SIONS." So there we have the beginning of this stream that has flowed and blessed the world from that time, and is still flowing today. Heaven alone will reveal all that has been accomplished from this beginning.

Why is this place called the birthplace of American foreign missions? On August 2, 1806, five young men, students at Williams College who regularly met on Wednesday and Saturday afternoons for prayer, were forced to take shelter under a haystack when a thunderstorm interrupted their time together. They continued their prayer meeting under that haystack through the noise of the thunder and lightning.

In the 1850s, Byron Greene, the only remaining living member of the "Haystack Prayer Meeting," revisited his alma mater. He gave an account of what had happened that day. He said that because of the thunder, rain, and lightning they huddled under the haystack and talked and prayed about the spiritual needs of Asia. They had been studying this continent in their geography class at Williams College. Through studying this subject, the five students saw the great need in Asia for the gospel of Jesus Christ. Then Samuel Mills said, "We can do it if we will! We ourselves can go!" Harvey Loomis objected. He said that they would all be killed. But Samuel Mills and the other students replied that God certainly wanted the advancement of His Kingdom. If they did their part, He could be counted on to help them. Samuel Mills, as he so often did, said, "Let's pray about it."

As they interceded and dedicated their lives, the thunder and lightning moved away and the sky cleared and sunshine broke over this spot. With the sound of the storm receding in the background, Samuel Mills prayed, "Lord, may the artillery of heaven be aimed against those who dare to lift one finger to oppose your heralds of the gospel around the world!" It was a "haystack" prayer meeting; but the emphasis was not on the haystack, it was on *prayer*.

As a result of these earnest prayers, streams of living waters poured around the world. I love the biblical phrase spoken by our Lord which is carved on the monument, "The field is the world" (Matt. 13:38). When Jesus saw people scattered abroad, and fainting as sheep without shepherds, He said, "The harvest is plentiful but the workers are few. Ask the Lord of the harvest, therefore, to send out workers into his harvest field" (Matt. 9:37-38). In our translations, I don't think "send out" is strong enough. The Greek word is *ekballo* which means "to throw out." When we pray, God will "throw out" workers! It takes that much to get a lot of us moving! The harvest will then be gathered for eternity for the glory of our Lord Jesus Christ who died on the cross for our sins, but not for ours only, "but also for the sins of the whole world" (1 John 2:2).

Samuel Mills took the matter of praying for and recruiting laborers seriously! He had been with Adoniram Judson at Andover Seminary in Massachusetts only one month by the time he convinced him that he should be a missionary. He persuaded him to sign up for the secret Society of the Brethren. This ended up with Adoniram Judson going to Burma. What a man of prayer Samuel Mills was! He was dangerous to be around! When people begin praying and taking Him seriously, God begins to work. After the Lord told the disciples to pray for laborers, at the end of Matthew 9, the beginning of chapter 10 tells us that the Lord sent the disciples themselves out. If you start praying for laborers, He may send you.

Two of the flood of missionaries that resulted from the Haystack Prayer Meeting were the Wilders who went to India. Two of their children, Robert and Grace, returned to the United States for their education. Grace Wilder attended Mount Holyoke College in Massachusetts, and her brother, Robert, went to Princeton University in New Jersey. They had a burden for India and the whole unreached world.

Robert Wilder started a mission band at Princeton University and had a pledge which he challenged different ones to sign. It stated, "God helping me, I purpose to be a foreign missionary." No halfway about it, you were signing your life away. Robert and Grace then heard that Dwight L. Moody had called a conference of 250 students from across the United States and Canada to gather at Mount Hermon, Massachusetts during the summer of 1886. This conference came about because Luther Wishard, who was a traveling YMCA secretary to college campuses, had knelt beside the Haystack Prayer Meeting Monument in the snow and prayed, "Lord, do it again! Where water once flowed, let it flow again!" He then persuaded the great evangelist Dwight L. Moody to call the conference.

It was to last a month. In those days they had a lot more time for meetings. Only one meeting was planned each day, and it was held in the evening. The rest of the time was to be spent in prayer, walks in the woods, and in conversations. The expressed purpose of the conference was for students to seek the infilling of the Holy Spirit for service even as D.L. Moody had received His power some time before on Wall Street, in New York City. He had been preaching in Chicago to the greatest congregation in that city. Two little old ladies, who always sat in the front of the church, told him they were praying that he would be filled with the Holy Spirit. It made him angry. Why were they not praying instead for pastors who weren't having the success he was having? Later, when he was on a visit to New York, he was walking along Wall Street and he says that the Holy Spirit came on him in such power that he had to rush to a friend's home so he could go up and lock the bedroom door and be alone. He prayed, "Lord, stop it!" He felt that the power was so great that he would be killed! From then on his ministry was singly blessed not only in North America but also in Europe as the Lord shook the rest of the world through him.

When Robert Wilder at Princeton and Grace Wilder at Mount Holyoke heard about the conference Moody had called at Mount Hermon, they prayed, "Lord, call 100 of the 250 students to sign missionary pledge cards." An impossible request! It wasn't even supposed to be a missionary conference.

When Robert Wilder arrived at Mount Hermon he found students there who had been in ten different countries. He went to Moody and asked if they could have an extra gathering included in the program—a meeting of the ten nations where those students had been; they would tell about the needs of these countries. Moody agreed. And it was this meeting that started a missionary awakening at the conference.

The slogan, "The Evangelization of the World in This Generation" caught fire. And before the end of the conference ninety-nine students signed the card that Robert Wilder had brought along. On the last day they were having a prayer meeting on a grass covered mound where the ninety-nine were kneeling, when the one-hundredth student rushed in and signed the card too! Their prayer was answered to the exact number. One of the students who signed that card was John R. Mott who later became a great missionary statesman.

A team of four students was selected to visit other campuses across the continent and share the vision. This meant that they had to give up one year of their education. Three of them were forced to back down because of parental pressures and other matters. Robert Wilder was the only one who was able to go. He got John Foreman, a seminary student, to go with him, and they started touring the campuses that academic year, 1886-1887. They had so many invitations that they had to separate so they could take twice the number of engagements! While they were apart, they prayed for each other at least once *every* hour that they were awake. This movement was not only born in prayer but was continued in prayer!

Grace and Robert Wilder had also prayed that over one thousand students would volunteer that year. More than seventeen hundred signed the pledge card!

When Robert Wilder got to Hope College in Michigan with his presentation, he displayed a big map of India. He set a metronome in front of it and explained that every time the metronome ticked, one person in India died who had never heard the gospel of Jesus Christ. Samuel Zwemer was a senior at Hope College that year. When he saw the map and heard the metronome he said that he could hardly stay in his seat. As soon as the meeting was over he rushed forward, asked for one of the cards, and signed it. He wanted to go to the hardest field in the world, which he concluded was to the Muslims in Arabia.

Dr. Zwemer pioneered in the Muslim world for years. When he arrived on the island of Bahrain in the Gulf area, he was single. But God brought a beautiful missionary nurse from Australia. She was going to work in Baghdad so the agency she was with wrote to Dr. Zwemer and asked him if he would meet her and help her along the way. He fell head over heels in love with her. When they decided to marry he had to pay her transportation from Australia, because she had a contract with the mission that if she resigned before two years she had to repay her passage. Dr. Zwemer said this was true to Middle Eastern custom in that he had to pay a dowry for his bride.

They had two little girls who were born in Bahrain. Both of them died of disease within a week's time. When these two little girls died, the Arab Muslims said they couldn't be buried in Bahrain because they would contaminate the soil. Finally, Dr. Zwemer was able to persuade them, provided he would dig the grave and bury them himself. On the tombstone he wrote these words, "Worthy is the Lamb to receive riches Rev. 5:12." The children's deaths broke the barrier with the Arabs because they saw Dr. and Mrs. Zwemer really loved them and were willing even to give up their children in order to serve them.

Later on at Keswick, England in 1923, Dr. Zwemer was speaking on missionary work in the Muslim world. He quoted Peter's words, "Master, we've worked hard all night and haven't caught anything" (Luke 5:5). He described the way his ministry among Muslims had similarly been an experience of fishing all night and of catching nothing. But he then heralded Peter's pledge, "But because you say so, I will let down the nets." Dr. Zwemer added that as by faith we obey the Lord, the time is coming when we will catch Muslims for Christ in such large numbers that the nets are going to break and the boats are almost going to sink. He died in 1952 before the great awakening, which started in 1965 in Indonesia, resulted in hundreds of thousands of Muslims coming to a saving knowledge of Jesus Christ.

In 1946 Dr. Zwemer was a keynote speaker at the first Inter-Varsity Student Foreign Missions Fellowship Convention at the University of Toronto which later became the Urbana Student Missions Convention. He was probably the greatest missionary to Muslims in history. He used to have his devotions in a different language every day of the week to keep up in them as a Christian scholar. He published forty-nine books in English and started the *Muslim World* quarterly which is still published today.

Dr. William Miller who currently lives in Philadelphia was also a student volunteer. When he was in seminary, he put a map on the wall above his bed and knelt and prayed, "Lord, if you tarry, and if you spare me, I'll be serving you somewhere in this world. Show me where you want me to go." God called him to the border of Afghanistan. He then began to pray for others; he also had a little prayer meeting in his room each noon from 12:00 to 12:15. Any student could come in and pray for laborers. Before he went to the mission field in

1919, he got more than a hundred others to sign the student volunteer card to go as missionaries.

One of them was David Howard's and Elisabeth Elliot's father, Dr. Phillip Howard, who went with the Belgian Gospel Mission. Two others were my mother and father who went to Iran. Jesus promised that if we prayed the Lord of the harvest, He would "throw out" laborers in His harvest.

Miss Margaret Haines, Dr. William Miller's sister-in-law, another student volunteer, served on the border of Afghanistan in what is now Pakistan. There she became very ill and had to come back to the States in the 1930s. Since then she has encouraged many to pray for Afghanistan. For years she sent out confidential monthly prayer letters with prayer needs for each day of the month to people who would intercede for that country. She also helped recruit and orientate those going to serve in that land. Besides serving on the Inter-Varsity board when it first started in the United States, she has held many student meetings in her home and has prayed many of them into mission fields all over the world.

Dr. Frank Laubach was another student volunteer who served in the Philippines and popularized a method of teaching illiterates how to read. By using pictures which depicted letters of the alphabet, he could teach adult illiterates how to read their own languages in a matter of hours. He put his system into over 350 different languages.

He was able to do all of this because of his prayer life. He practiced the presence of God and would pray every minute of his waking time. When he was writing a letter, he would be praying for the person to whom he was sending it. When he was reading a book, he would be reading it to the Lord Jesus Christ. When he was talking to a person, he would be praying for that person. It is estimated that over 100 million people have learned to read through Dr. Laubach's method. He then would get them reading the Bible. One book he wrote is *Each One Teach One and Lead One to Christ.* He not only taught them how to read, but sought to lead them to Christ. Dr. Frank Laubach, Samuel Zwemer and the others mentioned stood upon the heritage of the Haystack Prayer Meeting of 1806 since the Student Volunteer Movement was a natural outgrowth of that event. Our Lord Jesus said, "Whoever believes in me, as the Scripture has said, streams of living water will flow from within him" (John 7:38).

2
GO STAND IN THE MIDDLE
David Bryant

God loves drama! In the book of Joshua there's a
drama that was similar to one which occurred in 1806
at Williams College in Williamstown, Massachusetts.
The parallels are almost uncanny. Look for them as we
read the third and fourth chapters:

"Early in the morning Joshua and all the Israelites
set out from Shittim and went to the Jordan, where
they camped before crossing over. After three days the
officers went throughout the camp, giving orders to the
people: 'When you see the ark of the covenant of the
Lord your God, and the priests, who are Levites, carrying it, you are to move out from your positions and follow it. Then you will know which way to go, since *you
have never been this way before.* But keep a distance
of about a thousand yards between you and the ark; do
not go near it.'

"Then Joshua told the people, *'Consecrate yourselves, for tomorrow the Lord will do amazing things
among you.'*

"Joshua said to the priests, 'Take up the ark of the

covenant and cross over ahead of the people.' So they took it up and went ahead of them.

"And the Lord said to Joshua, 'Today I will begin to exalt you in the eyes of all Israel, so they may know that I am with you as I was with Moses. *Tell the priests* who carry the ark of the covenant: "When you reach the edge of the Jordan's waters, *go and stand in the river.*"'

"Joshua said to the Israelites, 'Come here and listen to the words of the Lord your God. *This is how you will know that the living God is among you*, and that he will certainly drive out before you the Canaanites, Hittites, Hivites, Perizzites, Girgashites, Amorites and Jebusites. See, the ark of the covenant of *the Lord of all the earth will go into the Jordan ahead of you*. Now then, choose twelve men from the tribes of Israel, one from each tribe. And as soon as the priests who carry the ark of the Lord—the Lord of all the earth—set foot in the Jordan, the water flowing downstream will be cut off and stand up in a heap.'

"So when the people broke camp to cross the Jordan, *the priests carrying the ark of the covenant went ahead of them.* Now the Jordan is at flood stage all during harvest. Yet as soon as the priests who carried the ark reached the Jordan and their feet touched the water's edge, the water from upstream stopped flowing. It piled up in a heap a great distance away, at a town called Adam in the vicinity of Zarethan, while the water flowing down to the Sea of Arabah (the Salt Sea) was completely cut off. So the people crossed over opposite Jericho. *The priests who carried the ark of the covenant of the Lord stood firm on dry ground in the middle of the Jordan, while all Israel passed by until the whole nation had completed the crossing on dry ground.*

"When the whole nation had finished crossing the Jordan, the Lord said to Joshua, 'Choose twelve men from among the people, one from each tribe, and tell them to *take up twelve stones from the middle of the*

Jordan from right where the priests stood and to carry them over with you and put them down at the place where you stay tonight.'

"So Joshua called together the twelve men he had appointed from the Israelites, one from each tribe, and said to them, 'Go over before the ark of the Lord your God into the middle of the Jordan. Each of you is to take up a stone on his shoulder, according to the number of the tribes of the Israelites, to serve as a sign among you. In the future, when your children ask you, *"What do these stones mean?"* tell them that the flow of the Jordan was cut off before the ark of the covenant of the Lord. When it crossed the Jordan, the waters of the Jordan were cut off. *These stones are to be a memorial to the people of Israel forever.'*

"So the Israelites did as Joshua commanded them. They took twelve stones from the middle of the Jordan, according to the number of the tribes of the Israelites, as the Lord had told Joshua; and they carried them over with them to their camp, where they put them down. Joshua set up the twelve stones that had been in the middle of the Jordan at the spot where the priests who carried the ark of the covenant had stood. And they are there to this day.

"Now the priests who carried the ark *remained standing in the middle of the Jordan until everything the Lord had commanded Joshua was done by the people,* just as Moses had directed Joshua. The people hurried over, and as soon as all of them had crossed, the ark of the Lord and the priests came to the other side while the people watched. The men of Reuben, Gad, and the half-tribe of Manasseh crossed over, armed, in front of the Israelites, as Moses had directed them. *About forty thousand armed for battle crossed over* before the Lord to the plains of Jericho for war.

"That day the Lord exalted Joshua in the sight of all Israel; and they revered him all the days of his life, just as they had revered Moses.

"Then the Lord said to Joshua, 'Command the priests carrying the ark of the Testimony to come up out of the Jordan.'

"So Joshua commanded the priests, 'Come up out of the Jordan.'

"And the priests came up out of the river carrying the ark of the covenant of the Lord. No sooner had they set their feet on the dry ground than the waters of the Jordan returned to their place and ran at flood stage as before.

"On the tenth day of the first month the people went up from the Jordan and camped at Gilgal on the eastern border of Jericho. And *Joshua set up at Gilgal the twelve stones* they had taken out of the Jordan. He said to the Israelites, 'In the future, when your descendants ask their fathers, "What do these stones mean?" tell them, "Israel crossed the Jordan on dry ground. For the Lord your God dried up the Jordan before you until you had crossed over. *The Lord your God did to the Jordan just what he had done to the Red Sea* when he dried it up before us until we had crossed over. *He did this so that all the peoples of the earth might know that the hand of the Lord is powerful and so that you might always fear the Lord your God"'"* (italics added).

In 1856 a plot of ground was dedicated at Williams College as the spot where substantial initiative was mounted for forming the first North American Protestant missionary thrust overseas. This "Haystack" location did not bear a monument, however, until 1866 when an alumnus of the school revisiting the campus remarked: "We really ought to have a monument at the site as well. I suggest we build an impressive concrete structure in the shape of a haystack!" Fortunately, a year later that suggestion was translated into the sculpture located there now, a weather-beaten pillar with a concrete globe on top. On the day it was dedicated, interestingly enough, a thunderstorm (as during the first Haystack Prayer Meeting) forced the crowd to retreat to the Congregational church a few hundred yards away.

At the dedication of the monument, Williams College President Hopkins said, "For once in the history of the world, a prayer meeting is commemorated by a monument. Monuments commemorate the past, and just as well, but only as such commemorations strengthen the principles that underlie the events and movement. The stress and struggles of the missionary are still upon us. The calls for help were never louder. I should only hope that this one memorial may serve to kindle and perpetuate on this ground a missionary spirit." It did. It still does.

Monuments and memorials can be important. God recognizes that fact in Joshua. But what were the twelve stones from Jordan a memorial to?

Six key elements in Joshua's drama parallel the drama at Williams College more than 175 years ago and continue today:

1. The mission before us
2. The immediate challenge
3. The people called
4. The power for the mission
5. The pioneers of faith
6. The memorial

Let me survey these parallels with you.

First, *our mission is very similar.* Biblical scholars hold varied interpretations of the symbolism behind the image of "Canaan." Some interpret it as a picture of heaven: entrance into Canaan is like our final entrance into heaven. Others parallel it to the deeper, spiritual life: the drama illustrates how we can enter now into the promises and blessings of God. In a sense, Canaan can represent both views.

In a more literal sense, however, the land best represents the *world of unreached peoples.* In fact, Paul tells us in Romans 4 that when Abraham believed God would give him the land of Canaan, his faith encompassed more than just a single piece of real estate. He believed he would become an heir to the whole world (4:13). He would have descendants scattered everywhere like stars throughout the sky. Entire nations would spring forth from his descendants.

Mark the similarities between taking possession of the land under Joshua and what we're considering in this book: planting bases of operation for God's Kingdom under Christ, among all the peoples of the earth.

For example, to the people in Joshua's day, Canaan could be rightly called the *"frontiers."* Joshua said, "You have never passed this way before." They knew very little of the people who occupied the land and very little of the struggle that lay ahead. Theirs was "frontier missions" indeed! The challenge entailed reestablishing a testimony for God's glory among tribal groups enslaved in the worship of idols, having little or no knowledge of Jehovah. In fact, some of the people groups mentioned in Joshua were so deeply deceived by the works of the Evil One they were eventually dispelled from the land. Joshua's mission called for assault on Satan's kingdom to reestablish a witness to the praise of the true and living God among those who had never believed.

Similarly, there was a strategy to plant communities of God's people where they had not been before in order to establish bases of operation for the saving work of God among the nations. Not only would this press back the darkness among the tribals currently in the land, but it would potentially turn the Land of Promise into a dynamic arena in which God's Kingdom could unfold for all the peoples of the earth to see and seek.

A mission that paralleled what Joshua faced was on the hearts of the five who first gathered around the haystack in 1806. We face it in our generation as well. God desires to use us to plant among the unreached peoples of our world, worshiping, witnessing communities within *every* tribe, tongue, and nation. They will, in turn, form bases of operation for the kingdom of God to bear its fruits of righteousness, justice, compassion, and light right where they live, among those who are their friends and neighbors and associates.

A second theme that I find in common in each drama is *the immediate challenge faced in fulfilling a "frontier" mission.* The greatest challenge for Joshua and Israel, surprisingly, was not the inhabitants of Canaan, but rather the Jordan River itself. It is interesting to note that God called them to cross the Jordan during the rainy season when the waters were flooding their banks, and that He brought them to the place of deepest entry. You see, God knew this would be the ultimate "battle" for them. Theirs was not, first of all, a battle with ungodly nations. The issue was not, first of all, planting bases of operation for God's Kingdom. The issue was, first of all, the obedience of God's people, the engagement of God's people with the *internal* forces of unbelief within their own hearts.

Joshua 4:24 tells us why God gave them the challenge of the Jordan River: (1) so that other nations would see how God was moving in response to the faith of His people and be convinced that they served an all-powerful God; (2) so that the Israelites *themselves* would see how faithful and mighty God would be on behalf of those who were obedient in faith. The Jordan experience taught the people to fear the Lord alone and look at nothing else but Him. What tremendous preparation this was for their mission to occupy the land!

To be sure, God told Joshua that "I will give you every place where you set your foot" (1:3). But God had a most unusual *first* step in mind. Not on the land, but into the water! What did God demonstrate by this? Simple. He was saying: "Are you, my people, willing to believe *me*? Are you willing to believe that what I did at the Red Sea I am able to do again here at the Jordan? Are you willing to take your first step into *me*, fully trusting that I can lead you in triumph even as you leave behind things secure, predictable, manageable?"

To take that first step of faith was, essentially, to have taken at the same time every other step God would place before them as they occupied the land. Faith for the Jordan was faith for the world mission.

Are you and I ready for this challenge of *faith*? Do we believe that the Father who brought our Lord Jesus out of the grave, purifying sin and throwing principalities and powers into disarray, is the same God who calls us to trust Him for every test of faith in the mission He's given us? What is our Jordan? Where do we struggle with faith right now in a way that could paralyze us from taking further steps of obedience as God leads us into more specific roles of sending or going?

Those who huddled against an August storm in 1806 had met many times previously to prayerfully grow in their knowledge of God. In those months they had discovered a deeper faith in all that Christ was for them. Even more, they had united in prayer for the revival of others on their campus, that others' faith in Christ would blossom as well. So, as they discussed under the haystack the needs of Asia presented in the past week's geography class, and resolved that afternoon to press Congregational churches into missionary action to meet such needs, their *greatest* challenge had already been overcome. *Their* Jordan had been conquered as they answered the question: "Can our God really use *us* to tackle such a compelling vision for missions mobilization in our churches?"

Quite obviously their youth and limited resources composed substantial reason for retreat from the vision. But they had already been revived with renewed faith in Christ for all He desired to do through them. So they stood firm that day in the midst of their greatest misgivings and fears, declaring: "We can if we will." "If we will" what? "If" they would simply fix their eyes on Jesus, author and finisher both of their faith and their ultimate vision for their churches and for Asia?

What Jordans are you facing this moment? In light

of the unfinished task, what very next step of obedience are you struggling with? Are you struggling with doubts of your own abilities? Maybe you're fighting unwillingness to risk or to make significant sacrifices in the face of the unknown? Are you possibly paralyzed by too many options for ministry so that you're not free in faith to take any bold steps toward any one of them? Are you overwhelmed by the immensity and complexity of the task? Or, are you hesitating at the Jordan of self-centered preoccupations, unwilling to turn back to the course at hand and press on through to occupy that which occupies the heart of God?

What Jordan does the church in North America face right now? Where is the log-jam of unbelief and what is creating it? What is the first step we must take together before God can do the greater works through us that He longs to do, miracles to penetrate the great "frontiers" remaining in world evangelization?

We find ourselves standing on the banks of a swollen current that challenges our faith about any new work God wants to do through us. Please hold on to *that* question as we explore some more of the drama.

The third parallel (and this is very obvious) is *the people for God's mission*. Who were they to be? Clearly the *whole* nation was to cross over to occupy the land.

Of course, the drama emphasizes the priests (we'll look at that in a minute). But, in Exodus 19:5-6 the whole congregation was charged to be a *nation* of priests. We see in that charge another way of stating the Great Commission: corporately they were appointed God's representatives before the nations around them. At the Jordan, that role remained intact.

The original generation from Sinai had now died off because of unbelief—because of disobedience to their commission forty years earlier. They had wandered aimlessly, fruitlessly, in the wilderness. They had no more mission as such. What a tragedy! But now a new generation had arisen. To all of them God reissued the commission to move forward to occupy the Land of Promise, and to begin by walking through the Jordan. I believe with all my heart that God is preparing a whole generation—of which you and I are a part—to be serving Him by the year 2000 as priests together—whether as goers or senders—in the fulfillment of the Great Commission.

In Christ's blood all of us have been released and set free from our sins to be a kingdom. All of us, Peter teaches, are living stones being built into a temple for the Lord. We in turn also act as priests for Him (1 Pet. 2). We are all together, he writes, a royal priesthood whose ministry is to declare to the world the excellencies of Him who has called us out of darkness into his marvelous light. So the task of world evangelization belongs to the whole people of God, not just to those who may actually go overseas.

The people of God in Joshua's day were clearly ready for their assignment. How well they had been discipled by Moses! (Read the book of Deuteronomy.) Those following Joshua had been discipled to go forward as people who were in love with God with all their mind, soul, and strength; circumcised in their hearts and fully leaning on the Lord. They were ready and prepared. Now the mission was in sight. It was just over the river. It belonged to *all* of them. They knew it. And, they were ready.

One of the great tragedies in North American evangelicalism is how we disciple people to put world evangelization into a compartment, off at the periphery of our walk with Christ. It never gets integrated into the way we pray, study Scripture, fellowship, worship, or plan for the future. I have used the term *world Christian* to describe what every Christian should seek to become as we take seriously the truth that Christ's global cause belongs to *all* who call Him Lord and as we integrate this into all we do for Christ. The mission before us requires a Church of world Christians!

However, as prepared as Israel was at this point to embrace the mission of God, they were still not fully mobilized. Somebody needed to lead them forward in the initial obedience of faith. Who would do it? The answer to that question comprises the heart of our study in Joshua.

Before looking at it, however, let's glance at a fourth parallel: *the power for the mission.* God's people were powerless before both the Jordan and the mission that lay beyond it. Powerless—unless they bore the Ark before them; unless they lifted up that Ark for all to see and follow. In fact, it says in two verses that the Ark, which represents the presence of God in covenant among His people, was the Ark of the "God of all the earth." This is who went before them. Here was their assurance that God was among them and among them with *all* authority and power. Later on, in chapter 4, we read that it was when *it* went into the water, when *it* passed through the Jordan, that God moved and worked His miracles.

The Ark of the Covenant was the Ark of which God says in Exodus 25, "There . . . I will meet with you and give you all my commands" (v. 22). It was the point of meeting with God, of reconciliation with God; the place where the blood was spread on the Day of Atonement; the focus of His glory revealed in the Holy of Holies. It was the Ark marking the covenant they shared with the God of the *whole* earth.

I guess you can see as quickly as I can the parallel to our Lord Jesus Christ Himself. He is the power for *our* mission. He is the assurance of its victory. Hebrews 1 says that in the past God spoke to us by the prophets but now He's speaking by a Son whom He has appointed heir of all things. Christ is Lord of the whole earth, by whom God made the world. He Himself is the glory and the image of God, fully expressing His radiance. It is He who has become our mercy seat, who has purified us in His blood and is now seated at the right hand of the Father, as Ruler over all the universe.

So, God calls us to exalt the Lord Jesus before one another and before all the nations. We have *no* mission unless He covers us, fills us, and goes before us. The power for our mission is the gospel of the Lord Jesus Christ. We must lift up Him and His gospel in every way possible.

Paul says, "I am not ashamed of the gospel, because it is the power of God for salvation to everyone who believes; first for the Jew, and then for the Gentile" (Rom. 1:16). He didn't say, "I'm not ashamed to be a Christian." (Of course, he wasn't.) He said, "I'm not ashamed of the *gospel* that I am lifting up with every fiber of my being, because God can use the message about His Son to bring salvation to all kinds of people, not only to people just like me (Jews) but also to those within languages and cultures not yet penetrated (Gentiles)."

Have you ever sung the old hymn by John Cennick, "Children of the Heavenly King"?

> Children of the heavenly King,
> As we journey let us sing;
> Sing our Saviour's worthy praise,
> Glorious in His works and ways.
> Fear not, brethren, joyful stand
> On the borders of your land;
> Jesus Christ, our Father's Son,
> Bids us, undismayed go on.
>
> Lord, obediently we'll go,
> Gladly leaving all below;
> Only Thou our Leader be,
> And we still will follow Thee.

There's the power for our mission!

But there's another parallel to explore between the drama at the Jordan and what happened at the haystack more than 175 years ago. In both cases there were *pioneers of faith.* Who were they for Israel? Who were the ones that first stepped forth? Who were the ones who lifted up the Ark and took it forward in front of the people of God, encouraging the rest, thereby, to follow? *The priests.*

Of all the people in the life of the nation, the priests most regularly represented the spiritual dynamics intended for all of Israel, both in her life of worship and of mission. The priests were totally dedicated unto the Lord. In fact they owned no land in Canaan; instead the Lord Himself was to be their inheritance. Consequently, they were a model for all God's people of what all should be in their *hearts.* The priests were literally "a movement of prayer" in the midst of Israel as they ministered before the face of God in the Tabernacle.

Now, at the Jordan, the priests were called to assume a unique role for the sake of the nation and its mission. Dedicated solely unto the Lord, nurturing the spiritual life of the people of God, they were now asked to be the pioneers of faith in Israel's penetration of the "frontiers" for God's glory.

This was not the first or last time they were given such an assignment. In fact, the priests are commanded to go ahead of the Israelites whenever they went into battle, blowing their trumpets as they led the people. This happened, for example, when they marched around Jericho. No wonder, then, that the priests were asked to take up the Ark, to cross over in front of the people of God and to *stand right in the middle* of the Jordan, right at the point of greatest spiritual paralysis and unbelief.

As a movement of prayer I'm sure they *remained* a band of keen pray-ers as they stepped into the swollen river. Wouldn't you have prayed pretty hard if you were asked to wade straight into a flood, making the center of its current your final destination?!

Let this parallel sink in deeply. What is the Jordan

for Christ's Church in our generation? What is holding us back, preventing us from releasing ourselves to the Lord that He might take the blessings He has given us in Christ and share them through us with the families of the earth? Are there Levites reading this who are prepared to step forward into our "Jordan"? Do not be afraid to obey. Look at what you can expect! It says in Joshua that the water stopped flowing. The priests stood firm on dry ground so that *all* Israel rose up in undiminished faith and crossed over to enter her mission.

I believe with all my heart, as I read this passage, that God wants those of us, who really have concern for God's missionary triumphs through His people, to couple that concern with a commitment of equal intensity to step out and serve as pioneers of faith—for the sake of the Church, the sake of the nations, and above all, the sake of the Lord Jesus.

What will that mean? Foundationally, it means to be fully dedicated to Christ ourselves, to see Him as our only portion. And then, in response, it means to become a people of prayer—and then a movement of prayer, even as the Levites were. It means we ourselves, as God shows us, must be willing to take steps of obedient involvement in the face of the fears of the unknown or fears of sacrifice and a cross. It means we will, we must take up the gospel of Christ with renewed dedication. We must sell our hearts out to the cause of the gospel by staking our lives on it as the power of God to bring men and women to know His Son and be reconciled to the Father, praising Him with us forever.

And, it means we must find others to join us. As the Levites were a select group within the nation, we must find others in our churches and Christian fellowships whom God is appointing to this critical work of pioneering faith. And, we must bind ourselves with them, launching out before the people of God together, not because we're any better or more spiritual but because

God is asking some of us, by His gracious Spirit's enablement, to be His pioneers of faith. He wants us to set the pace of faith in all He has promised to do *through* His people and thus help the whole Church so she can enter into the fulfillment of Christ's global cause.

Of the "Haystack Five," Samuel Mills worked to increase missions awareness in America and to establish missionary organizations, until his premature death at sea on his return from an evangelistic thrust in Africa in 1818. James Richard became a medical doctor and died of a hemorrhage in India in 1822. Harvey Loomis entered home missions, pastoring a church in a remote Maine town until he died of a heart attack while preaching in his pulpit in 1825. Francis Robins pastored a church in Connecticut; he died of old age. Byron Greene started out as a preacher but developed asthma and left the pastorate to work in the New York State Legislature. He finally died of old age while serving as a U.S. Congressman.

So, really, *only two* of those who prayed here in 1806 even found their way overseas. Of those whom God called to be pioneers of faith to launch the foreign missions movement of this country, only two were sent out themselves. Yet they *all* banded together as Levites in every sense of the word. They prayed for the spiritual life of God's people. And they were willing to press ahead, out in front, with the vision God had given them for spiritual awakening into a mission the whole people of God could embrace. As a result many, even their elders, followed their example and went forward in faith with them. Because of this, many unreached peoples in their generation, both at home and abroad, found salvation in Christ.

So, whether you sense God is calling you to go into cross-cultural missions; or, whether you're absolutely rock bottom sure that God has called you to sacrifice your energy to send those who do go; or, whether you're still in the process of exploring exactly what God has for you, you *can* plan to become one of God's Levites to lift up the Ark, standing in the midst of today's Jordans as pioneers of faith for the mission before all of us.

Finally, one last parallel in this incredible drama: *the memorial.* The pile of stones at Gilgal formed a memorial *for* the mission, more than one *to* the mission. Do you see the difference? When the memorial was erected in Joshua's day, the mission really hadn't started yet, except for that first obedient step of claiming the mission by passing through the Jordan. And *that* step is what Joshua embellished to encourage them to press on.

He had them select stones from right in the middle of the Jordan and pile them on the other side so that none would ever charge they had cheated in their obedience of faith. They got stones right out of the *middle!* Then they took the stones with them to where they camped that night. There they piled them up so that in the morning, when everyone awoke, they would immediately remember what had happened the day before. In the center of their encampment they'd find twelve stones to remind them (and future generations who carried on their work) how God's mission in Canaan had begun when twelve tribes of Israel were unconditionally obedient to the vision God had given them.

The memorial didn't commemorate possession of the land; it didn't commemorate the finishing of the task. Like the 1856 monument at Williams College, the stones commemorated a time when some of God's people moved forward with firmness, vision, and obedience of faith to fulfill His mission to the world. Recall again President Hopkins' words: "The stress and struggle of the missionary work are still upon us. The calls for help were never louder." He could be speaking today, right?

I remember when a student at a recent Urbana Onward conference was asked to give a book report on *Student Mission Power,* a volume which reproduces all the messages given at the first Student Volunteer Movement National Convention. (It was like the Urbana of the Student Volunteer Movement.) Matt was asked to give a three-minute synopsis. For one minute he told us about some of the chapters. Then suddenly, in the middle of a sentence his face changed markedly as he exclaimed: "You won't believe, gang, what God was doing through students just a few years ago!" At that point Matt stopped telling us about the book and started challenging us to have the same vision as students had ninety years ago. Pioneers of faith, memorialized in a volume of dated addresses, stirred up a member of the new generation of pacesetters that God is raising up at this hour. The SVM Levites became memorial stones that brought Matt alive to Christ's global cause, along with many others there that day.

As I walked alone around the weather-beaten Haystack monument in 1981, I got the strangest sensation. I really did. I had the feeling that Samuel Mills and the others who prayed there in 1806 were standing right beside me. I could hardly breathe. It was a holy moment on holy ground. Then I said to myself: "You know, in a sense, it's not wrong to feel this way because the same God who met with them then is meeting at the very same moment with me 175 years later. He knows the end from the beginning and all things are present before Him. Jesus who led them to stand in the middle of their Jordan by pioneering faith and prayer is the same yesterday, today, and forever." Surely, in the sweep of His eyes, the Lord of all, who encompasses all history in Himself, saw me standing there with the "Haystack 5" and they here with me. In one sense we were all there together then. Does that sound strange to you?

So it is that God's worldwide purposes move from life to life, and His ultimate memorial becomes the *people* who are linked up to His Son and committed to following Him right into the middle of the challenge of world evangelization, first by heart and then even by feet, even to the ends of the earth.

Look at the drama once again. When it was time for the priests (the pioneers) to cross over, time for all the nation to move out and take possession of the land, Joshua sent a message throughout the camp. What was it? *"Consecrate yourselves,* for tomorrow the Lord will do amazing things among you" (3:5, italics added).

At the beginning I said that the Lord is a God of drama. I believe with all of my heart that your reading this book is part of the fabric of God's preparation of a people to be consecrated to Him in a very unusual way. The *miracles* that must happen if over 2.7 billion unreached people are to clearly hear of Christ—the fulfillment of the task itself—can only come if *God* works among us and through us in great power. So, let us *consecrate* ourselves to Christ, saying: "Lord Jesus, pioneer and perfecter of all faith, whether I send or go, you will be my highest *passion.* Lord Jesus, what you sealed on the cross, and released by your resurrection, and what you want to carry forward in this hour among the nations, *that* will be my highest *purpose,* whether I go or send. Lord Jesus, whether I go or send, those billions who have yet to hear, for whom you died and over whom you weep and pray even now, they will be my highest *priority."*

Linked arm in arm, consecrated together as Levites of God, let us go and stand in the middle, and in so doing become His memorial stones for those yet to follow. Can we hesitate at such an hour as this? Who will from this day forward step out in front? Who will stand in the middle? Who will stand as God's Levites until *all* of His "holy nation" has crossed over, giving yourselves without reservation to the fulfillment of God's saving mission among all the earth's peoples? How can we tarry? The Ark which is Christ goes before us already!

3

JOHN THE BAPTIZER AND OBEDIENCE

Gordon MacDonald

Very few of us are ever consumed by a dream. We don't have a dream of what this world could be under the lordship of Jesus Christ.

Do you ever ask yourself, "Is it possible in a few generations to make such a forceful dent on the course of history that for a period of time, we literally roll back the forces of evil?"

Much of Christian literature today is constantly tearing the world apart, noting all the excesses and saying that everything is going down the drain, but recognizing that we will all be bailed out shortly, so let's look for that escape! That's possible, but isn't there some place in the middle of all this for a dream? Can we seize control of history in such a way that the power of the eternal Christ can capture the hearts and minds of men and women?

History could once again take a different turn. You must believe that, if you are to devote yourself to evangelism and mission. It's not enough to say, "I want to save people from the fires of hell." It's not enough to say,

"I want to get as many people under the Kingdom banner as possible."

There has to be a dream. I see in the Gospels a group of disciples and a group of people around them who are following the Lord and are captured by a dream. I see believers in the book of Acts captured by a dream and a belief that the Kingdom could be brought here, on earth, in their time. It drove them.

In the following centuries, the dream of the Kingdom seems to have dropped through the cracks. E. Stanley Jones said, "Unfortunately, the great creeds of the church do not reflect the dream of Jesus."

What is your dream? What would you die for? What is your fantasy about what could happen? Every great movement, secular and religious, that has ever gone far in seizing history was fueled by a dream and a dreamer.

JOHN THE BAPTIZER: MODEL OF OBEDIENCE

I have been influenced not only by a dream, but by a person who serves as a paradigm on the subject of obedience. I'm talking about John the Baptizer.

John the Baptizer is an interesting man. Very few of us know much about him. We know a lot about Paul; in a sense, he interpreted Christ for us. But John introduced Christ to us. Paul stands after Christ; John stands before Him.

I am flabbergasted by how much biblical material exists concerning John the Baptizer. You can find paragraph after paragraph about this man, his personality, his background, his preaching, and the effect he had on people. John is a magnificent paradigm, both of mission and the subject of obedience.

John had a dream. He dreamed of being a part of the introduction of that great kingdom. It had been the dream of his people for many, many centuries.

John the Baptizer was a man who obeyed God. He allowed the dream of God to trickle down into his innermost being.

There were a number of forces that shaped John. You can find evidence of the first one in Luke: "In the days of Herod, king of Judea, there was a priest named Zechariah, of the division of Abijah; and he had a wife of the daughters of Aaron, and her name was Elizabeth. And they were both righteous before God, walking in all the commandments and ordinances of the Lord blameless. But they had no child, because Elizabeth was barren, and both were advanced in years" (Luke 1:5-7, RSV).[2]

The first thing that makes obedience a great possibility is our family background. One of the reasons John became the kind of man he became was because of the kind of mother and father he had.

You may not have grown up in a home where discipline was exercised during your first ten or twelve years. It's possible that you were never taught to tell the truth and show respect for authority and elders. If you weren't, later, in your twenties and thirties, a lack of obedience could cause problems for you. You may now be asking, "Why do I have difficulty kneeling under authority, whether it is man or God?" Because you never learned it when you were a child. If you face up to that, you can at least know where the problem started.

Elizabeth and Zechariah were incredible people. Look at Luke 1:6: "They were both righteous before God." The word *righteous* was a common word in that generation. Everyone considered himself righteous. But the phrase "righteous before God" means they were special people.

Today, when we talk about someone we may say, "He's a Christian." But that's not quite enough, so we say, "She's a born-again Christian." But that's not enough either, so we say, "He or she is a Bible-believing, born-again Christian!" What we're trying to say is, "That person is really committed."

That's what the phrase "Elizabeth and Zechariah were righteous before God" means. Their piety was not just something that appeared in front of their peers. They showed their piety by reverencing the living God. Elizabeth and Zechariah had weaknesses, but they were very committed people.

John's birth is recorded in Luke 1:57. In verse 63 we read that, after many months of silence, Elizabeth and Zechariah name John. Starting in verse 67, Zechariah begins to give a Spirit-filled prophecy. Luke 1:68-75 gives the theological context of John's mission.

Zechariah says, "Blessed be the Lord God of Israel, for he has visited and redeemed his people" (1:68). And what has the Lord God done? He "has raised up a horn of salvation for us" (1:69).

The horn of salvation is a great military cry. It's similar to many of the plots of old television westerns when it looked like everything was going sour with four minutes left in the show. Then suddenly the cavalry galloped up over the horizon, rescued the troops and it was over. It's a similar event here. Zechariah is saying that history has been somewhat sour, but God is seizing history, and the horn is blowing, and things will happen.

In Luke 1:70-71, Zechariah says, "He spoke by the mouth of his holy prophets from of old, that we should be saved from our enemies" Why? To perform the mercy that He promised to our fathers.

In Luke 1:74, Zechariah says, "That we, being delivered from the hand of our enemies, might serve him without fear."

We're not saved just because we are lucky people. Zechariah is saying that when God saves, He saves that we might serve. We are not converted to collect an insurance policy keeping us from hell, but in order to reflect the glory of God and shine the light of God into dark places.

In Luke 1:76,77, Zechariah suddenly zooms his camera lens and says: "And you, child, will be called the prophet of the Most High . . . to give knowledge of salvation to his people in the forgiveness of their sins." Zechariah is aware that John's mission will be to open people's hearts, to prepare them for a choice they will soon make about the revealed God in Jesus Christ.

I picture Zechariah holding the baby. Maybe Elizabeth was holding John. Maybe there was a small crowd gathered around him. No one knows. But I can see Zechariah, with his eyes blazing, saying, "And *you*, child, will be called the prophet of the Most High God."

The prophecy continues in Luke 1:77-79: "To give knowledge of salvation to his people in the forgiveness of their sins, through the tender mercy of our God, when the day shall dawn upon us from on high to give light to those who sit in darkness and in the shadow of death, to guide our feet into the way of peace."

As John grew up, I believe Zechariah talked to him about these themes over and over. John had to get his dream from somewhere, and it came first from his father and his mother. I can imagine them walking across the hillsides and down the roads in their town, talking about these things to young John.

My point is this: Obedience begins in those earliest days. How might that apply to you?

First, if you are a parent, teach your children obedience. If you want them to grow up and make choices for the mission of God, breed obedience to yourself and then to God.

Second, if you have not grown up learning obedience, recognize that you may have problems with obedience. You will have to accept that you have a certain amount of crippledness which the Holy Spirit of God can heal. And He *can*.

If you have a problem with obedience because of early childhood struggles, for a while, perhaps, you need to deliberately submit yourself to a relationship in which some sense of human obedience can be reaffirmed. If we are not obedient enough to others, we will not be able to obey the voice of God.

IN THE WILDERNESS

"In the fifteenth year of the reign of Tiberius Caesar, Pontius Pilate being governor of Judea, and Herod being tetrarch of Galilee, and his brother Philip tetrarch of the region of Ituraea and Trachonitis, and Lysanias tetrarch of Abilene, in the high-priesthood of Annas and Caiaphas, the word of God came to John the son of Zechariah in the wilderness" (Luke 3:1-2).

Two statements are made here. (1) Luke is giving us a time frame; (2) here are all the offices, from Caesar of Rome down to the little local powers in the province. They're all doing their big, important things. But the word of God comes to John—not in Rome, not in the city of Jerusalem, but in the wilderness.

God is sure strange sometimes! We build Him big cathedrals, raise mighty organizations, and develop powerful pedigrees—and God chooses to speak in the wilderness! He doesn't speak to the powerful; He speaks to John.

In the Bible, God often speaks in the wilderness. He spoke to Moses, John, and Paul there. Why does God seem to like wildernesses?

First, He likes them because they are silent places. We learn obedience relationally, but we also learn it in silence.

We live in a world saturated with noise. We have Muzak, stereos, and Walkmans. We love to club ourselves with noise. But I am impressed with the number of times God speaks in silence. The great men and women of God through the ages have not been afraid to go to the wilderness. God does not shout at us, He whispers. But we live in a generation that often drowns out whispers.

God drew John into the wilderness to separate him from the influences of the structures and powers of his day. God lifted him out of the noise so John could be captivated by silence. It's time that we learned to be silent so we can hear God speak.

In the wilderness, God whispered more and more of the secrets of the Kingdom to John, so that later when John charged out of the wilderness he would speak boldly and firmly, with unmatched conviction, because he had first heard God's clear voice in silence.

Wildernesses do not have to be geographical. They can be experiences. Or they can be weaknesses or illnesses. A wilderness can occur because of a defeat. A wilderness is a place where our mouths are silent. You may struggle with hearing God's call because you are so busy talking to God and about God that you have no time to listen to Him. Obedience only comes to people who listen.

If you are currently going through a wilderness, do not resent it or resist it. Nearly every great man and woman of God through the ages has testified to wilderness experiences. It was in the wilderness where God spoke to them most clearly and succinctly.

THE SPIRIT AND OBEDIENCE

"The next day he saw Jesus coming toward him, and said, 'Behold, the Lamb of God, who takes away the sin of the world! This is he of whom I said, "After me comes a man who ranks before me, for he was before me." I myself did not know him; but for this I came baptizing with water, that he might be revealed to Israel.' And John bore witness, 'I saw the Spirit descend as a dove from heaven, and it remained on him. I myself did not know him; but he who sent me to baptize with water said to me, "He on whom you see the Spirit descend and remain, this is he who baptizes with the Holy Spirit." And I have seen and have borne witness that this is the Son of God'" (John 1:29-34).

Obedience is not possible unless we have been filled and moved by the Holy Spirit who makes us sensitive to the forces around us, both the forces of sin and the hand of God.

Do you remember watching old television movies in

which the safecracker sandpapers his fingertips so that
when he places them on the dial of the safe he can feel
the tumblers fall? As people of mission, you and I need
to develop sensitive spiritual fingertips so we sense the
tumblers falling around us. That means being aware of
the demons of Antichrist and the Spirit of God. Obedience depends on the man or the woman who sees the
Spirit at work. I do not think many people today are as
perceptive as John was to see the Spirit of God at work.
So they do not obey because they do not know what God
is doing.

Adrian Rogers, a Southern Baptist minister, said,
"Spiritual gifts are tools, not toys." Too many of us want
the gifts of the Spirit for notoriety, power, or good feelings. But the gifts and the indwelling of the Holy Spirit
are given to make us sensitive to the needs of people
and to what God is doing.

"Now when John heard in prison about the deeds of
Christ, he sent word by his disciples and said to him,
'Are you he who is to come, or shall we look for
another?'" (Matt. 11:2-3). Here we find John in jail.
This man who had known the sky as his roof and the
wilderness as his home for so many years, is now in a
6 x 4-foot prison cell. He is uncomfortable. He is overcome with the feeling of being penned up and not able
to do what he wants. I can almost sense him asking,
"Did I make a mistake? Did I spot the wrong person?"

John sends a couple of his disciples to ask the question. Jesus replies: "Go and tell John what you hear and
see: the blind receive their sight and the lame walk,
lepers are cleansed and the deaf hear, and the dead are
raised up, and the poor have good news preached to
them. And blessed is he who takes no offense at me"
(Matt. 11:4-6).

Matthew 11:5 is almost a word-for-word translation
of Isaiah 35:5. John, a student of Isaiah, picked up the
phrases and knew what Jesus was saying to him: "Yes,
John, the Power is here." During John's final months,

he struggled to obey and submit. He wondered whether he was on the right mission. So what does Jesus send him? A message from the Word; a message of power.

These are the items that help us to obey the voice of God: the people who raise us, the people that influence us, the wilderness experiences we go through, and the times when we are able to minister as power comes upon us. As these experiences form us with the influence of the Holy Spirit, we begin to say more easily, day by day, "Father, my rebellious spirit is quelled and I am obedient and ready to hear your voice and go wherever you send me."

4

WORLD MISSIONS IN THE PAST: WHAT CAN WE LEARN?

J. Christy Wilson

I once received a letter from Harriett Whitesides who is heading up a team of students serving in Quito, Ecuador. She grew up as a missionary's child in Mexico and, therefore, speaks Spanish just as well as English. For two summers she served with Mother Teresa's work in Calcutta, India as a registered nurse. Then she was my student assistant at Gordon-Conwell Theological Seminary. She wrote, "One of the greatest needs here is for people in the churches to remember their first love. Intellectuals and rationalists live by the thousands. There are so very few who really exemplify a life of prayer and holiness." And then she quoted 1 Corinthians 2:9: "No eye has seen, no ear has heard, no mind has conceived what God has prepared for those who love him."

DEDICATION

Just as the greatest need in Quito, Ecuador, is for Christians to regain their first love, so this is our greatest need right here—to regain our first love for the Lord Jesus Christ and to carry out His commission. As we look at world missions in the past and see what we can learn, *this* is what those who dedicated their lives then can teach us today. At Williams College, five students not only prayed but put their lives on the line in the Haystack Prayer Meeting. This is what we first can learn from their vision for world missions—utter dedication.

They said, "We can if we will." They didn't say, "The Church will, or others will." They said, "We can if we will." Let us look at the life of one of these young men, Samuel Mills, as an example of what God did through them. He is the one who said, "We can if we will." And what the Lord accomplished through this young man, in the twelve short years that he lived after the Haystack Prayer Meeting, is simply unbelievable. God did exceeding abundantly above all that anyone could have asked or thought through this young man because of his dedication.

When he, in 1808, established the Secret Society of the Brethren in East Hall on the Williams College campus, membership involved dedication for life. It was not just summer service. No, it involved signing away one's life. If there were any entanglements that would keep one from going overseas, they excluded such a one from membership. When Adoniram Judson joined this secret society, he did it for life. He spent the rest of his years on the mission field, and as a result of his and Anne Judson's ministry in Burma, there are over three million Christians in that area today.

Samuel Mills wrote to a friend in regard to his commitment. He said, "We need to give up all hope of domestic happiness, the one bliss as the poet says which has survived the Fall." He never got married. He lived until he was thirty-five, but he gave up the bliss of domestic happiness because of his utter dedication, which is why God used him in such a mighty way.

Like Samuel Mills, Dwight L. Moody of Northfield, Massachusetts, exemplified utter devotion. He heard someone say, "The world has yet to see what God can do through one person completely yielded in His hands." Moody determined in his heart, "God helping me, I'm going to be that man." He had only four years of semi-formal education. When he went to Boston at eighteen years of age, he couldn't even read. When he tried to read one verse in the Bible in his Sunday School class, he stumbled and got so mixed up that all the other boys poked each other, laughed, and joked so much that it broke up the class. From then on his teacher, Mr. Kimble, skipped over him and had the other boys read. But God used this uneducated man to shake the world.

The greatest revival that Cambridge University ever had was under the ministry of Dwight L. Moody. During his first meeting there, he used expressions like "he don't" and "she don't." Every time he made a grammatical mistake, all the students would pound their feet on the floor. At the end of the meeting one young scholar came up and said, "Mr. Moody, I jotted down every grammatical error you made tonight and I think this will help you in the future. Here they are." Dwight L. Moody looked at him and he said, "I know that I don't know much grammar. But I'm using all the grammar I know for the glory of God. Are you using all the grammar you know for the glory of God?"

The next morning the president of the student body came to D.L. Moody in his room and said, "Mr. Moody, we Britishers pride ourselves in being gentlemen. But last night we were all rude and you were the gentleman." Moody then led him to a saving knowledge of Jesus Christ. That started it. The dam broke and God brought the greatest revival in the history of Cambridge University. Why? Because of dedication. Even though he didn't have much in the way of education, D.L. Moody gave what he had to the Lord and, like the loaves and fishes, God multiplied his talents and influence.

INTERCESSION

These early volunteers not only demonstrated utter

dedication, but they were also powerful in *intercession*. It was the Haystack *Prayer* Meeting. When our Lord Jesus Christ saw the multitudes fainting and scattered abroad as sheep without a shepherd, His heart was moved with compassion and He said to the disciples, "Ask the Lord of the harvest, therefore, to send out workers into his harvest field" (Matt. 9:38).

The primary way to meet the mission need of the world is through believing prayer. Every missionary revival has been born in prayer. Before Pentecost, the disciples, along with the believing women, went into the Upper Room and gave themselves continually to prayer. And what happened? God poured forth His Holy Spirit and the great missionary movement which extends into modern times was initiated—because of prayer. Every other great movement in missions down through history has been the result of faithful intercession.

For example, Count Zinzendorf welcomed Christian refugees to his Herrnhut estate in Germany. They prayed and their differences were reconciled. Then in 1727 God brought a great revival. They continued interceding and had a prayer chain that lasted over a hundred years—day and night. As a result one out of every twenty-three church members went out as missionaries around the world. Prayer forced them out. One of them, Peter Bohler, went to England and was God's instrument in bringing John Wesley to a saving knowledge of Jesus Christ. This resulted in the Great Awakening that touched so many lives.

Every man or woman of God who has been used in missions has had a faithful, regular quiet time. Like the others, Samuel Mills of the "Haystack Five" had his usual devotional period every day. He would also set apart a day for fasting and prayer when he had some new plan of action to consider and when he needed a special gift of power from the Lord. His faithful intercession was one of the forces behind the great missionary thrust of the nineteenth century.

VISION

The Williams College volunteers had *vision*. In Proverbs 29:18 we read, "Where there is no vision, the people perish" *(KJV)*. And this is so true in regard to missions. When Christians have no vision, people all around the world perish. At the Haystack Prayer Meeting they were discussing what they had been studying in their geography class about Asia, about the Muslims, and about the other unreached peoples. They had a vision for Asia. In talking about it they said, "Oh, that we might be able to take light to that dark area of the world." This is the reason the Haystack Prayer Meeting Monument has a globe on the top. But the sphere was tilted as a student prank—New Zealand and Australia are on the bottom. I like to think that the repositioning of the globe is symbolic of these different ones being so powerful in prayer and in their missionary dedication and vision that they turned the world upside down.

Carved in stone on the monument are the words, "THE FIELD IS THE WORLD." You see they had a world vision. Below this the inscription reads, "THE BIRTHPLACE OF FOREIGN MISSIONS IN AMERICA." What started here sent streams of blessing to North America, to Asia, to Africa, to Latin America, throughout the world and to the islands of the sea.

EVANGELIZATION

Those mission volunteers were concerned about *evangelization*. When the Secret Society of the Brethren was started at Williams, they wrote their constitution and all of their minutes in code. Byron Greene, who lived the longest, and later was the one who located the spot where the Haystack Prayer Meeting took place, said that he felt this was done for two reasons. First, there was opposition to missions at that time. Christians really weren't interested. Many of them said that if

God wanted to save the heathen He would do it in His own way, in His own time, without human help. Secondly, Samuel Mills was such a humble man that he didn't want to be in the limelight. He wanted to work behind the scenes. These documents weren't decoded until 1818, the very year that Samuel Mills died.

One of the tenets of this secret society was that only those who had evangelical faith would be allowed to join. As Mills explained it, they wanted those who really believed the Bible, who really believed that people without Christ were lost. In writing to a friend he said, "Today, with seminaries teaching the Bible, we have no excuse to be in ignorance in regard to those who have been without Jesus Christ."

Inter-Varsity took a survey at Urbana a few years ago to find out what students there believed about those who had not heard of Christ. Sixty-three percent of them said they didn't believe that those who had not heard the gospel were lost.

The ones who started the foreign missionary movement here in North America believed that those who had not heard of Christ *were* lost. A lady, who is a professor in a university here in the States, when speaking to Corrie Ten Boom asked, "Are the people who have never heard of Christ lost?" Corrie quoted John 14:6 where our Lord said, "I am the way and the truth and the life. No one comes to the Father except through me." And she added that if anyone gets to heaven apart from Jesus Christ, His Word would not be true.

Our Lord Himself said, "The Son of Man came to seek and save what was lost" (Luke 19:10). He didn't come to save those who were already saved. He came to save those who were lost. Paul, in Galatians 2:16-21, brings out that if salvation were by any other means than through faith in Jesus Christ, our Lord would have died in vain. Peter also states this in Acts 4:12, "There is no other name under heaven given to men by which we must be saved." If everyone is going to be saved anyway, why bother about missions?

But the Bible says they are lost. It states that all have sinned and come short of the glory of God. Therefore the only way for them to be saved, to have everlasting life and the forgiveness of sins is through the gospel of Jesus Christ.

The book of Romans deals with this question in detail. In chapter 10 Paul says, "Everyone who calls on the name of the Lord will be saved. How, then, can they call on the one they have not believed in? And how can they believe in the one of whom they have not heard? And how can they hear without someone preaching to them? And how can they preach unless they are sent?" (vv. 13-14). This is the only way—that missionaries be sent, that they preach the gospel, that people hear, that they believe, that they call on the Lord, and then will be saved.

And so we see the need for evangelization. Samuel Mills realized this. He found a Hawaiian orphan boy named Obookiah in New Haven, Connecticut, who didn't have anything to eat or anyplace to stay. He took him to his home and his mother treated him like one of her own sons. Samuel Mills led him to a saving knowledge of Jesus Christ and then took him along with him to Andover Seminary as exhibit A. There could be no valid arguments that missions weren't effective because here was a living example of what God could do.

INSTRUCTION

Now from these early Haystack young people we learn not only evangelization, but also about *instruction*. Not only did Samuel Mills lead Obookiah to Christ, not only did he take him with him to seminary but, in 1815, he also started a school for Obookiah and other internationals in the United States. The purpose was not only to lead those from other nations to Christ but to train them to be missionaries to their own countries. He saw the need for instruction as Jesus Christ said in the Great Commission, "Teaching them to obey every-thing I have commanded you." This includes teaching internationals who come to the Lord that they should be missionaries as well.

ORGANIZATION

We can learn about the importance of *organization* from these who had world missions on their heart. In Acts 13, the Holy Spirit initiated a mission team. Similarly, mission structures are needed for Christians to be successful in cross-cultural witness. Samuel Mills saw the need for this back in the 1800s. Look at the missions organizations he established.

First of all, he was the main mover in the Society of the Brethren, in which the members dedicated their lives to establish "a mission or missions."

Secondly, he established the Society of Inquiry on the Subject of Missions. This organization to teach individuals and churches about missions continued until the 1930s, and has recently been started again.

Thirdly, he was the primary motivator in establishing, in 1810, the American Board of Commissioners for Foreign Missions. He planned to go with the first wave of foreign missionaries which included the Judsons and the Newells. But the directors of the new mission felt he was more needed as a recruiter, supporter, and organizer in North America.

The American Board of Commissioners for Foreign Missions sent hundreds of missionaries to other places. These included the first missionaries to the Sandwich Islands or Hawaii. Obookiah was planning and preparing to go as a missionary to his own people, but he died of sickness before he could leave. When the first missionaries were sent by the board to the Sandwich Islands in 1818, three of them were Hawaiians who had gone to the school that Samuel Mills started in Connecticut to train indigenous workers for their own nations.

As Ralph Winter has noted, these early missionaries were involved in the first era of modern missions and went mainly to the coastland areas and the islands of the world. The second era of modern missions involved reaching inland into the continents of the world. One of the missionaries sent out by the American Board, John Bingham, crossed South America from Brazil to Peru and Chile in 1824 on a missionary journey. David Livingstone went into the interior of Africa and Hudson Taylor pioneered the China Inland Mission. The third era today involves reaching the hidden unreached peoples, whether coastal or inland in location.

Samuel Mills rode thousands of miles on horseback in North America establishing Bible societies and planting churches in the frontier areas of this nation. He started the Marine Bible Society in New York City, and others in Washington D.C., Ohio, Pennsylvania, Tennessee, Mississippi, Louisiana, Indiana, Illinois, and Missouri. He also helped establish the Amerian Bible Society in 1816 to tie these regional ones together. Its constitution stated that it was not only to send Scriptures to the frontier areas, but also to the Muslims and other people all around the world.

Samuel Mills also established a school in New Jersey to train black teachers, pastors, and missionaries. Furthermore, in 1818, he got the Presbyterian and Reformed Churches to organize the United Foreign Society.

COMPASSION

Now not only did Mills see the value of organization, but he demonstrated the *compassion* of his Lord. Jesus Christ said "Greater love has no man than this, that a man lay down his life for his friends." Samuel Mills laid down his life really to help black people. When he went on missionary journeys to the frontier areas of the United States, he was moved with compassion for the slaves. He writes in his diary, "I long to have the time arrive when the gospel will be preached to the Africans and likewise to all nations."

He was deeply concerned with the needs of what he called "his poor African brethren." Notice, he called them "his brethren." He wrote, "If evil exists in a community, a remedy must be sought." He tried to seek a solution to the evil of slavery. He found owners who were willing to free their slaves, if only some right plan were made to assist them after emancipation. Therefore, Samuel Mills helped establish an organization to free slaves who could go and establish a colony in Africa.

He volunteered to go to Africa in order to find a suitable site to establish such a colony of emancipated slaves. He had two reasons for this. One was to do away with slavery in the United States by establishing a nation where freed slaves could go. Secondly, he believed those blacks who were Christians could be missionaries to Africa.

He first went to England and talked with William Wilberforce. (It is amazing how this young man got around. In his humility he could go to the highest people.) Wilberforce encouraged him in this project. From England he went to the coast of Africa by sailing ship. He explored fever-infested areas looking for a site for colonization; and he negotiated with the local chiefs in order to establish such a colony. Through his pioneering efforts the nation of Liberia was finally founded in Africa as a nation for freed slaves.

Samuel Mills got a Christian professor by the name of Burgess from the University of Vermont to go with him. In gratitude for the pioneering work of these two men, a town near Monrovia, Liberia, has been named Millsburg, which combines both of their names.

It was on the way back from this missionary journey to Africa that Samuel Mills contracted a fever and died on board the sailing ship crossing the Atlantic. On June 15, 1818 he was buried at sea. It had been just twelve years since he and the other had knelt under the haystack and dedicated their lives to the Lord Jesus Christ.

What can we learn from these who had the world on their heart? We can learn dedication. God isn't going to use us unless we are willing to do anything for Him!

I remember when I was Inter-Varsity missionary secretary and was going to different schools encouraging students to come to the first missionary convention which was to be held in Toronto right after Christmas in 1946. The war was winding down and we could tell that mission fields which had been closed during the war were going to open. This seemed to be a crucial time to challenge young people to volunteer to evangelize the world. As I spoke in different schools, I said, "Today we have a great opportunity to complete Christ's commission. Before Christ called His disciples, He prayed all night and then He chose His twelve. Where are our all-night prayer meetings?"

As soon as I said that, the Holy Spirit convicted me, because I never had prayed all night. I was talking beyond my depth, and I knew I was a hypocrite. So, at Prairie Bible Institute in Three Hills, Alberta, I decided that I was going to spend a night in prayer. It is one thing to decide to do this, but it is another thing to know what to do.

I had just read a book by Robert Wilder, whom God used to help start the Student Volunteer Movement. In this book he said that the Bible study which had meant more to him than any other was the tracing of the Person and work of the Holy Spirit from Genesis to Revelation. I thought that this is what I would do, I would spend half an hour in studying the Bible and half an hour praying. I had never before realized how wonderful the Holy Spirit is and how great His work is.

Toward morning as I was praying, I sensed the Lord asking me, "Are you willing to do whatever I want?" And I told Him that I was willing. I didn't hear an audible voice, but the thought came into my mind. I then had this question come from Him, "Are you willing to die for me?" I answered, "Lord you died for me, therefore I will gladly die for thee." As soon as I prayed that prayer, the Holy Spirit came on me in power. I wasn't expecting this—this was before I had ever heard of the Charismatic Movement. Things like that weren't supposed to happen any more!

But after that, God worked in a new way. Students volunteered in larger numbers. Years later in Afghanistan, when Betty and I faced death time after time, the Lord would remind me of the time I had covenanted, "Lord, you died for me, therefore I will gladly die for thee."

Bakh Singh, from India, gave a tremendous message at the first student Inter-Varsity Convention in Toronto. He based his address on Luke 14:27-33 where our Lord told us first to count the cost. He said don't volunteer lightly, it's serious business! It will cost you your life.

One of the young men at that convention was Jim Elliot. Nine years later, he was speared by the Auca Indians. It cost him his life. Jesus didn't say that He would preserve us under all circumstance. He said, "Be faithful, *even to the point of death,* and I will give you the crown of life" (Rev. 2:10, italics added).

A student in seminary with me told the Lord that he was willing to serve anywhere, provided it was in the United States. He candidated in one church after another and couldn't find out where the Lord wanted him to go. He was miserable. He became so desperate that he finally said, "All right, Lord. I will even go overseas if you want me to!" As soon as he prayed that prayer a wonderful peace came over his heart. For the first time he knew that God was calling him to take a church in his own hometown.

Until he was ready to go anywhere, he wasn't ready to go anywhere. Until he made Jesus Lord of all, He wasn't Lord at all. Are you willing to live 100 percent for Him? The time is short. We aren't going to be here much longer. The work out there is great, and we have the Lord's promise that He will be with us always. He didn't fail those under the haystack who dedicated their lives and prayed. He was with them! He will be with us always too, even unto the end of the world. Are you willing to go anywhere, to do anything, for the Saviour who has loved you and has given His life for you?

5

MISSIONS TODAY—A LOOK AT THE FUTURE
Ralph D. Winter

In a sense, the topic "Missions Today: A Look at the Future" seems schizophrenic. What is it—missions today, or a look at the future? I decided, therefore, to reword and condense this topic a bit in such a way that we would be looking into the future through the present. To do that I've employed in each of my four points the phrase "the new era." We're both in it, but it is also the era ahead of us.

THE NEW ERA IN CONFLICT WITH THE SECOND
Why do I refer to a "second" era? Did I mention a first or a third? And what do I mean by the "new" era? The new era is, in fact, the third era. It is also, in fact, the last era. In terms of the definitions I'm using, there is no other era beyond this third one unless you talk about an era beyond the end of the world!

To speak clearly of eras, however, we must recognize that each of them runs through four stages of missions. Everyone recognizes the term *Pioneer stage* as the beginning of missionary work in a certain field. Most have also heard the term *Paternal stage* and often assume that it is somehow undesirable. I view it as the logical, essential next stage beyond the pioneer. It is the stage when national leadership is being developed so that the church can function on its own. In the third stage the church is mature, but still welcomes the *Partnership* of missionaries. Leadership positions may be held by either nationals or missionaries who are equal in voice and vote in church councils. But in the fourth, *Participation stage*, missionaries are present only by the invitation of the national church under whose auspices they work. The church is fully mature, capable of running its own affairs, doing its own evangelism, and sending its own missionaries elsewhere.

A question arises: is it not possible for one mission field to be in one stage of development while another field is in another stage? The answer is yes, and this provides an apparent conflict of perspectives.

Let me explain. It is perilously easy to think that if most missions are in the process of turning things over to the nationals in Korea, missions should therefore also be turning things over to the nationals in, say, Zambia. This assumption may be true, but not just because it's being done in Korea. Willy-nilly to do so creates tremendous problems and produces confusion. Some assume, for instance, that perhaps the missionaries should never have run things in the first place, as they do during the Paternal stage. A few intimate that perhaps even the pioneering stage was never entirely proper. They wonder if instinctive feelings of superiority and the long-lamented colonial mentality are ever entirely put aside short of the partnership or participation stages. (On the other hand, isn't it true that we today, in fact, feel definitely superior about not feeling as superior as did the early missionaries?) One thing such people fail to recognize is that the Partnership and Participation stages are impossible without the previous Pioneering and Paternal stages. That is, since the original converts are made in the Pioneering and some of them trained as leaders in the Paternal stage, how could a national church be born, much less mature, without original converts and without the subsequent development of national leadership under someone's tutelage?

An apparent conflict of eras results when, as our question implied, one field may be in the Partnership or Participation stage of maturity while another, perhaps right next door but in another tribe or people group, is still in the Pioneer or Paternal stage. Now, when most of the mission work of all missions is in the latter two stages (Partnership and Participation), then that era of missions can be said to be closing.

Confusingly, however, at the very same time one era is closing, another era may be just beginning with pioneer work in a few new places. For example, Hudson Taylor began the second era of missions with his push into pioneering areas in the interior of China at the very same time the first era was closing, with missionaries being sent home from mature fields, such as Hawaii.

Today, once more, the Protestant tradition is in a slow, massive, agonizing transition between the second era and the third, or the final era—what I have referred to as the "new" era. Like two Kodachrome slides on the screen at the same time which cover each other up, the Partnership and Participation stages of the second era confusingly overlap and tend to obscure the logic and necessity of the Pioneer and Paternal stages of the emerging new era. By now, the churches begun by Hudson Taylor and those who followed him into the inland territories of all the continents on our planet are now mature and in the Partnership and Participation stages. At the same time around the world, hundreds of previously overlooked people groups are being penetrated for the first time, and we see work in a Pioneer stage.

Thus, William Carey's first era worked through the

four stages and gave way eventually after a long transition to Hudson Taylor's second era emphasis on inland frontiers. Today, after a long transition, the second era is giving way to a third and final era focused on the bypassed or unreached people groups.

Today, we are in the very end point of the second transition. We are moving out of the second era and into the third. Today the Africa Inland Mission (AIM), an outstanding second era mission agency that came into being at the turn of the last century, is entering all kinds of new fields. It is amazing! In a sense, the AIM is moving very smoothly into the new era. As a matter of fact, most missions are now shifting to a new emphasis on pioneering in new frontiers, but their supporting churches have been left far behind. No sooner have church people understood the concept of working in partnership with the national church, than they begin to hear about pioneering again—a concept they had understood to be obsolete.

But that's the problem with transitions. Most people understand best only one of the two eras that are going on at the same time during a transitional period. They either understand that there is now a national church to which they are sending missionaries, or they understand, say, the Wycliffe situation where there are people groups which are completely unevangelized and need pioneer missionaries among them. But the person is rare who understands how both these situations can be equally true at the same time in maybe even the same country.

Toward the end of the first era, at the time of the first transition, adjustment shifted both ways. Early, for example, Hudson Taylor's emphasis on new frontiers got very little hearing. Late in the transition, missionary activity in mature fields got very little hearing.

In other words, when young missionaries recruited by the Student Volunteer Movement at the beginning of this century rushed out overseas, they went in vast hoards by comparison to the earlier student movement initiated by the Haystack Prayer Meeting of 1806. Many of these new recruits were college graduates, much more so than in the first era, and when they got to the field they said, "Look at all these poorly prepared, poorly schooled pastors." However, by then, the first era missionaries had finally learned the hard way that they had to start churches with national Christians where they were educationally, and then lead them forward gently. But by the time the churches began to gain maturity in those first era fields, the second era was upon them, with wave upon wave of new missionaries. Most of these went inland, and wherever they bumped into first era missionaries, they more or less misunderstood their work.

Because of their tremendous zeal, we often tend to make champions out of those Student Volunteers. This rush of new recruits so outnumbered the first era missionaries that even in well-established fields they unfortunately sometimes failed to preserve the degree of nationalization and indigenous character already established by the earlier missionaries. In other words, it is possible for a new era to burst in upon an older one and even in the well-established fields to roll history backwards. Perhaps their college education gave them a false sense of superior wisdom. Whatever it was, these student volunteers didn't catch on for a long time.

Finally, they began to rediscover the principles so necessary to building a strong national, indigenous church. About 1940, all kinds of people were talking about the "indigenous church" as if it were some grand and glorious new idea. Yet almost a hundred years before, first-era missionaries had talked about the same thing. Obviously, not all brilliant ideas of strategy were born in our time!

Sam Hofman, a missionary friend of mine in Southern Mexico, has spoken of three of these same four stages and likewise pointed to the difficult transition between them on a given field.

> The picture of the missionary moving on to new
> and unreached fields will also be helpful for the
> sending church. Too often missionaries who
> are ministering to the needs of the national
> church have gone home with a message, "We're
> through. We've turned the work over. We're out
> of a job." The false message the sending church
> gets is that the job is done (with 2.8 billion peo-
> ple yet to be reached!). Our missionaries need to
> be challenged, Don't go home, move on.

I should add, though, that I personally feel it may be
asking too much to shift missionaries to another field.
After spending thirty years learning one language, it
would be extremely difficult for them to move on and
start all over in another field. It has been done. But I
believe that the point is not necessarily to shift the missionaries but to send more. It's the agencies, not the
missionaries, that need to move on. And the missionaries that stay can shift from evangelism and church
planting to helping the receiving church become itself a
sending church!

As I said before, one of the most spectacular modern
examples of a second era mission going into many new
fields in the third era is the AIM. That is an agency
that's moving on. One problem they face is that their
present missionary personnel are so dominated by their
work in well-established fields that when they recruit
new personnel while home on furlough, they encourage
them to join them in the older, established work. Yet
only younger people will be readily able to pick up and
go to the newer fields. And AIM is assiduously looking
for new people to go to the new fields they want to enter.

Wade Coggins of the Evangelical Foreign Missions
Association speaks about the fact that the new era, "the
era we face," must involve the participation of overseas

mission structures—the so-called third-world mission agencies. Thus, today, we not only should go overseas to plant churches but to plant mission agencies as well. Those new mission agencies will then join us, perhaps working alongside us, helping to penetrate those people groups no one has ever reached.

Because of the increased worldwide base from which to reach out to the lost, the presence of strong indigenous churches around the world is still the great new fact of our time. This new worldwide base has not yet assumed full responsibility for the unreached fields, however. The third-world churches are just now beginning to lift up their eyes and look out beyond themselves, planning how to send out their own people as missionaries to unreached peoples quite different from themselves. The existence of healthy, growing, third-world churches often tempts us to consider them the end product of our own missionary outreach. They cannot be that. Rather we must see them as the valuable and necessary basis for new beginnings of outreach to other bypassed people groups still without the gospel. Mission fields must become mission bases.

Early in 1980 there was a meeting in Thailand which, among other things, talked about the unreached frontiers. Later, in November at Edinburgh, Scotland, there was another meeting called the World Consultation on Frontier Missions, whose entire agenda was frontiers. In my lifetime I do not expect *ever* to attend a more significant meeting—past, present, or future. Fifty-seven different Asian and African agencies sent eighty-eight delegates to this second meeting. More mission agencies were represented at Edinburgh than at any consultation or meeting of any kind in the history of the world. Now, don't misunderstand! There are more than two hundred agencies in the world. But never in the history of the world have so many mission agencies participated in any one meeting. Yet close to two hundred different mission agencies sent official delegates to the World Consultation of Frontier Missions at Edinburgh.

For example, the Africa Inland Mission and its related, parallel, third-world agency, the Africa Inland Church Mission Board (the AICMB)—the mission board of the church established long ago by the AIM—sent more delegates than any other mission. At Edinburgh there were six Africans who had been sent, not by the AIM or the Africa Inland Church, but by the AICMB, accompanied by several missionaries from the Africa Inland Mission.

There were two very unusual additional features to that meeting at Edinburgh. One was that one-third of all the agencies participating (57 out of 171) and one-third of all the delegates (88 out of 270) came from *mission structures born in the third world!* That is how it happened that it was not the AIM which sent the six Africans, but the mission agency of the national Africa Inland Church. Never before in history have there been as many as 57 third-world mission structures represented in any one place, or as many as 88 mission executives from so many agencies. This is why Wade Coggins's statement is so true. We Westerners are no longer the only missionaries in the world. We can now definitely count on Koreans, Nigerians, Brazilians, Indonesians, and Kenyans to go with us. We can find new mission recruits out there just as we find European missionaries back here.

The other unusual trait about this meeting was the simultaneous, large, parallel, autonomous youth meeting called the International Student Consultation on Frontier Missions. That student consultation portends, I believe, the responsible, respectable, determined (and unable to be overlooked) participation of the younger generation in the halls of decision-making and strategy development on a world, as well as a national, level in the world of missions. And I hope that never again in history will there be a major, international mission meeting without a large youth contingent present from around the world. I further hope that this will be the last year that the IFMA and EFMA mission executives will meet together without a youth contingent there—a younger people's contingent. I think the way for that was paved at Edinburgh.

THE NEW ERA: THE NATURE OF THE NEW FRONTIERS

We've mentioned that the first era represented the impacting of missionaries on the coastlands and the second era their moving into the interior. What then is the nature of the new third era of missions? It is what is left—the residue—what you might call the "bypassed" peoples. These are those people groups who have been somehow overlooked, wherever and whoever they are. In terms of definitions, this era is more difficult. It is easy to say, "Let's go to the coastlands of the world." For the most part, that is all the earliest missionaries could do in the first era—to get out to the coastlands of the non-Western world. In the second era, Hudson Taylor pointed to the inland areas. Although there were other people who even earlier went inland (Livingstone, for example), Taylor was the first person to found a major mission focused precisely on the inland territories, the China Inland Mission. Almost overnight forty other missions holding central the very same word, "inland," sprang into existence. An example is the Africa Inland Mission. They are not embarrassed to admit that they got the idea from Hudson Taylor. Others, like the Sudan Interior Mission, wanted to choose their own word! Still other new mission agencies wanted to use more biblical terminology and called their mission the Regions Beyond Missionary Union. Or how about the Unevangelized Fields Mission? Or the Heart of Africa Mission? All these names imply moving inland geographically.

But in the third era, today, where are the frontiers?

They're everywhere. They're here in the U.S.A. A Canadian Baptist mission executive told me awhile ago, "You know, every year we used to have hair pulling contests at the annual meeting of our denomination as the home board of missions said that *its* work was the most important and the foreign board of missions said that *its* work was the most important. The people voting didn't know what to do, so they would take sides. Now both boards talk about frontiers, the 'hidden peoples.'" That technical definition of hidden peoples defines groups of people wherever you find them, so long as there is not as yet a missionary breakthrough into their culture.

Let me elaborate a bit because this distinction is very crucial. Why do we call the Apostle Paul a missionary? Because he learned a foreign language? He didn't! Because he went to a foreign country? He didn't, not really. Well, then, why do we call him a missionary? If he didn't learn a foreign language nor go to a foreign country, why should we call him a missionary? He himself answered this question in very technical terms when he said in Galatians 2:7 that Peter was called to minister to the circumcised and he, himself, was called to minister to the uncircumcised.

You might say, "So what? Why is that important?" Very simply, Peter was called to work with his own people, Paul with somebody else's people. Moreover, the unique thing that Paul did (which comes down across the centuries as the classical example of *missions*) is that he planted churches in cultures where there were no churches. He founded what were, in effect, Gentile synagogues. That really blew the minds of the Jews— both Christians and non-Christians, as a matter of fact. They couldn't believe the Gentiles could run their own synagogues, and so they called them churches! This differentiation of terms, unfortunately, didn't help very much. Relatively soon, still in the ancient period, there was intense warfare between the synagogues and the churches. In the early stages the synagogues won, and Jews (perhaps some of them Christian believers) betrayed the Gentile believers to the civil authorities who had them beaten, bound, and killed. As a result, Gentile Christians later gaining influence in the empire virtually did away with the synagogues, shifting the day of worship to Sunday, etc. Down through the centuries since then the church, so called, has taken its place, forgotten its swaddling clothes and become a natural worshiping unit within each new culture. It was Paul's special strategy that enabled this to happen. His approach might thus be called a strategy for frontiers.

Today our distinction between the reached people groups and the unreached people groups is the result of this difference between Paul's work and Peter's. Those groups which are reached already have a church in their culture; the unreached do not. It is a fascinating exercise to go around the whole world and instead of looking at individuals, to look (biblically) at people groups, units which the Bible calls "nations." India is a country of three thousand nations. Of those three thousand, less than a hundred have any Christians at all among them. Let me repeat that. *Of the three thousand nations of India, using the word in the biblical sense, less than a hundred have any Christians at all.*

Evangelicals are accustomed to talking about *individuals* or about *countries*. By contrast, the Bible talks about *nations* far more than it does about individuals. In the Bible it is the nations, the *ta ethne* that we are trying to reach, not individuals. Individuals are included, of course, since nations are made up of individuals. But the Bible talks mainly about *nations* and *tribes* and *tongues*. These are the people groups. These are the families referred to in Genesis 12 where all the families of the earth are to be blessed through Abraham and his faith.

If you were to look around the world and ask just one question about each nation, you should ask, "Is there an indigenous, viable, evangelizing church within this nation, this people group, or not?" If there is, you should call it a "reached" group and could add it to your list of all other reached peoples. Then you might take all the groups where there are one or two Christians who, like the God-fearing Gentiles in the New Testament synagogues, worship outside their culture. You may notice that there are some missionaries working among them, but they haven't made much headway yet.

There might even be a church in that geographical area, but it doesn't belong to that particular culture. All through the Middle East there are Christian churches of all kinds—mostly of ancient Christian traditions, but also some Catholic and some Protestant. There are 17 million Christians in the greater Middle East, and thousands of churches. But the majority population, the Muslims, are linguistically, ethnically, and culturally quite different from the people in those churches. For Muslim converts, therefore, such churches are not indigenous churches, even though they may be in their midst.

Thus, even those groups which might have a handful of Christians (perhaps worshiping in churches of another cultural tradition), which might even have a few missionaries but which have no indigenous church of their own—these we call "unreached" groups or "Hidden People" groups or "frontier" groups. They are a different category from those non-Christians who have an indigenous church within their culture where they would feel at home, should they yield their hearts and lives to our Lord.

Let me draw another distinction: there are cultural blocks of people that are mainly frontier groups. The lion's share of the Hidden Peoples—as a matter of fact, 15,000 out of 16,000 groups—are in this category. Of these, 1,000 are Buddhist, 2,000 Chinese, 3,000 Hindu, 4,000 Muslim, 5,000 are tribal, plus 2,000 others. But not all tribal peoples are "hidden" groups.

Some of them are, but others aren't. Not all Chinese groups are "hidden people" groups. Some are; others aren't. Likewise not all Hindu societies have no Christians among them; not all lack that essential, viable Christian church. Some do; others don't. The Muslims are the worst off in terms of any kind of a substantial invasion into any of their sub-cultures. Only in Indonesia has there been any effective penetration of Muslim people groups.

At first glance, the statistics of the unreached people groups are rather shocking. But there is another side to the picture. First of all, there are about 7,000 groups of people that *have* been penetrated by the gospel and that now has a viable, evangelizing, indigenous church planted within them. There are still 17,000 people groups who haven't. How many individuals are we talking about? In each case it is roughly 2 billion.

But, you ask, how is it that the unreached cultures have so many more groups and yet not many more individuals? The reason is that missionaries in the past have tended to go to the larger groups, leaving the number of individuals to be reached less than one would think when noticing the larger number of people groups to be reached. But the task is best measured in terms of the number of groups since it is the initial penetration, the initial founding of a viable internal witness, that is so very difficult. That is the missionary task. Once that is done, then ordinary evangelism within that culture can complete the job of winning the rest of the individuals, even though they may number in the thousands and millions.

How many people are there who have yet to be won? That is, how many unreached individuals are there? Well, the difference between those who have been reached and those still unreached is a bit greater here. That is, within the societies where there is a church, there are 1.7 billion non-Christians yet to be won. By contrast, in the unreached or Hidden People groups, there are 2.479 billion individuals to be won.

What about the number of true Christians? What hope can non-Christians logically have of hearing the gospel? There are 245 million true Christians within the reached groups. By contrast, there are less than a million, or $1/250$ as many Christians, among the unreached groups.

What about missionaries? There are 73,500 Protestant missionaries working with the reached groups and only 8,000 with the unreached groups. Half, or about 4,000, of these are Wycliffe translators. After 100 years of work by the Africa Inland Mission, there are not only 5,000 churches, but also 3,000 or 4,000 full-time Christian workers—people who work long hours. How many full-time Christian workers are there in the unreached groups? None at all—by definition—since there is no church.

How many well-established congregations? In the reached groups, 2.45 million. It would reduce us to tears if we could fully understand the significance of that number. They meet in small churches, but often in small grass huts all over the world. Just think of it! 2,450,000 well-established congregations! But how many well-established congregations are there within the unreached groups? Zero! Again, by definition.

Thus, the remaining frontiers are vast, yet the missionary task, when described in terms of people groups, can be done. We are in a time of transition, a shifting of emphasis from well-established work to frontiers. Now, how do we go forward? What do we do next?

THE NEW ERA: WHAT WE MUST REBUILD
Up to now what we have talked about may have seemed purely statistical, purely scientific, at best somewhat detached from everyday realities. But if these statistics shake you up (and I hope they do!), what will you do about it? What can God expect *you* to do in this

new era? That's my third point. And I have three answers.

First of all, we must rebuild a new perspective on the Bible. I believe the Bible is a widely misunderstood book. The best way for you to understand what I mean by that statement is to get a copy of Don Richardson's third book, *Eternity in Their Hearts.* That book is a bombshell. Its implications would blow the lid off the average seminary. The first half talks about the "general revelation" that's present in a culture before the missionary gets there, the second half about biblical revelation—what theologians call "special revelation" and what is precisely the missionary task. That book, brilliantly written, tells a story which will give you a brand new understanding of the Bible. I can only hint at this. If your Bible is like mine used to be, it is a Bible full of riches, with many good things here and there. You open it expecting to be blessed. Pastors have opened it and blessed you. You go to Bible study groups and you're blessed. It doesn't matter where you turn in it, there are riches here and riches there, every place you look. It's a wonderful book. But does it center on how you can be a blessing to all the peoples of the earth?

When I was a kid, a Sunday School teacher sternly said to our class, "This book will keep you from sin, and sin will keep you from this book." And this is true! It is a very special book. But, for most people, really, that's about all the Bible is—a book of good things, for them. For them it is almost like a "snack bar" Bible! For the new Christian the Bible is a book full of blessings which he desperately needs. For Christians who are a little further along in their Christian experience, it's a book they run to when in trouble. Many of us just get the basic stuff out of it, with a few remnants left over. We consult it in dire emergencies, or use it as a "medicine chest" Bible.

There are others who by profession *have* to study the Bible all the time. Often their minds work hard, trying to get interested in something about the Bible. For example, they might say to themselves subconsciously, "What can I do this time, studying Ephesians for the seventh time?" Or they might start thinking about, maybe, the future. People do get drawn into prophetic studies. They write books and books on what the Bible tells us about the end times. The Bible can become to them a "crystal ball" Bible!

All these people may really love the Bible. They use it; they dog-ear it; they think it is just great! But while the Bible is all of these things, it is not primarily any of these things. It is misused if we run through it and find little hints about missions here and there and call that talk, "The Biblical Basis of Missions." We proudly stand up with our long list of Bible quotations trying to see if we can find missions all through the Bible. But it will take you a long time, even as it took me, to come to the place where you realize that missions is the *only* subject of the Bible.

As I see so clearly now, the first eleven chapters of the Bible are the introduction—not to the book of Genesis, but to the entire Bible. It talks about the beauty of God's creation, the invasion of sin, and the hopelessness of fallen man. It merely sets the stage for the Bible itself, which is a single book. The various books of the Bible, as we commonly call them, should really be called chapters, unless your concept of inspiration is faulty. God put this book together as one unified whole. Beyond the introduction, then—beyond the first eleven chapters of Genesis, that is—the rest of the Bible could be called in modern language *The Kingdom Strikes Back*. That is what the rest of the Bible is all about— God's relentless intent to push back the kingdom of darkness across the next four thousand years leading right down to the year 2000, just a few moments away. Four thousand years of single-minded, unchanging, unswerving, consistent, durable purpose to reach out to all the nations. I used to think, "Oh, isn't it wonderful that God hinted about the future in Genesis 12?" I felt then that it contained a little glimpse of God's purposes to be fulfilled later—a "hibernating" mandate, as it were. No one ever told me that Genesis 12:1-3 is the Great Commission, and that it wasn't merely a hint about what was going to happen in the future. It was a commission that went into force right then, when God first enunciated it. That is, from the very beginning God intended Abraham to be His witness to the various nations listed in Genesis 10. And when he didn't perhaps fully live up to what God wanted, he was forced into Egypt *as a missionary.* Eventually his whole lineage stayed in Egypt for four hundred years. When Joseph revealed himself to his brothers after their crime against him and his subsequent long years of suffering, he said to them, "You sold me, but God sent me." All through the Old Testament, this is a missionary book, but it is the story of a disobedient missionary nation.

But what does this insight mean to us? It throws light immediately on America today. America is called by the Great Commission just as much as Israel was by the Abrahamic one, or Armenia during the first centuries of the Christian era. (How is it that Armenia, the first Christian nation, has a history so parallel to that of the Jews?) Will God not require of us what He required of those other nations? He has given America many wonderful blessings, which we have only reluctantly shared with the rest of the nations. For them to hear about Him and His love, will it be necessary for Him to send us also into exile? Do you somehow think that American citizens will never be dragged off into foreign countries? Why not? Do we deserve greater favor than other nations before us which were blessed with the Good News and failed to share it with the heathen nations round about? Ah, yes, for me this book is a very different Bible from what I used to think, and I cannot see that our nation is excused from God's commission.

Secondly, we need to rebuild a new movement to prayer. I have been involved with others in a campaign to win a million American evangelicals into a daily prayer discipline called "The Frontier Fellowship." All of my early ministry was what I would have to admit was mainly a hit-and-run ministry. What I mean is that in spite of all my speaking, there was little I could leave behind that could nurture a person daily in God's purposes for the nations.

I received a letter from a fellow who was at my seminar at Urbana in 1976. He said that after he got into the seminar, he wished he hadn't come because he couldn't find a seat. He was wedged between two others, sitting on the curb of the concrete steps, but he was too embarrassed to get up and walk out in front of the crowd. He saw this funny little fellow up front, no hair, a bow tie . . . and he told me how much that seminar had changed his life. Thus, I don't mean to say that everything I've ever done and every place I've ever gone has been a hit-and-run ministry and that it has had no impact at all. I don't mean that. But during these last two years, every place I go, I leave behind this challenge: **"Will you dare to pray every day for the frontiers?"** That's a very innocent, simple, yet threatening question! You will be quite able to avoid the frontiers—unless you start praying daily for those very real people out there across the world.

At the U.S. Center for World Mission we're involved in a nationwide campaign to win a million people to this kind of daily prayer. We've asked every Christian organization to join this campaign. Africa Inland Mission, North Africa Mission . . . a number of mission agencies have already joined. We're asking a hundred Christian organizations to promote simultaneously a daily devotional discipline of this sort, characterized by a very interesting mechanism—something like a string tied around your finger to remind you. It's a mechanism called "Loose Change." Every day, at the end of the day, you reach into your pocket or purse and set aside the loose change for new advances into unreached people groups. It isn't setting aside the money that's important. That is only a little interruption, a reminder, a nuisance that helps to form a new habit. The habit involves study. It involves prayer. A little booklet called *Global Prayer Digest* introduces you to the facts, the glories, the challenges and the tragedies of the remaining frontiers of our world. But these frontiers will never hear the gospel unless first there is a vast movement of Christians praying daily for these frontiers.

Thirdly, we need to rebuild and renew the entire mechanism of society. I don't mean that we need a lot of new mission organizations. But we do need new vision, new excitement, a veritable "greening" of the sense of purpose of all kinds of Christian organizations.

For example, the Sunday School materials today are devoid of any reference to missions. They didn't used to be. And the Christian college curricula are just as bad. Oh, lots of courses are there which will be helpful to missionaries, but maybe not a single course describing the past, present, and future of the missionary movement as a concrete cause. The seminaries may be even worse. And the congregations of this country are still worse by a million miles. Our country right now is practically devoid of any mission knowledge of even the most rudimentary nature.

On the other hand, the mission agencies are, in fact, generally the most alert of all the Christian organizations. Almost all of them now have a new emphasis on unreached frontiers, even though for some it's like trying to turn a massive ship. Did you know that it takes twenty-five miles for a major ocean liner or a battleship to turn around?

On the other hand, if you think the answer is to start your own mission agency, let me warn you. It takes a long time to get a new agency going. It may take thirty years before it will hit its stride. Wycliffe Bible

Translators is a good example. It is one of the most progressive, bright-eyed, ready-to-go mission agencies that ever existed. Cameron Townsend, Wycliffe's founder, was a young college dropout who rushed off to Guatemala, went around selling Spanish Bibles to people who couldn't even read their own Indian languages, much less Spanish! Finally one of the village elders said to him, "If your God is so smart, why doesn't He speak our language?" You know the story. But young, seemingly foolish Cameron Townsend went on to become an early prophet of the third era by pointing out those unreached tribal frontiers.

But even with all the brains and brawn of those early Wycliffe translators—the Cameron Townsends, Eugene Nidas, Kenneth Pikes, etc., all brilliant people—it took Wycliffe thirty-five years before they completed the first thirteen New Testaments. Did they do something wrong? Absolutely not! And I warn you: Think twice if you want to found your own mission agency. You will need at least thirty years of patience. Finally, ten years after those first thirteen translations were complete, Wycliffe workers completed not thirteen more, but a hundred more. Two years later there were another hundred finished.

The point is, don't you think it would be far better to join a major agency that has finally mastered the details of what it's doing rather than to start out from scratch and fumble around, perhaps for years? If you must build your own house, then build it! But take seriously the existing mission agencies. Don't lightly write them off.

We're going to have to rebuild the school system in this country, also. Perhaps you didn't consider this as part of the greening I referred to, but it must be. I'm involved in an experimental university in Pasadena. We expect to take people right out of high school and put them into an eleven-year work/study internship where they'll come out with a Ph.D. A Ph.D. is not worth much more than a college degree was fifty years ago. Under the present circumstances, of course, when you have to waste half your life getting a Ph.D. and then don't have time to make use of it, it would be a tragedy if everybody decided to get one. But if one is working while learning, then the discipline of the Ph.D. may be of great value.

So, as I see it, we have to also rebuild the educational system. Though the William Carey International University had been in existence only six years, by 1981 we already had over seventy people who had asked about our graduate training leading to the Ph.D. Such students need not come to the U.S. There are Ph.D.s all over the world who can be their graduate mentors. In 1980 in the city of Nairobi alone there were twenty-five missionaries with Ph.D. degrees. Why should Kenyans have to come to the States to work under some professor who may know a lot less about Kenya than one of those missionaries equally well qualified academically? Today the field is the world, and the campus is also the world. We have to readjust our thinking to this fact.

Then, young people themselves need to be rebuilt in terms of the distinction between a career and a cause. Our educational system programs people to be heroic individuals. For perhaps fifteen, eighteen, twenty, or twenty-five years of schooling we are programmed to work all by ourselves, not as a team. As a result, we're almost hopeless if what is required for a certain task is a team. (That's another caution to remember if you intend to form your own team: are individualists able immediately to work that closely together?) Consequently, we need to rebuild our educational system to train us to work together.

Moreover, we are trained to think that our talents, our interests are what is most important. It matters little if some other task is urgent and there is no one to do it. We have to be true to our own talents. I don't know how we justify this viewpoint theologically. Certainly it is not biblical. To interpret the parable of the "talents" in this way is really rather loose exegesis. Throughout the New Testament the emphasis is to lose our lives rather than to refuse to help unless we feel it fits our specific gifts.

You may think I've really gone astray from the whole subject of missions. Why am I talking about the educational system? Do I think it is that bad? Who cares how bad or how good it is in and of itself? I don't! But I earnestly do not believe we can win the world to Christ if young people do not get to the field at least as students by the time they are sixteen. You can't really master a foreign language if you don't start learning it that young. There has to be a way in which young people can get experience overseas while they are still young, still learning.

THE NEW ERA: WILL YOU AWAKEN TO IT?

I seriously believe that young people are crucial in the rebuilding I spoke of—a new mastery of the Bible, a new movement to prayer, and a new mechanism for renewal. Now the question is, will you awaken to the new era of missions? Or are you merely "dating" the subject of missions? Most young people I know who are "interested in missions" are merely dating. They're leery of engagement. You can't pop the question and get any very positive response. It's too early; they're merely dating. There's nothing wrong with merely dating. After all, we shouldn't rush into things. On the other hand, it is an absolute fact that most young people, even some of the most mission-minded in school, are glad to graduate because they know that no one is going to follow up on them and see what they do with their mission vision. No one can. So long as they are in school, they don't mind going to the meetings and taking part. They're not just pretending interest. They are just grateful for that neat little fire escape: they know that as soon as they graduate they can really decide for themselves without peer social pressure. Then they won't be

held to college enthusiasms or idealism. Thus, students
can get involved in a very subtle phoniness. Usually on
campus, if students are interested in missions at all,
they're probably mainly dating. I have a daughter who
was one of the student leaders in the Inter-Varsity
group at UCLA. Like my other three daughters, she is
very, very involved in missions. (Through no fault of my
own. All our girls picked up their mission interest elsewhere. My wife and I never crammed this nor pushed
this at all.) Well, this daughter looked forward to that
one-night-a-year mission emphasis in their IV group,
but, unfortunately, someone mentioned in advance
that that particular night would be dedicated to a mission theme. Instead of the usual seventy, only twenty-
five came.

What I am saying is, will we really awaken to the fact
that a new era is upon us? Or will we toy with it? I have
been caught up in the task of breaking into all these
16,750 unreached cultures by the year 2000. I hope
that before you finish this book, you will also be caught
by this same vision. But I know that none of us has
really faced the music yet. We have not yet "resisted
unto blood," as the book of Hebrews says.

Did you know why those students back in 1806
didn't come in out of the rain but had their prayer meeting under a haystack? Have you ever stopped to think
about that? Pretty dumb students! Have you ever tried
to pray under a haystack? Those of you from the farm
might understand how it is possible. I couldn't until I
went to live in a rural area of Guatemala where they
have haystacks. The cows come along and eat away at
the haystack. But they can't eat from the top down; they
just nibble away at the bottom, in some kind of a para-
bolic curve, so the haystack ends up looking something
like a huge mushroom. If you're out in the rain, you can
sit back into that concave part at the base of the haystack and be perfectly protected. The rain runs down
and drops right in front of your feet, but you are in your

own private little cave. If it's a fairly large haystack, there will be space for a number of people to sit around the bottom, and in a prayer meeting like those five students had back in 1806, they could see the others around the bend and continue in prayer together.

But the startling question is why they did not simply come out of the rain. Why didn't they go into the wonderful Williams College Chapel Memorial Building, or whatever? Why were they praying outside in the first place? The answer is they went outdoors because it was *too dangerous* to pray in the dormitory. I wonder if you understand the significance of that. Is it dangerous for you to pray in your home, church, or dorm?

In that same year there was no place where it was safe to pray at Yale either. At that school, founded to train ministers, there was not a single student on campus who would even admit he was a Christian! This was right after the American revolution when French revolutionary atheistic philosophy was sweeping this country. But later on Yale got a godly president, Timothy Dwight, a grandson of Jonathan Edwards, and he won a few students to Christ. Because there was no place else where they would be safe, he invited them into his office to pray, and a revival swept the whole campus. That was later. Quite different was the background of the first Haystack Meeting which resulted in the first student movement into missions and the formation of the first American board of foreign missions. It all began because a few students dared to pray.

Think about that. If you get excited about the new frontiers, you may find yourself opposed by fellow students, parents, pastors . . . and also by all the principalities and powers and the workers of darkness of this world. You're not joining a majority cause. But this is not the light that failed. This is the one sure cause!

6

THE CHURCH AND WORLD MISSIONS
Paul McKaughan

I was raised in a missionary organization. My father formed a mission which later merged with another mission, so we lived in missionary headquarters all across our United States. Missionaries were all around me from the time I was very small. I can remember the stories they told, the wonderful things God had done through their lives and ministries. I also remember the biographies. Some of the first books I read were stories of Hudson Taylor, Watchman Nee, C.T. Studd, and many other great missionaries of past eras.

In the midst of all that talk about foreign missions and all the stories of missionary heroics, an image of what a missionary was began to evolve in my mind. The only way I could picture it was like the Lone Ranger and Silver, where the missionary went galloping out to do battle with the evil one, firing silver bullets and always vanquishing the bad guys and coming back unscathed.

Then I became a missionary in the interior of Brazil. My wife Joanne had never lived outside of Boston or Minneapolis, and I took her to a "house" in the middle of the Brazilian jungle. It really wasn't a house—it had been a corncrib. We soaked down the walls with insecticide and moved in. I didn't know enough to pursue language study. I had grown up in a mission that never talked much about cultural adaptation and all the things we take so much for granted today.

All of a sudden I found myself in the middle of the jungle trying to start a church. For the first time in my life, I had to face the reality of what the Church of Jesus Christ really was. I had studied many things in my missionary formation, but I didn't know anything about the Church. Somehow my orientation had been me and then God and maybe my wife also, and we were going to do it!

It was a faith mission. We felt we should trust the Lord for our support, and He supplied in a wonderful way. Funds were no problem. But relationships with the other people around us were a big problem. I really didn't know how to cope with them because I had just begun to learn to get my guidance from the Lord and not worry too much about other people.

My feelings about denominations could best be expressed through an experience I had while growing up in Chicago. We had moved there with a missionary organization and were looking for a church home. There happened to be a Presbyterian church near my grade school, and we attended their services for three weeks. The pastor did not mention the name of Jesus Christ, but he gave some very interesting book reports. I filed that away in the back of my mind as denominationalism. So, if my view of the Church was negative, my view of denominations was much more negative.

I thought of the Great Commission. This was the great missionary mandate, but somehow the Church was not there. As I began to get to know my fellow missionaries, I discovered the myth of the Lone Ranger was nothing more than that—a myth. Instead of always being victorious, missionaries were bruised and battered people who were hurting.

I began to see that many times toward the end of their ministry, even the rugged individualists—those very strong personalities God had used in such a wonderful way to go out and start churches—had to leave the churches they had started because the people couldn't stand them. Personality quirks had arisen, or colleagues who had welcomed their leadership at first saw they were beginning to lose some of the forcefulness of their personality or leadership skills. There was no net to catch these men, and they were more or less put on a shelf.

It has only been in the last few years that I have come to see the importance of the Church. Through working with a team of people, I began to see the necessity of the Body of Christ functioning together. The concept of "team" sounded romantic to us. It was new when we started out in Brazil about fifteen years ago. We hadn't heard of it and thought we were inventing it, but as we began to search the Scriptures, we discovered that the rules for governing our relationships to one another were found in Christ's teaching of how the Church should function. It wasn't something we were discovering or inventing. It was what God had always intended the Church to be.

Now I'd like to talk about missions and the Church. I will be covering three points:

1. The Church and its mandate for missions
2. The Church as God's structure for interdependence
3. Some practical points about the Church and our relationship to it.

THE CHURCH AND ITS MANDATE FOR MISSIONS

As I was reading through J.H. Bavinck, the great theologian and missiologist, I came across a phrase that burned its way into my mind during the preparation of this chapter: "The glory of Jehovah and not the need of the heathen is the overriding motive for missions." Missions didn't start with Matthew 28; it was in the mind of God from the very foundation of the world. Missions is not something we do; it's something we are. In 1910, Robert E. Spear said the following in a talk about the missionary mandate:

> That duty is authoritatively stated in the word of the Great Commission. It is of infinite consequence to have it so stated by our Lord Himself. But if these particular words had not been spoken by Him, or if having been spoken they had not been preserved, the missionary duty of the church would not be in the least affected. The supreme argument for missions is not found in any specific word. It is in the very being and character of God that the deepest ground for the missionary enterprise is found. We cannot think of God except in terms which necessitate the missionary idea. Though words may reveal the external missionary duties, the grounds are in the very being and in the very thought of God.

As you think about missions, think of the covenant God, the God who created man and wanted to enter into a relationship with him to show what He was like to all the powers of heaven and earth. That's what missions is about.

The first point of the catechism that a Presbyterian learns as a child is that the chief end of man is to glorify God and enjoy Him forever. Let me say something—it's impossible to do that by yourself. Even as we start out, we must recognize that God initiated the relationship with man and then placed him in a fellowship of believers. When God chose the man Abraham and promised His blessing to a tribe and nation, He was seeking to demonstrate His own personality. He was seeking to show all of heaven, all the principalities and powers, what He was like. That is what the Church is to be, and you cannot do that alone.

The Psalms are a great book of hymns. This is the hymnal of Israel. I am always blessed by the fact that hymns are not only wonderful for the people of God, but they are also a great testimony to a watching world. Psalm 67 is a missionary hymn:

> May God be gracious to us and bless us
> and make his face shine upon us;
> may your ways be known on earth,
> your salvation among all nations.
> May the peoples praise you, O God;
> may all the peoples praise you.
> May the nations be glad and sing for joy
> for you rule the peoples justly
> and guide the nations of the earth.
> May the peoples praise you, O God;
> may all the peoples praise you.
> Then the land will yield its harvest,
> and God, our God, will bless us.
> God will bless us,
> and all the ends of the earth will fear him.

The greatest reason for missions is that God wishes to demonstrate Himself through His people.

In 1 Peter 2, we read that we are a chosen race, a royal priesthood, a holy nation. The Church is God's chosen successor to Israel in that great job of demonstrating what He is. The Church isn't optional. In Acts 2:47, we read that the Holy Spirit added to the Church those who would be saved. When you come into a right relationship with God, you are automatically a part of His Body. There is no other way about it. If you are born of the Spirit of God, you are a member of each and every person who is born of God. A negation of that fact is a negation that you are really born of God. The two cannot be separated.

Peter Barnhouse has said that people who are converted want to be part of the Body of Christ; that is part of the gospel, an essential manifestation of God's power to redeem man and society. The gospel reveals that the living Lord is the liberator not only of individuals but also of the group. Somehow we've lost this whole aspect of salvation.

The Church is the redeemed in the redeeming society. The Church of Jesus Christ demonstrates to a watching world what God is like and how He reacts. It is incarnational truth. In John 16, Christ says that by this men shall know we are His disciples, if we love one another. Galatians 5 speaks of faith actuated by love. John 14 says that love results in obedience. First Peter 3 states that if we don't want our prayers to be hindered, we must be careful of our relationships with our wives. You see, that aspect of relationships comes from God and has to be expressed through us.

Once again, Bavinck says the success of the Church in missions and the work of evangelism depends on the ability of the Church to arouse envy. Is your relationship with brothers and sisters in Christ before a watching world demonstrating the presence of God in such a way that people are provoked to envy and want to be a part of that fellowship, want to be in a right relationship with God as you are with your brother? A watching world cannot see much of your relationship with God, but people can see a great deal of your relationship with other Christians. Those relationships and everything about them are only made possible as a sovereign God works on our hearts and gives us the power to live in a supernatural way.

THE CHURCH AS GOD'S STRUCTURE FOR INTERDEPENDENCE

Let's move on to the Church as God's structure for interdependence. Notice I did not say "independence." We are very proud of our independence, but independence is really a quest for self-sufficiency. It cuts across everything we see in Scripture about our need for God and for other people. Independence is egocentrism and sin, yet somehow in our individualistic society we have so raised up this standard of individuality and independence that we've lost the corporate nature of the Body of Christ, which is really dependent on each and every member of that Body.

One of the great truths of the gifts of the Spirit is my need for you and yours for me, because a sovereign God has given us gifts for the mutual upbuilding and completion of His Body. Without the gift that God in His sovereignty has given, I am incomplete. Without the gift God has given me, you are incomplete. This can only work as the Church functions.

I am not locked into form and I don't mean to say we ought to have a Church that looks exactly like my little square box. However, I do say this: If you are not in a fellowship that is holding you accountable, and if you're not in a worshiping fellowship where the Scripture is preached and discipline exercised, you are bypassing God's primary means of missions and of demonstrating to the world who He really is.

Paul seems to indicate at least three things that give a commonality in the Church: (1) a shared teaching, a gospel coming directly from our Scriptures, which came directly from God; (2) a common responsibility for one another; and (3) a necessity to extend the Kingdom to the uttermost parts of the world that is inbred in the Church and is part of its genetic engineering.

The Church has been a great success story. Many of us are prone to reject the Church, as I rejected it as a young person, viewing it as a has-been. It seemed to me the action was not in the Church—it was somewhere else. I never could define where the Church was because I knew it wasn't with me. Somehow I felt God had set the Church on a shelf. However, as you study missions and what God has done, you find it is probably the most successful enterprise in all of history. If you just look at what God has done pragmatically through the Church, you see some fantastic things. The hundredth anniversary of the Christian Church in Korea is being celebrated in 1984. In Korea there are three Presbyterian denominations with over a million adult members in each one. There are seminaries committed to the Scriptures, just as you are, with six to seven hundred students. The goal of the Korean church today is to send out ten thousand foreign missionaries in the next hundred years.

In East Africa, churches of the Anglican confession in Kenya, Tanzania, and Uganda have approximately one million adult members. There are Lutherans in Madagascar and Tanzania. The Assembly of God is a vibrant denomination in Brazil with over three million adult members. Baptists in Brazil number about five hundred thousand. The United Presbyterian church was so effective in Guatemala that, in the near future, this country could become the first Latin American country to be 50 percent Protestant. God has used His Church in wonderful ways, yet it is so easy for us to write it off as something that really isn't all that important.

It is interesting to note that missions like Sudan Interior Mission, Africa Inland Mission, and many others have been mightily used by God in the establishment of His Church. Just as I am related to God and to you, it is very natural to me that a connectional relationship should result from churches being formed around the world. I find it very interesting that people who were congregational by nature, and successful overseas, found it very natural to be related to one another and draw strength from one another, because that is the natural flow of Christianity—the establishing of these relationships.

The term *para-church* distresses me because it is a negation of terms. If what I have been saying is true, a person cannot be a believer without being in the Church. How can someone be para-church? It seems impossible to me.

On the other hand, God in His sovereignty has raised up certain structures over the years. In the modern missionary movement, the Bible Society followed close on the heels of the early denominational boards. There are also organizations with a special focus that are raised up by God at specific points in time. These organizations are wonderful and can do things that we, as denominational missions, could never do and perhaps would never try to do. Their ministry cuts across the whole Body of Christ. Organizations of this kind are sodalities, called of God to do a specific job at a specific point in time.

If you are feeling called of God to be a part of one of these agencies, don't think of yourself as a second-class citizen. At the same time, don't think you can live your life apart from the Church of Jesus Christ. In my opinion, it is unfortunate that many of these special missions brought into existence by God as a part of the Body of Christ have tried to operate as though they had no relationship to His Church. In so doing, they are living out before a watching world something that is sub-biblical.

SOME PRACTICAL POINTS ABOUT THE CHURCH AND OUR RELATIONSHIP TO IT

What have we stated thus far? The Church is God's expression and comes from His very nature. Being part of the Body of Christ, of His Church, is not optional, because the Holy Spirit baptizes us into His Church and it is impossible to be a Christian without also being part of the Church. The extension of the Body of Christ through churches relating to one another is a further expression of the oneness and wonderful unity in the relationship we have through a covenant God. God has brought into being many specialized structures to meet specific needs, yet they too are part of the Church. What does this mean for you and me?

After my first term in Brazil I joined a mission by the name of Overseas Crusades (O.C. Ministries today). Fortunately, this mission stressed the importance of the Church and insisted that we relate to the Church. While I was seeking to raise support, Dick Hillis told me, "Paul, don't worry about support. You minister to people, and then God will supply your needs through His Church." I heard what he was saying in my head, but I didn't hear it in my heart.

Even at that time, in my mind the Church in America was something to be used. I had seen the need of the Church in Brazil, to which I related and to which I was in submission. The Church in America was going to further *my* vision. I suffered through itineration/deputation/fund-raising simply because it was something I had to do in order to go back to Brazil and do what I really wanted to do. The idea of ministering to the Church was manipulative in my own heart. Yes, I preached, and I hoped God would bless the Church. But if God didn't bless the Church in terms of money in my pocket, I didn't care what else happened. Those of you who have been missionaries or done itineration know what I am talking about. Those of you with para-church organizations know also.

I do not believe the Church of Jesus Christ is meant to be used. I believe that, as a part of that Body, we must in practical ways submit to the discipline of the Church, even in our own country. How does that work? In the Presbyterian church in America, our missionaries travel to congregations throughout our denomination, and individual churches respond in several ways. Some may consecrate the missionary, have a dedication service, and send him off to the field. This says, "We think you are a good guy." Others offer a tangible response—financial support. Still others give a less tangible and harder to measure response—they pray.

I find there is a great myth about missionaries, and as missionaries we talk about it a great deal. We talk about the superhuman missionary who is great on the field but can't tell spectacular stories, so he never gets his support. But this has not been true in my experience. If you are ministering effectively to people here in the United States, God, through His Church, will give you all the support you need. I think in particular of one of our missionaries at Mission to the World. If she were to stand before you, she would not impress you as a public speaker, yet she always has money in her account.

If you minister to the Church of Jesus Christ as a part of her—not as an outsider trying to exploit the Church or as if you are doing others a great favor by giving them the privilege of investing in your ministry, if you go into the churches of America with a heart to serve the people of God and identify with them, then you will see your support provided in wonderful ways.

Many times people don't want to raise support through itineration to individual congregations because they find submission to the Church for the validation of their ministry a frightening prospect. It does seem terrifying, but if God can't use you to touch hearts here in America as you visit churches across the land, you are probably going to have a hard time overseas. So let me urge you to be a part of the Church, right here at home, from the beginning of your ministry.

There is also a Church overseas to which you must relate, and it's a pretty complex Church. There are three kinds of reaction to the national church. I have talked to missionaries (myself included) who have experienced all three at different times in their ministry.

The first is an attitude of superiority. We think we are an established Church with our mature theology and sophisticated ways of doing things, and we see a young Church in need of our sophistication, technology, and theology. We think we are there to bless the local church, but this kind of attitude doesn't work very well. Let me give you an example. I spend about five months each year overseas with our missionaries. On a visit to one of our teams, I noticed there were children running around unsupervised during the morning service, and our missionaries were irritated by it. Afterwards a conflict developed among the team members about who should take care of the children and why something hadn't been done before. But who was bothered by things like children running around? Was it the nationals or us? Somehow we have come to think that a church must have a graded curriculum for the younger children. If you have a church, you must also have this and that and all kinds of neat little things. So this attitude of superiority comes out in many very subtle ways.

At the other end of the spectrum are those who think everything God has given us in the United States is bad and everything He has given the national church is good. They end up turning against the Church in America. This is what I did. I disassociated myself from every American missionary I knew except the members of my own team. They walked down one side of the street and I walked down the other. I didn't like Americans at all. God had to deal with me. He said, "*I* love them." Then I realized He meant I had to love them too. But it took a long time to do it.

People talk about the great and wonderful prayer meetings in Korea at daybreak. Tremendous spirituality! I've heard missionaries put down the Church in America and extoll the Church in Korea because they get up so early to pray. But they fail to mention the politics of the Korean Church. They have warts just like we do. They have members who are immature and in the process of being formed into the Body of Christ and made into the image of His Son just like us. There is no difference—we just know where our warts are and don't yet see where theirs are.

These then are the two extremes. You can think you

have all the answers for the Church overseas, or you can think, "They have all the answers for us, so I'm going to become just like them and cut myself off from my roots." I think the balanced view, and this is the third response, is to realize that God in His sovereignty has allowed them to be what they are and you to be what you are, because together, He wants to bring all into a fuller expression of what the Body of Christ is meant to be.

When we are born of God, we have His Spirit and the promise that He has given us all we need for a particular point in time. But He has also given us ample indication in His Word that we need one another, with all the various gifts God has given us, if we are ever going to reach that fullness of stature in Jesus Christ. Let me issue a challenge to you. If you go to the field, look at the local church not as something inferior or superior, but as something unique that God has created and is allowing you to be part of. He is allowing you to be a part of that church because He has a unique contribution for them to give you and you to give them.

There is another problem as we go to the Church overseas that I feel constrained to mention. (This will sound negative, and I have wanted to be very positive.) I feel an imperialistic mentality has arisen in the Church overseas. They are fallen creatures just like us, and just as we are ethnocentric and think America or Canada is great, they think their own country is great and want to be rulers over all they survey. This leads them to think they are lords over great unoccupied geographic areas.

Over and against that attitude is the liberating concept that has come out of the Lausanne Congress, which is the idea of reaching people groups. You can truthfully say the sun never sets on the Church of Jesus Christ, and you can also say there is probably no country on the face of the earth where the Church of Jesus Christ does not exist. But to say the job we have been talking about is finished is quite a different thing. I believe it is wrong for us to delegate or relegate all of a particular country to a national church just because its members occupy a small part of it, especially when there are vast numbers of people groups in that country that need to be reached with the gospel of Jesus Christ.

When I speak of being committed to the Church, I don't mean going to Brazil and being blindly under the domination of Brazilian ecclesiastical structures to the point of forgetting the millions of hidden people who may exist in the metropolitan areas of that country. I don't mean being in subjection to the Korean church or any other church and overlooking those vast numbers of people for whom the national church has no vision. I am saying that today, more than anything else, we need pioneer missionaries to plant the Church of Jesus Christ. I am surprised by the people who come to the Presbyterian church in America wanting to be every other kind of missionary: fliers, computer technicians, engineers, nurses, and everything under the sun except people who are really involved in the nitty-gritty of seeing the Church planted in difficult places. It may be difficult, but still that is where the greatest need in mission is today. We need people there, at that particular point, where the rubber hits the road. It doesn't matter how good the radio station is or how relevant the gospel presentation is. Unless somebody forms those who hear the message into worshiping and living communities, the job isn't done. The watching world has not yet been shown who God is.

I would like to challenge you today, as you look at the Church, to also look at the possibility that God might be calling you into the very difficult job of seeing churches that will add to the wonderful mosaic which is the Body of Christ from among the people groups of the world.

I'd like to turn briefly to Revelation 3:7-12 and read something that was said to the Church:

"To the angel of the church in Philadelphia write:

'These are the words of him who is holy and true, who holds the key of David. What he opens, no one can shut; and what he shuts, no one can open.'" Remember, our missionary mandated vision comes from the very personality of God, the God who opens and the God who shuts.

"'I know your deeds. See, I have placed before you an open door that no one can shut. I know that you have little strength, yet you have kept my word and have not denied my name.'" Is that true of you and the Body of Christ with which you worship? This word was not given to an isolated individual. It was given to the Church.

"'I will make those who are of the synagogue of Satan, who claim to be Jews though they are not, but are liars—I will make them come and fall down at your feet and acknowledge that I have loved you.'"

There is apostasy in the world. "Since you have kept my command to endure patiently, I will also keep you from the hour of trial . . . '"

None of us has any kind of hope that God will take us through scot-free, but those hours of testing will come, and when they come, He will keep us. "' . . . I will also keep you from the hour of trial that is going to come upon the whole world to test those who live on the earth. I am coming soon. Hold on to what you have, so that no one will take your crown.'" Hold fast, don't let it slip.

Think about the great movements throughout history as Christians have walked through open doors and been faithful to the Word. God has kept them true and blessed them in a wonderful way. God says to us today: "Hold on to what you have so that no one will take your crown. Him who overcomes I will make a pillar in the temple of my God. Never again will he leave it. I will write on him the name of my God and the name of the city of my God, the new Jerusalem, which is coming down out of heaven from my God; and I will also write on him my new name."

The revelation of God and missions started when God revealed Himself. God built a nation and a Church. He is saying that the goal of His entire revelation is for those who are faithful to be built into the habitation of God and become a part of the holy temple of our Lord. That expression of worship and of what God is, is a marvelous calling.

"He who has an ear, let him hear what the Spirit says to the churches." I believe this is true for us today. I believe God wants us to sense, as never before, that He is calling us together to express the fullness of His personality to a watching world, calling us together as the Church of Jesus Christ to occupy lands and peoples never before occupied with the gospel, in order that our God might receive great glory. It is the glory of God and not the need of the heathen that is the heart of the whole missionary enterprise.

7

REFLECTIONS ON THE DEATH OF FIVE MISSIONARIES
Elisabeth Elliot

My husband, Jim, and I were missionaries in South America. Back in 1956 five American missionaries made an attempt to reach a tribe of Auca Indians who had never been contacted by any outsider, let alone by anyone with the gospel. They were speared to death in the attempt. One of those men was my husband.

I think most Christians would assume that these missionaries would not have been doing what they were doing and they certainly would not have been privileged to have a chance to lose their lives for the sake of the gospel of Jesus Christ if they had not been *called* by God.

Were they called? Did they obey? Was it worth it?

Were they called? It's been twenty-eight years since my husband was killed. A great many things have happened in my life and I've had a chance to do a lot of reflecting in the light of that incident.

Back in 1953, two dugout canoes moved slowly down a little river in the eastern jungle of Ecuador. In one of the canoes was a young missionary by the name of Jim Elliot. In the other was his brand-new wife. We had been married three weeks. Each canoe was poled by two Indians: one in the bow and one in the stern. They were Quichua Indians. This was the tribe among whom Jim and his colleague, Pete Fleming, had been working. They were reducing an unwritten Indian language to writing, had started a boys school, and were preaching the gospel. They already had a group of about a dozen or so believers at that time.

I had been working on the other side of the Andes among a small tribe of Indians, the Colorados. They were not related in any way except racially, we might say, to the Quichuas. Their language was totally different. There's no more connection between the Quichua and Colorado languages than there is between Chinese and English.

Jim and I were married in Quito, the capital city of Ecuador. Now we were on our way down the river to our first honeymoon cottage—a tent. Just before Jim and I were married, he and two other missionaries had made a trip down another river, the Bobonaza River, seeking possible new sites for mission stations among Quichuas who had never been reached by missionaries. They were particularly eager to establish new stations because their one station had just been completely demolished by a flood. Jim had spent the entire first year not only learning the language and preaching and starting a school and a church, but also rebuilding the dilapidated buildings that had been abandoned for some time. His work was all destroyed by flood. We were married shortly after this.

On their trip down the Bobonaza River, the three men met an Indian named Atanasio in a little place called Puyupungu. Atanasio was unique among Quichuas because, as far as I know, he was the only Quichua that had two wives. He lived on the border of another tribe where polygamy was customary and might have gotten the idea from them. He thought it was a good one, so he had two wives and about fifteen or eighteen children. Atanasio said, "I have a family here that will make a school but we need a teacher. Would you missionaries ("evangelicals") come in and put a school here?" Well, to get an invitation from an Indian to open a mission station was virtually unheard of, so the men felt they could not possibly turn him down.

Jim and I answered the call and started Puyupungu as a mission station. We lived for five months in a 16 x 16-foot tent which was leaky to begin with and much leakier by the time those five months were over. We had two seasons in that area of the jungle: the rainy one and the rainier one. This was in the rainier season. This tent had been given to Jim by somebody who probably wanted to throw it out but decided instead that: "The Lord laid it on my heart to give it to the missionaries." So Jim pitched the tent. He had not yet gotten around to digging a trench around the outside of it to keep the water from running into the tent when it rained, let alone put a floor in the tent, when he came down with hepatitis. Our honeymoon was over. The hepatitis lasted a good six weeks. It poured rain for the entire six weeks. I had no place to cook, no place to do much of anything. The legs of the bed that we'd brought along (a roll-away bed) were gradually sinking into the mud floor. It was what you might call a rigorous first six weeks of any marriage, let alone any missionary experience.

But there wasn't any question in our minds that we had been "called." What kind of a call would be necessary to get two people to a place like that? If it's the will of God, He has all kinds of ways of making that known to anyone who is listening. He cannot make it known to you unless you are listening. Nine times out of ten the call of God comes through human beings. It might seem like heresy to you, but if you study your Scriptures you'll find out that that's the way it happened most of the time. We do like to think about the pillars of cloud and fire and the angel visitations as the ways in which God is going to lead us, but God doesn't generally lead people that way. He didn't generally lead them that way even in Bible times.

When I wrote my little book on the guidance of God, *A Slow and Certain Light,* I read through the entire Bible to find out how God led people. I found out that He leads, generally, through other servants of His, and generally, while they are in the course of doing *ordinary* work. In the course of our duty God gets to us. When we are being obedient to the things that we *know,* then God can get our attention to show us the things that we don't know.

Jim had been called to Ecuador to work with Quichua Indians. The very fact that this Indian named Atanasio, who was not a Christian, expressed a need and said, in effect, "Come over into Puyupungu and help us," was all the call that was necessary. The three men considered it together. They knew that they could not possibly decline the invitation so they prayed about which one of the three should go. It was very simple. The call of God was narrowed down to Jim Elliot, first of all because Ed McCully did not speak Quichua at that time and he needed to live in a more civilized place so he wouldn't have too many other duties while learning Quichua. Pete Fleming was on the verge of going back to the states to get married and bring his bride back to Ecuador. He didn't think Puyupungu would be a very good place for her to start out since she had never been in the jungle. So it didn't leave many possibilities. Jim and I were the ones who went.

We then went to Shandia (where Jim had worked before) and continued with the work of the school and the literacy program, the translation of the Scriptures and teaching the believers. The call of God there was also a matter of very simple and very obvious needs. Neither Jim nor I had any medical training of any kind. When people came along with desperate medical needs and there weren't any doctors or nurses available, we found ourselves doing medical work. So one looks back on it and says, "That's what God called me to do." God also called us to do translation work and the school and the church and all these other things.

The day came when Nate Saint, pilot of the Missionary Aviation Fellowship, came to our station with a tremendously exciting piece of news. He had been serving our station and many others for years and, in the course of his flights over the jungle, was always looking out of the corner of his eye for Auca communities. Missionaries had been praying for Aucas for years. They had known the Aucas were there; they knew their reputation: they were savages. They killed all outsiders; no one had ever gone in there and come out alive. Many people had been praying for an opening for the gospel, so Nate was watching for Auca houses. He had seen several over the course of the years but they were abandoned. So, on that day in October of 1955, Nate told us that he had found an inhabited Auca house. There was no question that they were Aucas—they were stark naked and there were no other naked Indians in Ecuador. He could also see that their haircuts were different and the type of houses and plantations was different.

Jim was immediately "called" to the Auca Indians. How? By a very obvious, undeniable need. He was on the spot; he was in a place where he could participate in an attempt to reach the Aucas; he was willing, as he had heard about the Aucas many years before; and he was excited. It was exactly the kind of thing that Jim had always wanted to do. He had a very strong streak in him of what I would call romanticism, just as the Apostle Paul had. He wanted to name the name of Christ where it had never been named before. There's no reason why God should not take our personalities, our tastes, our particular propensities and desires and channel them in the course of His will. When we have already presented our bodies as a living sacrifice, everything in us has been given to God. Why shouldn't God use those dreams and romantic notions?

Jim had prayed that God would send him to the Aucas, so he believed he was called. Nate's call came because he saw the Auca houses. We might say that Jim's call came because Nate said, "I've seen an Auca house."

Nate and Jim were not going to do it by themselves. They needed a team. Who could go? There was already a team of men working with the Quichua Indians which included Ed McCully and Pete Fleming. Let me tell you what kind of men they were.

When I think of the men I knew on Wheaton campus, back in the 1940s, I can think of very few people that I would have considered less likely to become a missionary than Ed McCully. Ed was what we called a BMOC: big man on campus. I mean, everybody knew who Ed McCully was. To start with he was six foot three and dazzlingly handsome. He was a great football player; he was even a track man and, I think, a high jumper and a hurdler. I've forgotten all the things he did in sports (I wasn't the least bit interested in sports), but he was also president of the senior class and won the national championship in oratory. He was going to be a politician, and planned to go to law school. He majored in business administration. We all thought he would make a great politician. I remember when my brother, Dave Howard, was married we followed the bride and groom from Wheaton into Chicago, blowing the horns. Ed sat on the back of his open convertible, while somebody else drove, waving his bowler hat. Everybody in the Chicago slums that we drove through thought he was a politician. When the car stopped for a red light, Ed would jump out and shake hands with whoever was standing there and say, "Vote for Howard!" That's the kind of man he was.

Ed had become a very close friend of Jim's at Wheaton, but Jim was endlessly needling him. He

would say things like, "Well brother, how come you're
not going to the mission field?" Ed would say, "Well, I
don't believe God's called me to the mission field. I'm
going to be a politician." Jim would say, "You don't need
a call, you need a kick in the pants."

After Ed graduated he enrolled in law school and
took a job as a night clerk in a hotel in order to spend
some of his time studying. Jim visited him there and
said, "Brother, why aren't you spending about half of
your time during these long, quiet nights reading the
Bible?" So Ed began to do that. In a sense, Jim Elliot
called Ed McCully to be a missionary. Ed ended up in
the jungle.

Jim was hoping that Ed and he would be sent out
together. The Lord sent people out two-by-two, so Jim
had been praying for a long time for someone to go
along. He was quite convinced that it was not to be a
wife; not at least until he had spent some time in the
jungle, so he prayed for a buddy. Then Ed disappointed
him by getting married, so Jim prayed for another partner. He knew a man in Seattle who had a master's
degree in literature from the University of Washington
and was headed for a teaching career. His name was
Pete Fleming. Jim went to visit him and said, "How
come you're not going to the mission field?" Pete was
called to missions.

These three men in 1955 were working together
with the Quichuas. After a good deal of prayer and con-
sideration and discussion with their wives, they all
agreed to go to the Aucas. It was not a frivolous or light
decision, by any means, because the men were fully
aware of the risks they would be taking. They did go.
And they were killed.

Were they *called*? Were they called to *Ecuador*?
Were they called to the *Quichuas*? Were they called to
the *Aucas*? Were they called *to be killed*? Were they
called to stir up people back in the United States?

I believe that we can say yes to all of these questions,

but I think it's very easy for people to think that there has to be something terribly esoteric, terribly spiritual, terribly unusual about the ways in which God calls people.

In Acts 11, beginning with verse 19, Luke says, "Now those who had been scattered by the persecution in connection with Stephen traveled as far as Phoenicia, Cyprus and Antioch, telling the message only to Jews. Some of them, however, men from Cyprus and Cyrene, went to Antioch and began to speak to Greeks also, telling them the good news about the Lord Jesus. The Lord's hand was with them, and a great number of people believed and turned to the Lord. News of this reached the ears of the church at Jerusalem, and they sent Barnabas to Antioch. When he arrived and saw the evidence of the grace of God, he was glad and encouraged them all to remain true to the Lord with all their hearts. He was a good man, full of the Holy Spirit and faith, and a great number of people were brought to the Lord. Then Barnabas went to Tarsus to look for Saul, and when he found him, he brought him to Antioch. So for a whole year Barnabas and Saul met with the church and taught great numbers of people" (Acts 11:19-26).

Who called people to Phoenicia, Cyprus, and Antioch? It was God, wasn't it? But it was through the persecution that arose over the death of Stephen, what might be called an ordinary human circumstance. The persecuted Christians were scattered to Phoenicia, Cyprus, and Antioch. There they managed to bring the message to Jews. But there were some natives of Cyprus and Cyrene among them. When they arrived at Antioch these began to speak to Gentiles, telling them the good news of the Lord Jesus. So God "called" these Gentiles *through* the Cypriots and the Cyrenians.

Then verse 22 says, "News of this reached the ears of the church at Jerusalem, and they sent Barnabas to Antioch." *Who* sent Barnabas to Antioch? It was God, wasn't it? God sent Barnabas to Antioch *through* the operation of the church in Jerusalem. When he got there he set to work. Soon he was off to call Paul to Antioch.

That looked like quite an ordinary sequence of events, didn't it? When I think of the way in which God called me to the mission field, it was quite similar to that, really. But the call starts with a willing heart. It starts with a person who gets down on his knees and says, "Lord, here is my body. I present it to you as a living sacrifice. Everything in it, everything I've got, everything I am or will ever be is yours forever." You've got to be willing and you've got to be listening.

These early church people were called. They were Christians, already committed to Christ. Cypriots and Cyrenians went to Antioch and spoke to Gentiles. The Gentiles believed. The news went to Jerusalem. Barnabas was sent to Antioch to get Saul. He brought him to Antioch. They had the willingness to do.

There has to be the life of obedience which starts the minute you get up off your knees. You don't get down on your knees and say, "Lord, here I am: all of me for you forever," then get up and start doing your own thing. You say, "Lord, what is it you want me to do?" and you go out and you do that thing *now*. God is not going to call you to the jungle of Ecuador today, that is, He doesn't want you to *go* today. He might call you today. Maybe He's already called you. But He does call you to do *something* today in obedience. It is the doing of *that* thing that puts you on the road to the will of God. You are already there. You are in touch with God. That obedience will open the way for the next thing He calls you to do, and the next thing, and the next thing.

Were these four men called? Yes, they were. Nate, Jim, Ed, and Pete responded to God's call. As they began to plan their strategy for reaching the Aucas they felt they really needed a five-man team. They were going to camp on the edge of Auca territory, letting the Aucas know they were there, hoping the Aucas would come to them. They all felt it was a good idea to have three men on the beach all the time and two flying in and out. Nate, the pilot, couldn't spend the night there with the plane because the river might rise in the night. Landing a plane on a sand spit is a very touchy business, so Nate wanted a man to fly out with him. Nate said, "You know, the guy I have the greatest respect for among jungle missionaries is Roger Youdarian. He's working with the Jívaro Indians. He's just opened up a new area among the headshrinkers that has never been touched before." Missionaries had been with the Jívaros for years, but nobody had ever been to this area. "Rog is a man with a heart for the Lord," Nate said. "I think he would want to participate, so I'll ask him." And guess what? God called Roger Youdarian.

The second question is, *Did the five men obey the call of God?* God's call starts with a willingness to do. But it continues with a life of obedience in everyday duties. Obedience includes a whole lot of things besides preaching the gospel and translating the Bible and landing on sand spits in the middle of nowhere to reach naked savages. Obedience to Jesus Christ means saying no to yourself.

There's no question in my mind that these five men obeyed. Here was a need that they were capable of meeting. They were in the right place to meet it. They were willing. It is as simple as that.

Are you willing to go? Do you see a need? Are you capable and willing to respond to that need?

Romans 1:6-7 says, "And you also are among those who are called to belong to Jesus Christ. To all in Rome who are loved by God and called to be saints: Grace and peace to you from God our Father and from the Lord Jesus Christ." The word *call* occurs twice. How did Paul know that they were God's called and dedicated people? Because he'd heard evidence of their faith and of their obedience. When you start obeying God, you will *know* you are called.

It can get very confusing to try to sort out the theological problem of the sovereignty of God and the free will of man. His sovereignty is His business. It is a wonderful thing and it's a very fortifying and steadying doctrine to hang onto, and I'm grateful for it. But I also know that when it comes to the call of God, my response, my obedience, and my willingness are bound up with the gift of freedom that God has given to me to choose. I may choose to obey and I may choose to disobey. When I have obeyed, then, of course, I look back and say, "I sought the Lord." But afterward I knew He moved my soul to seek *Him* seeking *me*. He called me. The only reason I was willing, the only reason I was obedient, the only reason I responded was because I had been called—already called—by God. But I didn't know that *until I started moving in that direction.*

Are you interested in missions? Are you willing to go? Is there an opportunity presented to you at this particular juncture in your life when you have to make decisions, to meet a need that you just conceivably might be able to meet? I've told you about five men: Pete Fleming who was going to get a Ph.D. in English; Ed McCully who was a champion orator; Jim Elliot—I didn't tell you all of his qualifications, but he was a champion wrestler among other things; Nate Saint who was a very skillful pilot; Roger Youdarian who was a paratrooper in World War II. They all sound like fantastic people. But they were very ordinary guys most of the time. They had very ordinary sins and very ordinary difficulties. Not one of them thought to himself, "I'm really cut out to be a missionary. I'll make a good one." I'm sure of that. I've read their journals; I've known all but Roger personally. They had the same doubts you may have: "Oh, but what if this happens?" "I'm not so sure I can take that!" "Who do I think I am, going out to be a missionary? I'm not sure if God has really called me. What if I make a mistake?"

Second Corinthians 3:4-6 says, "Such confidence as

this is ours through Christ before God. Not that we are competent to claim anything for ourselves, but our competence comes from God. He has made us competent as ministers of a new covenant—not of the letter but of the Spirit; for the letter kills, but the Spirit gives life." *"Not that we are competent to claim anything for ourselves."*

In the very next chapter, 2 Corinthians 4:7 it says, "We have this treasure in jars of clay to show that this all-surpassing power is from God and not from us." "Jars of clay!" If ever there was a missionary who was painfully and acutely conscious of being a clay pot, it was I when I lived with those Auca Indians; the conditions under which I lived; the apparent hopelessness of ever getting *anything* across to these people, let alone the gospel, made me believe that my "competence comes from God" and God alone. I was a clay pot. There was no question of being qualified in myself but I heard the call of God. I was willing. I had put my life on the line and what did I have inside? This first verse tells us: a treasure. Phillips translation calls it a "priceless" treasure. This proves that the transcendent power does not come from us but is God's alone.

Did we obey? Yes, by the grace of God. Nothing else. Not because we were so spiritual; not because all our lives we had seen visions and heard voices and had any terribly unusual qualifications, but we have a priceless treasure.

Finally, was it worth it? Five men with those kinds of qualifications had to die? Five men who were the husbands of young wives and four of them the fathers of very small children? (Nine children were left fatherless when they died.) The Auca group that was responsible for killing the men numbered exactly sixty people altogether. I know; I counted them. Five men did the actual killing. I know each one personally. I have tapes that they've given me. Does that make sense to you—that God would let Jim and Ed and Pete, the only male missionaries in Ecuador who spoke Quichua at that time and were in contact, potentially, with ten thousand Quichua Indians; Rog who was in contact with ten thousand Jívaros; Nate who served all the jungle stations—does it make sense that they should die for the sake of sixty people? By whose standards can we answer that question?

Well, we say, lots of Aucas got saved. You've probably heard stories about all the Aucas becoming Christians. I've heard stories of thousands of volunteers to the mission field. I'm not sure where they are. I know there are some. I know that thousands of people were stirred up. I still meet people everywhere I go who tell me that they remember the story: they were moved by it; they've been changed by it. Hundreds of young men have told me that the book *Shadow of the Almighty* has changed their lives, that it had a greater influence on them than any other book outside of the Bible. I don't deny that for a moment. Suppose it's all true. Suppose every Auca got saved. Suppose there were thousands of volunteers for the mission field of which several hundred got there. Does that make it worth it?

Let's suppose, for a moment, that not one Auca got saved; that not one person ever heard the story of those five men, let alone was changed by it. Would it be worth it? Yes! Why? "Unless a kernel of wheat falls to the ground and dies, it remains only a single seed. But if it dies, it produces many seeds" (John 12:24), or as King James puts it, "much fruit." Now, you and I are accustomed to thinking of fruit in terms of souls or volunteers for the mission field. That is one kind of fruit, but that's not the only kind. Some of the fruit is invisible. Some of the fruit we're never going to hear about until we get to heaven. Probably most of it. That's my conviction. Here's a little handful over here that were stirred and went to the mission field. Wonderful, praise God for that! Here's a little tribe of Indians, maybe a 100 percent of them got saved. I don't know. Praise God for that, but that is not my business. The results of my obedience to God are the business of Almighty God who is sovereign. My part is to be willing to be that seed that falls into the ground and dies.

I've heard people say, "I think I'd just die if the Lord asked me to go to the mission field!" Know what I'd say to that? You won't be much use out there unless you do. Nobody wants you out there if you're not willing to die, and I mean to die daily. You're not going to be of any use to anybody if you haven't already died to yourself and presented your body as a living sacrifice. Don't bother to go to the mission field.

There's a little story in *Those Strange Ashes* that I heard an African tell. I wish I could track down the source of the story. I'm sure it's only a legend about Jesus and His disciples.

"One day Jesus asked each of His disciples to pick up a stone to carry for Him. John took the biggest one he could find, while Peter picked a small one. Jesus took them up to the top of a mountain and commanded the stones to be made bread. Each was allowed to eat the bread he found in his hands, but of course Peter did not get enough. John then shared some of his with Peter. On another occasion Jesus again asked the disciples to carry stones for Him, but this time, instead of leading them to a mountaintop, he took them to the River Jordan. "Cast the stones into the river," was His command this time. The disciples looked at one another in bewilderment. What could be the point? They had lugged those stones all this way (and you know who picked the big one this time, don't you?). Throw them in the river? Why? But they obeyed. Jesus turned to them and said, "For whom did you carry the stone?"

The love of Christ constrains us. There is no other motivation for missionary service that is going to survive the blows of even the first year. You do it for *Him*. The love of Christ constrains us. Get that straight.

"Lord, I'll do it for you, regardless of whether I see the fruit, regardless of whether I get the bread to eat myself, regardless of what disposal you may make of my gifts."

God disposed of that mission station which Jim had worked on for a whole year—all those buildings right down the river in one night. He disposed of five men who were, according to some other older missionaries in Ecuador, among the finest that they had ever known. One older man said to me, "Why didn't God take me? I can't do anything compared to what these men could do." God knows what He's doing.

Were they called? That's my question. The answer is: they were called. Are you?

Did they obey? They did. They knew that they had been called. Will you obey?

Was it worth it? "The world and its desires pass away, but the man who does the will of God lives forever" (1 John 2:17). It was worth it.

"Teach us, good Lord, to give and not to count the cost; to toil and not to seek for rest; to labor and to ask for no reward, save that of knowing that we do Thy will, O Lord our God. Amen" (the prayer of Loyola).

8

THE MISSIONARY'S PERSONAL WALK WITH CHRIST

Robert B. Munger

How important is a personal walk with God, a close relationship, a fellowship with Him, a life lived in and by and for and with Jesus Christ? A walk that is expressed in Psalm 27:7-8 (RSV),[1] "Hear, O Lord, when I cry aloud, be gracious to me and answer me! Thou hast said, 'Seek ye my face.' My heart says to thee, 'Thy face, Lord, do I seek.'" The *New International Version* says it this way, "My heart says of you, 'Seek his face!' Your face, Lord, I will seek."

The importance of a walk with God, a personal relationship to God, can be seen in *creation, redemption, intercession,* and *fellowship with the Body.*

CREATION

The wonder of the world and humanity was forced upon the astronauts on their return to earth from their moon walk. Nearly all of them came back from the moon impressed with the contrast between the moonscape and the beautiful orb of earth. The moonscape, which is drab, colorless, absolutely lifeless, was surrounded with darkness and the vast emptiness of space.

Then, as they approached earth, the astronauts saw this beautiful blue and white orb floating there in space. It was fragile, delicate, and yet, in this envelope of atmosphere, it was protected both from the frigid cold and intense heat and also from the lethal rays of the atmosphere. They knew, under that envelope of atmosphere and that blue and white globe, that it was pulsating with life. It was full of color. It was teaming with multiplied forms of life and, most marvelous of all, on that little speck of cosmic dust were human beings, capable of intelligence, love, and purpose, who could, in their creativeness, bring about a spaceship and travel to the moon. As far as we know, there is nothing like earth anywhere in the solar system or in the universe.

What was the purpose of this creation? Why is this unique earth here? Above all, if there is a purpose to anything, why is human life, personality, here? This was what impressed some of the astronauts upon their return. At Christmas one of them read the first verses of Genesis: "In the beginning, *God* created the heavens and the earth."

So we go back to God's purpose in creation and we understand that the highest level of His creation was human personality—with a capacity to know Him, to walk with Him; not with only intelligence, and emotion, and volition, but a spiritual being who could grasp the concept of a personal God and respond, in trust, love and obedience. Human personality is the climax in Genesis 1:27: "God created man in his own image, in the image of God he created him; male and female he created them." Theologians have pointed out that the grace and the love of God are as evident in the creation of man as in the redemption of man, because why else would God want creatures if not to respond to Him and to be in relationship to Him? The fact that we are alive is sheer grace, there is nothing compulsory in natural law to bring about human personality. Even the evolutionist is perplexed. How does he account for this?

REDEMPTION

On this marvelous spaceship earth are human beings. What is implicit in creation is explicit in *redemption*. Ephesians 1 has a great concept, beginning with verse 3: "Blessed be the God and Father of our Lord Jesus Christ, who has blessed us in Christ with every spiritual blessing in the heavenly places . . . [By the way, I think that "in the heavenly places" might be understood as "in the *real* world of God," not the world we so often think is real, but in the *real* world of God.] "He destined us in love to be his sons through Jesus Christ, according to the purpose of his will, to the praise of his glorious grace which he freely bestowed on us in the Beloved" (1:3,5-6). He purposed us to be sons and daughters. So, on this tiny planet Earth, whirling about in cosmic space, God has brought into being human beings with a capacity to love Him, to respond to Him, to be creative, to serve Him, and to reflect His nature.

Why do parents desire children? Some of you have children; some of you are anticipating, in due course, that God may grant you children. Why would you want children? To do the errands? Mow the lawn? Wash the car? Help you with the housework? Well, that may help, but if that's what you want children for, you're going to be disillusioned sooner or later. The reason you want children is so they may respond to you with some understanding of how you feel about them, that they might be with you in relationship as trusting, loving children and grow into adulthood to return to you as peers in close relationship. I believe that's what God is after from His created beings.

Then we need to understand that though God is a missionary God, and He calls us in grace to be part with Him in His redemptive work, that is not, in my humble judgment, the most important thing He's after. He's after your heart. He longs for *you* because He is Father. This is where His desire lies.

This desire is seen in our redemption, "God so loved the world that he gave His only begotten Son." "God shows his love for us in that while we were yet sinners Christ died for us" (Rom. 5:8). The gospel came to the first Christians with an overwhelming sense of the sheer, incomprehensible love of God for them. They discovered that they mattered to God. They were important to God. He wanted them with Him. Out of the relationship flowed their eagerness of service.

"The love of Christ controls us; because we are convinced that one has died for all; therefore, all have died. And he died for all, that those who live might live no longer for themselves but for him who for their sake died and was raised" (2 Cor. 5:14-15). There arose a tremendous sense that they mattered to God. They understood that the Father who had stood waiting, looking down the road to the far country, longing for His prodigal race to return, had embraced the prodigal, returned him to the Father's house, washed, cleansed, welcomed, and renewed. He was seated at a banquet table, recognized as the son of the household, not a servant but a son, celebrating with joy that they were together again in the family.

Let us never substitute work for worship; service for fellowship; commitment to His cause for companionship with His heart. Early in my ministry I recognized that I was being forced to make a decision. What would be primary in my relationship to God? Would I be a son or a servant? If I was going to be a son, then relationship is primary. God wants sons to be with Him.

We should pity the elder brother who so misread his father that he thought his only worth to the father was work in the field. If you get on that kick, you're going to be just like the elder brother: working, sometimes resentful that God doesn't give you the goodies you'd really like to have in ministry, not seeing that He is giving you Himself and calling you to His own heart in order that, from that, you may go out. I'm sure the prodigal worked in the field, but he also sat at the table. We do not want these reversed, no matter what the task, what the challenge, what the crisis, what the difficulty, what the urgency. Let me hear it again: "Thou hast said, 'Seek ye my face.' My heart says to thee, 'Thy face, Lord, do I seek'" (Ps. 27:8).

If that's true in creation and redemption, it's true also in the call of Christ for those to follow Him. We see this portrayed in the life of our Lord. He models this. Our Lord had a very responsible task—to fulfill for us all righteousness and to accomplish the work of redemption. Three short years of ministry after His anointing and the entrance into the ministry (even Jesus was anointed for ministry before He entered it) Jesus sought the Father's face a great while before day out in a desert place, again in solitude, but with the Father. I'm sure He had much, redemptively, to pray about.

INTERCESSION

I think the ministry of our Lord flowed out of the life of *intercession*. Luke makes that very clear. He always relates prayer and the Holy Spirit together, never separate. Jesus prayed not only for ministry in the Spirit but, in a sense, to commune with the Father. The disciples saw Him praying. They were so moved at both the reality of His prayer and what flowed from it that they said, "Lord, teach us to pray. We want to pray just like that. It's so hard for us to pray, so difficult for us to have anything happen there and you seem to be in converse with God, with your Father. Teach us to pray like that." Jesus said, after this manner (and Luke is so marvelous here), "Say Abba." Say, "My own dear Father, Abba": not "High and Holy One" or "Oh, Mighty Creator." We need to have reverence, true; but "Abba" right here with me, knowing me, caring for me, loving me, hearing me, embracing me, being a Father to me. Say, "Father" and let prayer and ministry flow out of that.

In that dark night before His crucifixion, His fearful disciples gathered around Him and He said, "The hour is coming, indeed it has come, when you will be scattered, every man to his home, and will leave me alone; yet I am not alone, for the Father is with me" (John 16:32). At the deepest level of His consciousness, Jesus knew He was never alone. He confessed that the works He did, the words He said, were not from Him, but from the Father. He was with the Father.

In that terrible hour when He bore our sins, when fellowship with the Father was ruptured as He endured the pangs of hell for us, there came that cry, "My God, why have you forsaken me?" He endured that hell for you and me that we might never be forsaken of the Father and never have the Father's face turned from us. This is the glory of our sonship in Christ: the Father's face is always there, looking at us, loving us, knowing us, *for* us. You can count on that. Jesus died for that and rose again. Say, "Father." He's yours.

Are we too busy to seek the Father's face? Is there too much work to do today to spend a little time at the Father's table, talking about our day, seeing it in the perspective of His understanding, looking to Him for resources? You say, "But, I have so many things . . . there's a lost world out there." Notice how Jesus walked through His three brief years of ministry? I don't see Him hurrying under a pressure of time, saying, "Man, if I don't get out of Capernaum, over there to a certain town by tomorrow, then umpteen people are not going to hear the Word." No. He spent a morning apart, early (Mark 1:35-36), and then He said, "We must go to other places. We don't need to stay here now. The Father has another place on our agenda." He was free in spirit to move without feeling guilty.

Theodore Bovier, the Swiss psychiatrist who is now gone to be with the Lord, has a little book on *Take Time and Be Free.* We are all under the tyranny of time. He

said that the only way we can transcend time and be
free is by fellowship with the Eternal. Isn't that good?
You want to be free from time? Then spend time with
the Eternal and look at life through His perspective. Too
busy for One who really cares about you?

My colleague at Fuller, Bill Panell, had his office just
across the hall from me. When he was in Detroit ministering in the innercity, he said that one day he was playing with his two boys, ages six and eight, in the fresh
snow, making a snowman and wrestling. He had a
great time with his two boys. He then came in and had
supper and was refreshed and went out to the assignment of the evening. While he was driving his car he
thought to himself, "How great my children are! Isn't it
just great? They really turn me on." Then he meditated
a bit and raised a tremulous question. He said, "Oh,
God! Do I turn you on?" Yes! What turns the Father on?
Work? Well, He's pleased when the son or daughter
takes responsibility and helps Him in the work, but
what a father wants is the joy of being with his child.

I think this is seen even in Jesus' call to the disciples. He said, "Follow me and I will make you fishers of
men." He calls us to be colleagues in the work and
makes it clear that it is in relationship with Him that
our ministry finds fulfillment, not apart from Him. In
respect to the vine and the branches, a branch does not
bear fruit apart from the vine. Jesus said, "Apart from
me, you can do nothing," nothing redemptive that lasts
for eternity. He is the giver of life. He is the mighty
worker. Who do we think we are anyway? If I have
brains enough and energy enough and dedication
enough, I can build God's Kingdom! Don't kid yourself.
There's only one builder of the Kingdom—that's God,
Himself. We are permitted to share in that through
Jesus Christ our Lord.

Too often, you know, we get a keen sense of mission.
Thank God for that. Then we think that we can accomplish the mission by hurrying off to some far corner of

the world and working ourselves to death for Almighty
God and for the gospel, only to find that we've burned
out or something. We don't see the mission realized. We
wonder, "Where's God?" No, you see, it's reversed. We go
to God and *with* God into ministry, not first into ministry and then ask God to help us. That's why solitude,
the wilderness, alone with God, time with God to get
acquainted with Him, to know who He is, to know who
you are, are so important.

FELLOWSHIP WITH THE BODY

If it's true with the branch and the vine, it's true
with the member and the Body. How does the hand
respond to the impulse of the mind? It's related organi-
cally to other members of the body but it's connected
with the head. A hand cut off from the body and separated from the head simply does not function.

So He calls us to be colleagues in ministry and mission and He calls us to be comrades and companions of
the heart. Mark 3:14 says that He chose twelve that they
might be with Him, or it could be translated "that they
might be His companions." John brings this out so
beautifully in the thirteenth chapter of his Gospel:
"Having loved his own which were in the world, He loved
them to the end," or, in the *New International Version*,
He "showed them the full extent of his love" (v. 1). He
laid aside His robe, took the towel and basin, washed
their feet and gave them a model of how they should
love one another. But He did this because He loved
them. "Greater love has no man than this, that a man
lay down his life for his friends" (John 15:13). I don't
catch from that that we are to be dutiful servants. In
fact, Jesus makes that quite clear, "No longer do I call
you servants, . . . but . . . friends" (v. 15). Charles E.
Finney used to storm the woods with the gospel. He
said, "God has no slaves." Are you slaving in the work?
Do you get up in the morning oppressed with the feeling of duty, "I've *got* to do this; I've *got* to do that"? Then

you're not free. I'm a son. I'm not a servant. I do what my Father bids me to do; what I see my Saviour wanting me to do out of the constraint of desire, of love.

Do you know the difference between a housekeeper and a housewife? You better know the difference! A housekeeper may do everything in the house that a housewife may do, but she may not do it out of love, out of companionship of the heart.

Friends identify with the same purpose and with the same mission. So, when Jesus calls us friends, it's not as though we have no part in His ministry. The closer I am in friendship, the closer I am to the responsibilities, the visions, and the burdens of my friend. I want to be with my friend. Even as Jesus wants to be our Friend in our lives, I want to be with Him in His life.

Looking back at the Student Volunteer Movement, we see surfacing, again and again, a personal devotion to Jesus Christ. Samuel Zwemer was one of those in the later years. He was a great Christian layman, one of the early Christian strategists and missionary leaders for nearly fifty years. Editor of the *Moslem World* magazine, and a prodigious scholar, he was a faithful, hardworking missionary. Do you know how he penetrated Arabia? I found out during my last year in seminary.

Samuel Zwemer retired from the field and accepted a position as a professor of missions. He gave a course on the unoccupied fields of the world, which I took in my senior year. There were only six or eight of us in the class so he invited us to meet in his study. We sat in a little circle around this veteran missionary and he told us story after story of those early years on the field. You couldn't get any visa into Arabia at the time. There were *no* Christians allowed in—none at all. Neither could he get a passport from his own government, no official permission granted. So, he said, "If a board will not let you go, punch a hole in the board!" He got into Arabia by taking a steamer down through the eastern side of Arabia. When they came to the town of Bahrain (no Europeans there at all at that time), the captain said, "We have to leave at high tide. Be back here by a certain time—3:00 P.M.—if you're not here, we're going to sail without you."

Zwemer left the ship to stroll through the town. He got one of the people on the dock to get his belongings from the ship when nobody was looking and to carry them far enough away so they wouldn't be looking for him. He waited until he saw the ship sail out of the harbor. That's how he entered Arabia! Here was a pioneer! You know what he told me and the others in that class? "There's only one reason that I was able to stay forty years in Arabia and see only as many converts as I can count on the fingers of one hand. I did it because I loved Jesus and I wanted to please Him." If you are going out in mission and this is your motive, you're going to be looking for Him. You're going to seek His face. You're going to want Him and you'll find Him.

It's never been my privilege to serve on the mission field. I tried to go out and they wouldn't let me. I didn't punch a hole, I stayed! But I can remember when I moved from a fraternity house at the University of California, Berkeley, to the Moody Bible Institute. Now *that* was a culture shock! I didn't know anybody who was engaged in any kind of full-time Christian work. I had seen some, but I didn't know them. I didn't know anything about Chicago or about ministry. I can remember taking an evening train; when the train went around the corner around Richmond, I saw the lights of San Francisco and the Bay disappear and I knew I was away. I sat there all alone in the car, feeling very sorry for myself. I didn't know where I was going. I didn't know what was out there. I felt very depressed; but it was a gift of God, I think. My mind got ahold of the words of Jesus, again burned into me. He said, "All authority in heaven and on earth has been given to me . . . and lo, I am with you always" . . . any place, any time, any situation, "I am with you always."

That was a long time ago. He has kept His promise. I can't say that I've always sought His face, but I do know that when in repentance and faith and prayer I have sought His face, His face has come. My highest desire is not souls. It's not even establishing churches (I'm speaking for myself). The thing I want above everything else is the smile of His face, "Well done, I'm glad. This is what I want you to be." That's held me steady, even in times when I couldn't see anything around me that would be encouraging. Count Von Zinzendorf said it long ago as that marvelous Moravian missionary movement really sprung from Zinzendorf's leadership: "I have one passion. It is He, Christ."

"Thou hast said, 'Seek ye my face.' . . . 'Thy face, Lord, do I seek" (Ps. 27:8).

Note
1. Unless otherwise indicated, Scripture quotations in this chapter are from the *Revised Standard Version* of the Bible.

9

FIRST YEAR ON THE FIELD AS A MISSIONARY
Warren W. Webster

I spent sixteen years as a missionary living in Sind. That's the name of a desert province in Pakistan where we worked among the Sindhi people. Before going we spent some time preparing linguistically to work with people whose languages were not fully written or who didn't have complete Bible translations. Through my studies in linguistics, anthropology, and communications, I became convinced that all of us as Christians are called to translate the gospel into life. Some Christians are better translators than others, some are more effective than others, but every believer is called to communicate the gospel of Jesus Christ in his sphere of influence. Perhaps you recall the unknown poet who put it this way:

You are writing a gospel, a chapter each day
By things that you do and words that you say.
Men read what you write, whether faithless or true.
Say, what is the gospel according to *you*?

EARLY LESSONS IN COMMUNICATION

I want to begin by sharing some lessons that will stand you in good stead as you prepare to be an effective translator of the gospel into life.

The Most Important Dimension

The first lesson I learned really came to me as part of my preparation before going. It was while I was at the Summer Institute of Linguistics in Norman, Oklahoma. In a chapel service one day, a veteran Wycliffe missionary from Mexico said to the young students studying linguistics: "The most difficult part of missions is not slogging up the jungles of the Amazon or crossing the deserts of Central Asia. The most difficult and most important aspect of communicating the gospel is in getting it across the last eighteen inches, after you get there."

The journey in getting to the destination and staying there may be rigorous and demanding, but you and I succeed or fail as ambassadors for Jesus Christ—on American campuses, in our U.S. neighborhoods, or overseas—in terms of how well we get the gospel across the "last eighteen inches" that separate us from lost men and women everywhere. It's in those face-to-face personal situations that communication really matters.

Seek to be a good communicator, not just through the impersonal use of literature and the media. Learn to be an effective communicator in one-on-one, face-to-face, "eighteen-inch" situations separating you from people who need to know Jesus Christ. That was the first lesson I learned in effective communication: the importance of the last foot and a half. A missionary really doesn't accomplish much to go halfway around the world to central Asia if he fails to get the gospel across the last foot and a half. He might as well have stayed home and spared himself the difficulty and the expense of the first ten thousand miles of the journey.

Love—A Universal Language

The second lesson that I learned is that love and friendship are a universal language and they are basic to effective communication of the gospel. You can go overseas working for a company or for the government and communicate without loving people or being particularly friendly. You won't enjoy it as much. You may not be a great success, but you can be a communicator of sorts. You cannot, however, be an ambassador of the King of kings without speaking the language of love. The gospel is communicated best through love and through friendship.

I became convinced of this before I went overseas. I think I learned it from my father. He was a godly man, president of a mission board, and pastor of a large university church. During his ministry he saw scores of young men and women go into the ministry and into missions. I remember Dad telling about one of his pastorates in the midwest where he saw a young couple come to Christ. They didn't seem to have a lot of gifts and abilities. They weren't the kind that you would pick to be the sponsors of the youth group, or even be Sunday School teachers, at least not as such young Christians. But they had a concern for their friends who didn't know Jesus Christ. Shortly after they became Christians they set a goal to reach another young couple they knew. They invited them into their home. They did things with them. Their children played together; the wives sometimes went shopping; the husbands went fishing or hunting. They had family picnics. Pretty soon the Christian life that had so changed this one home began to rub off on the other family as they heard thanks given before meals and saw the children tucked in bed at night with Bible stories and prayer. Gradually the first family began to bring the other couple to church with them. Within about a year they saw their friends accept Jesus Christ.

What did the first family do then? Did they drop their friends as new Christians? No, they went on befriending and discipling them, but they also showed them how to reach out to others through friendship and love. In the meantime, they turned toward another family of their acquaintance and began to spend time with them until within about a year they won that family to the Lord. During the seven years my father was in that church in Iowa, he said that on an average of once a year, that first couple won another couple to Jesus Christ, through friendship and evangelism.

I went to Pakistan convinced that love and friendship are basic to gospel communication.

Language Learning

We arrived in Sind shortly after the partition of India and Pakistan. Millions of Muslim refugees had flooded into the country and filled all available space so that housing was very difficult to find. Three families of us went as a team to begin work and witness among the Sindhi people. The only place we could locate for living accommodations was an old house that Hindus had left when they fled to India. It was in a bad part of town across from a large brothel. The old house was owned by one of the prostitutes who used it as a barn to house water buffalo. She sold their milk to the tea stall in the brothel to earn extra money. We offered her about fifteen or twenty dollars a month (which must have been more than she was making from the milk she was selling) and she agreed to move the buffalo. We scooped the place out, white-washed the walls, and then three families moved into a house that had three rooms. One room became a bathroom with a commode and a tin tub for bathing. Alongside we stacked the baggage and supplies for three families. One family had two children so they got a whole room to themselves. The other two families—my wife and I with our two-year-old daughter, and the other couple with their two-year-old son—

divided the third room by putting a canvas tarpaulin across the middle. We lived communally out on the porch where our wives did the cooking and we ate meals together. That was how we began in Pakistan.

I remember one day working out in the courtyard in front of our house. I was turning a packing crate into a simple little desk that I could work at—pounding it apart, sawing it up, and putting it back together. Some of the neighborhood children, who really should have been in school but weren't, came around and walked into the open courtyard. They were amused to see these white-skinned foreigners who had just moved in. They were very friendly, chattering among themselves, looking at me and pointing and smiling. I tried to laugh and smile back! But that was all I could do. They were talking away and I didn't know what they were saying. It was really very frustrating. I wanted them to know that I wanted to be their friend. But how do you tell people that in your first week in a new country with a strange language?

After a bit I decided that since I couldn't speak their language I'd speak my own. So I turned to the boys, smiled real big and said, "Hello!" You should have seen the reaction I got! Their smiling faces turned to frowns; they jumped back like I'd shot them with a gun; and they looked at each other in perplexity. I couldn't figure it out. There I was convinced that friendship is a universal language but when I tried to be friendly all I did was turn them off! I really wrestled with that. I went back sawing my boards and pounding away and after a while, when they saw that I wasn't dangerous, they grouped around again. I had to try being friendly once more. Again I turned to the boys and smiled even bigger than before and said, "Hello!" When I got the same startled reaction I gave it up as a bad job, took my saw and hammer into the house and the boys went away.

A couple of nights later, the Lord sent to our place a Pakistani visitor. He came by night, like Nicodemus. He was a businessman who spoke English and said he wanted to meet us and welcome us to the community. But he was quick to add, "I had to come at night because you live in such a bad neighborhood. I didn't dare be seen in this street during the daytime." He did prove to be very friendly and very helpful. He told us where to buy milk that didn't have water mixed in it. He told us how to get a rope-strung bed made and what we ought to pay for it.

He answered many questions that we had and asked if there was anything else we wanted to know. I immediately thought of those boys I tried to be friendly with: "The other day some boys came in here playing. They were very friendly until I began to speak to them and then they suddenly became silent and very serious. I don't know why."

"How could you speak to them?" he inquired. "You don't know our Sindhi language."

"No, I spoke English."

"Well, what did you say?"

"You know, in America, when we meet someone we often say, 'Hello.' It means 'Hi, how are you?' or 'Good morning.'"

"Oh yes," he said, "I know. The unusual thing is that we have a similar sounding word in our Sindhi language. But in Sindhi it doesn't mean 'Good morning,' it means 'Scram! Get out of here!'"

Then I began to understand. There I was a big grinning American, smilingly saying, "Hello, Hello" which came across to them as "Scram! Get out of here!"

That was the day I learned my third lesson in effective communication. I still believe in the importance of getting our message across the last eighteen inches. I'm still convinced that love and friendship are basic to doing it, but that day I learned that a missionary had better get to work and learn the language of people if he eventually hopes to communicate the gospel to them.

This is true even on the American scene. To reach

another with the gospel you've got to talk his language. That's why students, for example, are more effective in witnessing to fellow students than some of us missionaries may be who come back from another culture or from another era. Identification calls for learning the language of people in order to communicate to them effectively.

So, we went to work to learn the Sindhi language. There was no language school available. Several of us had received Wycliffe training and had some idea how to go about learning a language. Let me say, for your encouragement, that even if you got a *C* in Spanish or French and did poorly with Latin, it doesn't necessarily mean you'll be a failure in learning the language once you are immersed in another culture. If you've learned to speak English, one of the world's hardest and most irregular languages, you can probably learn any language in the world. Be encouraged!

The way languages are taught in many high schools and colleges in America is not very effective. On the other hand, some of them are quite up-to-date in their methods. Linguists know that, in general, the best way to learn a language is the way you did as a child. You should hear it before you try to speak it. You should be able to speak some of it before you try to read it. You should be able to read it before you try to write it. That might not be as necessary if you are learning a European language written in the Roman alphabet, but if you are learning Arabic or Japanese or Chinese or Korean, those principles are basically valid.

Drs. Thomas and Elizabeth Brewster wrote a book titled *Language Acquisition Made Practical*. One of the things they call for in THE LAMP method is to get away from the "junk pile" approach (dictionaries, grammars, and vocabulary cards) so as to get out among the people and begin to use what you are learning.

One of our young missionaries was on his way to Zaire and had to go first to Europe to study French. He took a couple of hours in a standard language school each morning but he supplemented it with the LAMP approach which, for him, involved an afternoon tour of an area along the River Seine where he disciplined himself every day to try to converse in French with at least twenty people. He stopped at the flower vendor's shop, next at the bookstore, and then at the milk seller's shop. Sometimes he took his little son or daughter along and used them as the subject of conversation. When you are learning a language if you'll get away from your books long enough to go out and talk with ten or twenty local people every day, you'll make some phenomenal progress.

Paying Attention to Details

As we started to work on Sindhi we found it to be a rather complex language with strange implosive sounds. We were challenged by its intricacies. I studied with an informant each day and tried to prepare a lesson utilizing what I learned. My wife typed the lesson that night and the next morning I met with our other missionaries to teach them what I'd learned the day before—sort of a pulling-yourself-up-by-your-own-bootstrap method.

In most languages it takes a good part of a year or so before you can get beyond carrying on a conversation, to the point where you can teach and preach, and even then you are limited in what you can communicate. I remember one of the first little messages I gave in Pakistan. It was in an eye hospital on the edge of the Sind desert where both glaucoma and trichoma are endemic. Dedicated mission doctors from England and America came for two or three months each year and removed several thousand cataracts during the season that the eye camp was open for treatment. But the doctors didn't speak Sindhi so it was our responsibility to translate for them and the patients while ministering both physically and spiritually to the patients and their families. Before the doctor came into the examining hall, we would gather a group of fifty, eighty, or a hundred patients and share with them why we'd come—we loved them because God loved them.

Details of Pronunciation. On this occasion I chose to present the wonderful story of our Lord's feeding the five thousand. Remember the little boy with the two small fish and the five loaves of bread? I read a simple Sindhi translation of that passage in the Gospels and then I made a few comments, but I sensed that I was not getting my message across. People weren't particularly attentive. Worst of all, they seemed to be laughing! Snickering! It seemed that whenever I talked about the fish it triggered a little ripple of laughter. They smiled and nudged each other and I was beginning to feel very uncomfortable in one of my first attempts to preach in the Sindhi language.

Those of you who teach or have to communicate before audiences may be aware that two things are very painful for public speakers. One is if you tell a joke and nobody laughs. That's the situation I found myself in. There I was telling a wonderful, but very serious, account of our Lord feeding the five thousand and they were laughing at me! I stumbled on through, doing the best I could, but I was relieved when it was over. I quickly moved out of the room, glad to get away from that situation. I didn't do well and I knew it.

After awhile, I got up the courage to ask one of the Pakistani male nurses what went wrong. He tried to encourage me: "You know we appreciate your coming here. Hardly any white people have ever tried to learn the Sindhi language. You're trying and some day you're going to learn it. But you did have a little trouble today. I noted especially your problem with our word 'fish.'" (Ah, now we were zeroing in!)

"Yes," I said, "I thought maybe that was it. But what precisely was my problem?"

"Well," he said, "we have two words in our language

that are very similar."

"Oh?"

"Yes, one of them is *kurady,* our word for the little boney fish that swim in the irrigation canals which flow from the Indus River. The people catch them in nets and put them in their curry."

"Yes," I replied, "I know that."

"Well, you didn't say that."

"I thought I did. What did I say?"

"You said, *kirady.*"

"Okay, fish is *kurady* and I said *kirady.* What difference does it make?"

"Well," he said, "it makes quite a lot of difference because while *kurady* is our word for little fish, *kirady* is our word for little lizard!" (He was talking about the kind of little household lizards that are very common in Pakistan and much of South Asia. They scamper up the walls and then wait quietly in the corners where they eat flies and mosquitoes. Sometimes they scoot across the ceiling, lose their footing when they hit a dusty spot and come falling down on your table or your bed. When they do they look frightened and surprised and quickly run away. They are quite harmless and wouldn't hurt you.)

But I did get his point. You see, lizards don't belong in a little boy's lunch! He went on to say, "We really couldn't help laughing when you told us about the boy that brought a lunch with bread and lizards in it. We wondered what kind of a mother would pack such a lunch! Then you told about the sacrifice he made in giving it to Jesus. We thought he probably was glad to get rid of it. Next you told about Jesus praying over the bread and the lizards and breaking them into pieces. When the disciples passed them out to the people it was no wonder there were twelve baskets full left over!"

Right there I learned my fourth lesson in language communication. It not only involves getting across the last eighteen inches, using the language of love, and determining to learn their language, but it also involves paying attention to detail.

There's a very small difference between the short vowels *ĭ* and *ŭ*. It has to do with how you shape your lips and where you put your tongue. It's a rather minute difference, but failure to differentiate the two spoiled the message I was trying to communicate and made my whole attempt ineffective. As Christian communicators it makes a difference how we use our tongue and our lips. The reason that you are not a more effective communicator of the gospel may be that you're careless about the way you use your lips and your tongue and your life as well. Carelessness leads to inconsistencies that undercut your verbal witness. Both spiritually and physically, you've got to watch the details of your tongue if you're going to be a good communicator for Jesus Christ.

Details in Translation. I've referred to my failure to pay attention to the details of pronunciation. It is also important to pay attention to details in translation. The history of missions is replete with classical incidents of missionaries who have not paid adequate attention to details in language learning and have done translations poorly. Some years ago the Bible Society sent a translation consultant to Liberia and discovered that one of the early missionaries had translated the Twenty-third Psalm, the Lord's Prayer and a few other passages to be used in worship. But he had done a rather poor job of learning the language and translating it. As a result, these people had been repeating the Lord's Prayer every Sunday morning, but instead of praying "Deliver us from evil" their translation read, "Do not catch us when we sin." They prayed it with great vigor every Sunday morning. You can be sure that the Bible Society made the correction in a hurry!

I think of another illustration in a rather obscure verse of the New Testament. First Peter 1:13 says, in the King James Version: "Gird up the loins of your mind."

What does that mean? How would you translate it into another language? In one situation, a well-meaning missionary who had to translate that verse without the advantage of knowing the original language of the New Testament did the best she could. She came out with a translation which read: "Put a belt around the hips of your thoughts." That's hardly an improvement. If she had studied New Testament Greek, she would have understood that what it really means is: "Be alert in your thinking." It helps to know the details of biblical language and culture in order to communicate effectively as a missionary.

We Americans sometimes get uptight. We get worried and anxious. People in other cultures do, too. Among the Uduks of the South Sudan, along the borders of Ethiopia, people also worry. They sometimes get anxious. But they don't get uptight in their minds or troubled in their hearts. When they are worried, they "shiver in their liver." For them the liver is the seat of the emotions. As a result, when translators prepared the New Testament in the Uduk language John 14:1 does not say, "Let not your heart be troubled." In their Bible it reads, "Do not shiver in your liver. You believe in God, believe also in me." That's the only way you can translate it to get the original meaning across effectively for the Uduk people.

Details of Cultural Understanding. In going abroad we need to observe details not only in language learning, pronunciation, and translation, but we need to become lifelong students of the details of cultural understanding. We begin learning about a people by observing patterns in their behavior. Dr. Paul Hiebert of Fuller Seminary's School of World Mission reminds us that some of the things we generally learn most readily when we go to another culture are patterns for exchanging greetings:

For example, we have all seen two American

men on meeting grasp each other's hand and shake it. In Mexico we would see them embrace. In India each puts his hands together and raises them towards his forehead with a slight bow of the head—a gesture of greeting that is efficient, for it permits a person to greet a great many others in a single motion, and clean, for people need not touch each other. The latter is particularly important in a society where the touch of an untouchable used to defile a high-caste person and force him to take a purification bath. Among the Siriano of South America, men spit on each other's chests in greeting.

Probably the strangest form of greeting was observed by Dr. Jacob Loewen in Panama. On leaving the jungle on a small plane with the local native chief, he noticed the chief go to all his fellow tribesmen and suck their mouths. When Dr. Loewen inquired about this custom, the chief explained that they had learned this custom from the white man. They had seen that every time he went up in his plane, he sucked the mouths of his people as magic to insure a safe journey. If we stop and think about it a minute, Americans, in fact, have two types of greeting, shaking hands and sucking mouths, and we must be careful not to use the wrong form with the wrong people.[1]

Now there's a classic illustration of cultural differences and the way our customs may appear to others.

In seeking cultural understanding you need to remember that people in different cultures do not simply live in the same world with different names or labels attached to the same thing. It isn't just a matter of learning somebody else's name for an object or an experience. We must realize that people live in different conceptual worlds. For example, they may divide the color

144 The Unfinished Task

spectrum differently, view space relationships differently, and see time from a very different perspective.

Take, for example, the Quechua Indians of Bolivia. They readily speak of the future, but they always talk about it as if it were behind a person rather than in front of him. We talk about looking into the future as though it were out ahead of us. The Quechuas talk about looking back into the future. As a result, where the English translation of Luke 1:48 has Mary saying, "From now on all generations will call me blessed," the Quechua New Testament reads, "From now on behind me all generations will call me blessed."

You say, how did they ever get mixed up like that? On the contrary, their usage reflects a highly intelligent view of experience. If I should ask you, "Which can you mentally visualize more readily—yesterday or tomorrow?" you laugh and say, "Well, obviously yesterday. The events of yesterday are quite clear in my mind. They are all easily visible. Tomorrow is not." That's exactly what the Quechuas say: "Yes, the past—yesterday—is right out in front where you can see it. The future is still behind you, hidden, and you won't see it until it comes around and enters the past." From their perspective it makes good sense. But you have to know how they view time in order to meaningfully communicate with the Quechuas.

STAGES IN CULTURAL ADJUSTMENT
Dr. Paul Hiebert in a chapter on "Culture and Cross-Cultural Differences" describes three stages in adjusting to a new culture.[2]

The "Tourist" Stage
First of all, there is the stage which some of you have already experienced in going overseas as tourists. You're excited about getting on the plane in Los Angeles, Chicago, or New York. You anticipate strange places, exotic smells, interesting people, nice food—all

the things that are supposed to be part of the tourist experience. Once you get there you find the people quaint, the food interesting, the marketplace colorful, and the bargains not as cheap as you had hoped.

Hiebert points out that tourists don't generally experience real culture shock as they launch out from American style hotels on daily forays that bring them back at night to a little America whether in Cairo, Karachi, or Jakarta. Tourists go out to see the local people but they don't have to settle down among them and build stable relationships. Moreover, they know that in two days or two weeks they are going home! That's why tourists seldom experience real culture shock.

But the new food you tried might not seem so interesting when it becomes a steady diet—

> You mean to say the people here eat it twice a day, every day? And so will I when I move to the village? For three years? In this house with no running water? No doctor? No one who can talk decent English? How did I get into this anyway?[3]

That's when culture shock begins to set in. It comes after the tourist stage when you realize you are there to stay.

"Culture Shock"

Dr. Hiebert reminds us that culture shock is not a reaction to poverty or lack of sanitation. People who come to America from other lands experience culture shock without being exposed to poverty, filth, or primitive conditions.

We suffer culture shock when we begin to realize that most of the cultural patterns we have learned during twenty-five years of growing up in America, now suddenly are meaningless in the middle of Pakistan. They don't work. They don't hold the keys to anything;

they don't explain anything.

Culture shock comes from realizing that we are reduced to the level of children once again. The local Pakistani boys who wandered into the courtyard to meet me knew more about how to live in Pakistan than I did as an educated adult more than twice their age. It may be awkward or embarrassing to admit that the local people know more about their language and culture than you do. But you've got to accept it. You have to begin to learn the elemental things of life all over again—how to speak, to greet, to eat, to buy and sell, to travel, and many other things.

Hiebert observes:

> It is when we realize that this now is going to be our life, and for a long time to come, that the shock comes. Disorientation, disillusionment and depression strike, and we would go home if only we did not have to face the folks there.[4]

The Adjusted Bicultural Person

Pretty soon you'll begin to pick up a few phrases so you can greet people and make friends. You learn the number system so you can count money. You find out you can keep your health and you begin to fit into the new cultural setting. At this stage, you need to avoid the temptation to withdraw, to become quiet or sullen instead of going out and mixing with people. You won't get through culture shock readily if you withdraw. Most of all, avoid the temptation to create a little America in which to live. That, too, impedes the process of cultural adaptation.

As you learn to adapt to the new culture you find yourself becoming a bicultural person. The provincialism you felt as an American, thinking that American ways are the only way to do things, will begin to disappear. You'll learn to deal with cultural variety and discover that for the most part cultures are neither good nor bad; they're just different. The people you're living among probably believe that their culture has the best way of doing things and, for many things, they may be right. You'll find that, aside from a little curiosity about your foreignness, most people will not be interested in learning your way of doing things and you might as well recognize it and get on with learning their ways.

Of the bicultural individual Hiebert makes a rather amusing comment:

> In one sense, bicultural people never fully adjust to one culture, their own or their adopted one. Within themselves they are part of both. When Americans are abroad, they dream of America, and need little rituals that reaffirm this part of themselves—a food package from home, a letter, an American visitor from whom they can learn the latest news from "home." When in America, they dream of their adopted country, and need little rituals that reaffirm this part of themselves—a visitor from that country, a meal with its food. Bicultural people seem happiest when they are flying from one of these countries to the other.[5]

Maybe that gives you some understanding of the cultural adventures ahead for the new missionary.

POTENTIAL PROBLEM AREAS

I have said a good deal about linguistic and cultural orientation because it is so important to successful adaptation to another culture. But there are other potential problem areas as well.

A conference of EFMA personnel secretaries—people that work with missionary recruiting and counseling—focused on how to make first-time missionaries maximally effective by helping them face problems and make adjustments. They listed some twenty or thirty problem areas that first-termers sometimes experience: things like loneliness, depression, fear, insubordination, health problems, fatigue, and so on. They concluded that those things were generally symptoms and not the causes of missionary frustration and failure. What are some of the problem areas you need to be aware of!

Cultural maladjustment. In a study made of missionaries who withdrew from the field over a ten-year period, none of them cited cultural maladjustment as the reason why they left. They may have been unwilling to admit their problems in that area or too culturally insensitive to recognize one source of their frustration. About 40 percent said they terminated their service because they didn't get the language. Language is a very important part of culture and has been called "the shrine of a people's soul." This underscores the necessity of putting prime time and effort into learning the language well enough to use it effectively. I encourage men to see that their wives have adequate time and opportunity to study the language. Study is frequently complicated for the wife by the birth and care of children. If for those or other reasons, a wife doesn't get the language well enough to enjoy living among the people, to communicate with them and have a ministry, she'll be dissatisfied and her dissatisfaction in time may result in the whole family returning home prematurely.

Interpersonal relationships. In the study cited above about 13 percent of the former missionaries suggested that problems in getting along with nationals were a reason for leaving. Three times as many said problems in relating to other missionaries were a reason why they withdrew.

Philosophy on finance can cause problems. The potential missionary should sort this out with the mission agency and his spouse before he goes, know what the mission's policies are and be sure he is in agreement with them. Financial differences between missionaries, or between missionaries and the mission, or missionaries and the national church can cause problems. But they can generally be prevented by clear understandings ahead of time.

Communication breakdowns between husband and wife, or between the missionary and the national church, or the missionary and his supervisor, or the missionary and the mission board can appear. To be forewarned in this area is to be forearmed. The channels of communication should be kept open on all sides.

Family problems are a potential cause of frustration due to unsettled family life, uncut ties to home, children's educational concerns, and even marital difficulties that sometimes arise.

Spiritual immaturity can be a problem. Here in America Christians tend to be spoon-fed. First we lean upon our parents, then upon the pastor of our church or a godly professor. We are fed by television and cassette tapes from famous speakers. I've been told that there's a program now being developed so you can play videotapes for your personal devotions! If a potential missionary hasn't learned to feed himself spiritually, he is going to suffer when overseas. One thing some missionaries complain about is the lack of opportunity for spiritual stimulation. While learning language they may not understand enough to get much help from the sermon. They wish somebody would preach and minister to them in English. Some missions send visiting pastors and board members or staff to help minister in those ways.

Another problem is the lack of spiritual examples at home. *The missionary* becomes the spiritual example. That's why it's important to be able to stand on your own feet spiritually.

Relationship with the mission agency. You should ask the mission agency you're dealing with what they do about orienting and supervising personnel during the first year and beyond. This is important to a good start.

FIRST-TERM OBJECTIVES

There are a number of positive objectives which I think every first-term missionary can be expected to realize. He ought to go with some goals and objectives clearly in mind.

First of all, he should aim at a *good foundation in the language.* Some will become quite proficient within the first term. Others won't reach the same level of proficiency until sometime into a second term, depending on the difficulty of the language and the skill and time applied to acquiring it. I have already mentioned the importance of the wife getting the language as well as the husband. They both should be prepared to keep learning and growing in their ability to communicate in one or more languages in addition to their own.

Secondly, he should aim at *a satisfactory integration* into the life and culture of the people. During this first term he ought to become adjusted to the climate, the customs, and all that's going on.

Thirdly, he should aim at *a realistic understanding of the work* he is in: its problems, its demands, its potential. He ought to aim at a healthy relationship with his mission organization and with the national church that may be there.

He should aim at *a growing awareness of his gifts* and his role in ministry. He should not insist on having a major ministry from the day he arrives. He should be content to learn the culture and the language over a period of time, while looking for opportunities to share Christ in word and deed with those he comes in touch with. In time, and with the help of his colleagues, he will begin to see the ministry the Lord is preparing.

Another objective should be *a deepening confirmation of his call* from the Lord: a sense of belonging in that place, a consciousness of being in God's will and the satisfaction of making a real contribution to the work of the Lord.

Finally, one of the objectives in a first term ought to

be to *set goals for a subsequent ministry.* Then lay the foundation for reaching them. This may include continuing education and further study.

TRANSLATING THE GOSPEL INTO LIFE

I have shared from my experience a number of principles and suggestions that could make the first period of service as a cross-cultural missionary both effective and satisfying. Everything I have talked about from principles of language learning and cultural identification to the resolution of problem areas and the accomplishment of objectives is all focused on one major purpose: that you might be effective communicators translating the gospel into life.

There is a little poem that says:

You are the only gospel the careless world will read.
You are the sinner's Bible, you are the scoffer's creed.
You are the Lord's last message, written in deed and word.
What if the print is crooked? What if the page is blurred?

Lest you think that is simply a fanciful idea of the poet, I would remind you the concept is a very biblical one. It is found in 2 Corinthians 3:3 where Paul says, "You yourselves are our letter, written on our hearts, known and read by everybody, . . . written not with ink but with the Spirit of the living God, not on tablets of stone but on tablets of human hearts." You and I, as born-again believers, are intended to be "living letters" telling others of Christ. Long before Ken Taylor ever thought of *The Living Bible,* God had planned that His children should be "living letters" for communicating the gospel to the world.

As you think about missionary service in another

culture, how well are you translating the gospel into life here and now? Don't project into the future the great things you are going to do for the Lord some day when you get "over there." Instead, discover as many ways as you can to communicate the gospel to others now!

I'll never forget our trip to Russia as a family on our way back to Pakistan. In Moscow we made an effort to attend several services at the Evangelical Baptist Church. Every service was crowded out with people standing in the aisles for two to three hours at a time. They graciously gave us a seat in the balcony where we could see. An interpreter sat next to us and cued us in on what was happening. I especially remember the third speaker on Sunday night. (They had three preachers in every service!) He was an evangelist from the Ukraine and he had so much of the joy of the Lord about him that I turned to the interpreter and asked what he was talking about.

"Oh," the interpreter replied, "he is speaking from Revelation 22:13."

I opened my English New Testament to the verse that reads, "I am the Alpha and Omega, the First and the Last, the Beginning and the End." Then I thought what I would say if I were preaching on that verse. As my thoughts carried me away, several minutes went by before the interpreter nudged me and said, "Now he is telling the people that while Jesus is the beginning and the ending of God's divine alphabet, we believers are the other letters He wants to use to spell out His message today."

Are you that kind of living letter, spelling out God's message of love, joy, peace, and salvation? Remember:

> You are writing each day a letter to men;
> Take care that the writing is true;
> It's the only gospel some folks will read—
> The gospel according to you.

You may one day be engaged in a cross-cultural ministry. My prayer is simply that God will lead you to be a good communicator of His truth. May He help you to be effective in translating the gospel into life, whether at home or abroad, for lost men and women to see and hear and obey.

Notes
1. Paul G. Hiebert, "Part II: An Introduction to Mission Anthropology," in a book by Glasser, Hiebert, Wager and Winter, *Crucial Dimensions in World Evangelization.* (Pasadena: William Carey Library, 1978), pp. 45-46.
2. Ibid., pp. 50-52.
3. Ibid., pp. 50.
4. Ibid., pp. 50-51.
5. Ibid., pp. 52.

10

BECOMING A FRONTIER MISSIONARY
Elizabeth Cridland

There were 243 tribes without one word of the Word of God in their language—243 tribes! In those days, it was the Anglo-Egyptian Sudan, equally ruled by Egypt and Britain. The two ruling nations allowed only a very few missionaries into the country, and Sudan Interior Mission was one of them. The Sudan was my frontier.

As I describe what being a frontier missionary was like for forty years, I want to let another frontier—2.7 billion souls—file past your subconscious mind. I can't get away from the fact that God wants us to get to that frontier! Keep that in the back of your mind while I share about the frontier where people still live as they did a thousand years ago.

The Anglo-Egyptian Sudan was a large country territorially speaking, but not in population. There were about 12.6 million Arab-related people in the north who wanted to make it an Islamic state. In the south lived 5.6 million animistic people (pagans). The line of demarcation was 10 degrees north of the equator. Our station was just a little below that 10-degree line. No

Muslims could come below it and no pagans could go north of it. So we were restricted on both sides; however before we were forced to leave the country we did get north of the line and started a church.

Mary Beam had gone in with the first missionary party of six that opened the area for the Sudan Interior Mission seven years earlier. People still lived as they did a thousand years ago. It was just like going backward a thousand years. And when I arrived seven years later nothing had changed. Mary was in another station further south but she joined me because it was not safe for a woman to live alone at the station. Much of the time Mary and I were alone; much later, three more women missionaries joined us. It turned into a ladies' station.

After a long sea voyage our ship finally disembarked in Egypt and I continued the next part of my journey up the Nile River on a wood-burning steamer. The Nile is the longest river in the world flowing north. We stopped at many places along the way to load on wood for fuel. The steamer pulled barges that carried all of our goods and other cargo. It was an exciting trip—strange people, strange animals, strange languages. But I was never afraid. I knew I was where God wanted me to be.

When we got to a place 200 miles from the inland station to which I was going I disembarked. The rest of the journey would be made on a mission truck that was much the worse for wear. We loaded everything onto the truck—rope beds, rope chairs, gasoline tins filled with sorghum, ten months' worth of food, medical supplies, and personal belongings. Everything I would need for the next several months had to be brought with me; the nearest grocery store was 500 miles away.

After everything was loaded on the poor mission truck it wouldn't start. It needed a part that the driver didn't have with him; so we improvised. We used the coffee pot spout and made the part! After traveling in the overloaded truck for a while we finally bogged down in the mud (because the rainy season had started early that year). We unloaded everything off the truck and put all the supplies in village huts; then we drove on to the mission station. We would have to depend on the village chiefs to get women head carriers to bring everything to the station.

It was the middle of the rains by the time they arrived, and I never will forget the day. I looked out and saw a parade of Mabaan women (the tribe Mary was with before she joined me at my station) coming up our road, balancing tins of food and other supplies on their heads. Their bodies were covered with a red, oily mixture made out of soft stone, ground on a grindstone and mixed with nut oil. The women looked as if they'd been dipped into a barrel of red enamel and stood out to dry. Ornaments of all kinds were sticking out of holes in their ears and lips and from their nostrils.

Our tribe, the Uduks, also wore those ornaments. It was terribly tempting to me, when I first went there (being entirely out of culture), to pull one of those grass ornaments right out of one of their nostrils; they really bothered me—just bobbing up and down. But I didn't!

What a joy it was to see that strange parade. Enameled women balancing bags of flour and gasoline tins of sorghum. As they drew closer I could see that the tins of sorghum had bulged in the red hot sun of the Sudan and were leaking. Sorghum dripped down the enameled faces and the women were having a great time catching the sweet stuff with their tongues. I asked Mary, "Do you think we'll have enough left for a few cups of tea by the time they get here?" But it was wonderful to see them coming with our supplies and personal belongings.

I remember that the flour was full of weevils. Every week we would put the flour out in the sun until it got so many webs in it we couldn't pull them out. The frontier!

Just as in the days of Joshua, there were giants in the land that had to be driven out. You read in the Old

Testament about the "sons of Anak," giants of the land that Joshua drove out of his frontier, the Promised Land. The frontier we were in also had sons of Anak— the fear of evil spirits. This is where evil spirits were worshiped. All these people knew was their deep-seated fear. No one ever went to sleep for a full night. They slept like chickens, they said, with one eye open. They were afraid because of the evil eye of people all around them.

Some German psychologists from Heidelberg came to the Sudan to work on a documentary about the effects of Christian education on a primitive tribe (as they called them in those days). They visited us four times. We had such wonderful opportunities to share with these wonderful Heidelberg psychologists until two and three o'clock in the morning. They told us that the greatest fear they had ever come across in all their research was in the Uduk tribe. The psychologists divided the people into groups: those who lived farthest away from the station; those who lived a little closer; a little closer still; and the people who heard our message through our very halting language—since we were just beginning to learn the language at that time.

We provided men to help them in their research. But the psychologists said that the helpers we gave them were not really Uduks, we were misinformed; they couldn't be Uduks because they exhibited none of the deep-seated fear that was typical of the Uduk tribe. "Oh," we said, "you don't know the reasons for this." And we were able to share what the power by which God raised the Lord Jesus Christ was able to do in those people who lived as their ancestors did a thousand years before we arrived there. We saw that Power at work.

When I took my first trip away from the station I visited the district commissioner, John Long. His spotted hunting dog sat under the chair and looked straight at me the whole time I was there. Mr. Long said, "And Miss

Cridland (English, you know), what do you suppose that you have come here to do? Would you tell me what brought you to this place? I can understand your coming to work among the Mabaans, but what do you think you might do among the impossible Uduks?"

I answered, "Well, Mr. Long, I believe God has sent me here."

"Oh? Do you know that the British government has been working with these Uduks, and we have been trying to do something with them? We even took two men out to try to train them to be ordinary policemen at the border. They wouldn't even stay!"

Of course, they wouldn't! They were scared to death to go out of their territory, but he had not figured on that. He said, "Well, if you think you can do anything with them, more power to you."

You know what I wanted to say? "WE'VE GOT THE POWER!" And later we saw it work.

So the first thing we had to do was to drive out the "sons of Anak," the deep-seated fear. We learned later that the Uduks had talked among themselves when missionaries first arrived. "Are those white people going to live close to us? Are those shiny white faces going to be near us? We can't have those people coming so close to us!" So they got together with the British appointed chiefs controlled by the witch doctors and said, "If they want to stay with us we'll let them build up by the baobab tree, right at the top of the hill."

That was perfect, because it was the highest level of ground there was. We wanted to get away from the millions of malaria mosquitos down by the river—which ran only during the rainy season. There was tall grass everywhere; right by our house it was fourteen feet high—I measured it. Down by the river it was even higher. The mosquitos were worse down there, so we were glad to be higher.

They let us build at the foot of the baobab tree. Why? The baobab tree was the center of all evil-spirit worship.

"Let's see what the evil spirits will do to them. We've had them all our lives. Let the white people live with them and cope with them, then the spirits won't do anything to us." So the mission station was called, "The village at the foot of the baobab tree."

How did I come to be at this strange frontier? My parents died when I was a teenager and my younger brother and I were orphaned. I thought, after graduating from high school at sixteen, that my duty was to put my brother through college. I had been awarded a wonderful position in the suburbs of Philadelphia where I lived. A fifteen-minute walk from the suburban train station to my lovely office amidst the trees gave time for daily meditation. Those times of meditation led me to wonder about life.

There were several of us who went everywhere together. We were good, clean young people, although not always church going. We just lived from one good time to the next glorious time. I always smiled and laughed and had fun with my friends at the dances and other activities. But, deep down in my heart a struggle was going on that nobody, NOBODY except God knew about.

I didn't realize then that I was a David, but I was. I think David was seeking when he was out on the hills playing his harp in worship of God as he watched the sheep. The Scriptures say that David was a man after God's own heart. I believe that I was having a desire created in me to be a woman after God's own heart, but I couldn't have put it into those words at that time. I would wonder, "This is just a merry-go-round life we're living: getting on at one place, going round and round, getting off where we got on, getting nowhere. Is this all that life is about?" Many people are troubled with thoughts such as these, but when I was young I thought I was the only one who had them. So I didn't dare tell anybody. But God knows the seeking heart. God always sees the seeking heart and He meets everyone who is seeking. He met me and brought across my pathway those who would lead me out of that merry-go-round life I was living.

Amy Carmichael tells about a vision she had. She saw young girls gathered in a lovely meadow, making daisy chains. In the vision streams of people were walking along behind the girls, paying no attention whatsoever to where they were going, just walking along until, one by one, they all fell into an abyss. But the young girls went right on making their daisy chains, oblivious of the fact, not recognizing that an abyss was swallowing up all the people.

God saw that one day I might be willing to do something about those who were falling into the abyss. He has His ways of speaking to people, and He began to speak to me through different people.

The first person who spoke to me was Dr. Robert McQuilkin, founder of Columbia Bible College. Dr. McQuilkin said that God has a plan for our lives. We should pray every day until we are sure that God wants us out where 500 million have never heard the gospel. By the time I went, the numbers had increased to 700 million. Oh, how that pierced my heart. God was saying to me, "Set your face like a flint."

That's what God wants you to do too. As you meet God every day, ask Him to show you the plan He has for your life, what He wants you to do. He has the very place for you. A weed is a plant out of place. It might be a good thing, but if it's out of place, it's a weed. I sure didn't want to be a weed. So I said, "Lord, I just want to be the plant that's in the right place, and can grow."

I learned that God wanted me to go tell His Good News. Another thing I learned was that I didn't have to do it by myself. The Lord Jesus became the greatest reality in my life; He became my Master to tell me what to do. I learned then that I didn't have to live this new life all by myself but I had the most tremendous thing there ever was. I had the power by which God raised the

Lord Jesus Christ. The way I learned to appropriate that Resurrection power was to look to God every day for His promise to me. That has always been my practice. He started me off with a promise when I first met Him: "As thou goest, step by step, I will open the way before you," and every day He still has a special promise for me. That's what I live on.

Ten months after my father and mother died, my brother also died. Since my goal had been to put him through college I had to reevaluate my future and make new goals; so I decided to go to school myself. I enrolled at Columbia Bible College. I had to disown those who were caring for me. They thought I was going crazy, enrolling in a Bible college. I had heard Dr. McQuilkin speak at a conference and decided that I wanted him to teach me Bible since he was a professor at Columbia Bible College.

After graduating from Columbia Bible College I worked with Dr. McQuilkin, organizing his office, during the days when the Student Foreign Missions Fellowship was forming. We're still being blessed by the prayers of those who started this movement. God is still answering them. And I believe He's still answering Dr. McQuilkin's prayers for the young people of this generation to get into the last great push, the excitement of being one of those who would have the privilege of going to the frontiers where people have never once heard the gospel message.

Those basic truths which I learned from the time I became a Christian at the age of eighteen are the things that kept me all through those years on the frontier. Not once during the seventy-seven days on the sea during my first trip out, dodging submarines and getting into a lifeboat and waiting until it was safe to board ship again; not once when fanatical Muslims marched on our station to desecrate the church and "get rid of the missionaries"; not once when problems came up involving evil spirits, did I ever have a doubt but that I was where God wanted me to be. Oh, how I thank God that He is such a safe and sure God. When I was willing to say, "You are my Master; what you say, I do," I was showing obedience. As I learned to do His will, I believe (I'm not saying this to praise myself, I'm saying this is how God wants you and me to be) that my heart was like David's. David was a man after God's own heart. God also blessed me with a seeking heart each day. So I never had any doubts; I never said, "Oh, I guess I came to the wrong place. Oh, the loneliness is getting me down." It never did. I wanted more! Oh, it was just wonderful. The rainy season, when we never saw another white face for six or eight months, was wonderful. We got so much more done! There were never any tourists to come and say, "Why do you try to keep these people from their wonderful own religion and try to change them? Look at them dancing, three days in a row. Look at how happy they are."

I wanted to give them the Word of God in their own language. I knew that true happiness comes only from knowing God through His blessed Son. We'd push through the tall grass and, as we drew near a village, the dogs would bark. The villagers knew that they weren't barking at the lions or any other wild animal. We had those around us all the time. It was a different bark that announced our coming. We'd get to the village and everything was quiet; maybe there would be a spear stuck into the ground in front of the opening that led into a hut, and it was still quivering as if somebody had stuck it in the ground quickly and dashed inside the hut, telling everybody inside, "Be quiet. Those white evil spirits have come to our village." Oh, how we prayed for an opportunity to get close.

One time I moved up to some women with water gourds on their heads; we had to haul all of our water two and a half miles. I tried to let them see that I wanted to go to the water with them. Finally, I got enough of the language to tell them that I wanted to go with them.

They said, "Are you willing to learn to spit?"

"I'll try," I said. So they showed me how I could get enough saliva. This was sort of a problem for me because it didn't exactly fit in with my upbringing! They finally said to me, "You didn't have your two front teeth dug out with a spear like we did. You haven't got a place for the water to go through. That's why you can't do it. You don't have to learn to spit to go with us."

The women didn't tell me their right names; they didn't want the evil spirits to know that much about them. Everything they weren't familiar with was from the evil spirits. The "white things the wind blew," our papers, scared them all away from us because they were from the evil spirits. So we used to take tiny little pieces of paper and little stubs of pencil to try to write. We wrote everything down. We tried drawing pictures for communication.

Neither of us, Mary nor I, were very good artists. But Mary one day took a larger piece of paper. They all ran away at first, and then they came back. She said, "I'm drawing a picture of Mally." Mally was one of the men standing nearby holding his spear; his right foot rested on his left knee, which was a most comfortable position, one which Uduk men could stand in for hours. As he stood there, as if in a pose, Mary drew a picture of Mally. It didn't look too much like him but she said, "Here's Mally." Then they *gradually* came up and looked at it. Grinning they said, "Why, that's Mally!" To the day we left, we had people coming from miles around to see Mally on the "white thing the wind blew."

We were in the process of starting schools for the chief's sons. Oh, what a time! We were trying to get some of the adults to learn too. We used construction paper of all beautiful colors on which we wrote simple little words of the language that we were beginning to learn. We made these into little booklets that they could take to their homes, thinking that if we could get them to take the paper in their hands and go home with them, they would then show them to the women. The women were the hardest. We were in a matrilineal tribe, not matriarchal. The woman was not the ruler, but it surely seemed like it. The old women sitting back smoking their water pipes were the ones who controlled everything. They would wait at home for their husbands to come, and when they did come home, carrying the small purple or red or orange pieces of paper, they would say, "Where have you been? Up to that white lady? Get out of here!"

In the meantime, we had one person with whom we were able to communicate. He sat in our class and, from the little simple teaching we had been able to give him, he decided that he wanted to buy cloth to wrap around his body. We didn't tell him to do so, but he wanted to. Well, how could he earn money to do it? We agreed that he could come and work for us for half a day and then try to learn to read the other half a day. But as other men would learn about wearing cloth and try to do it too, the women would take their husbands hard-earned cloth and tear it to shreds and put it in the fire to keep them from coming to us.

We were grateful to God for the one person who was responding to us. People were praying. Mary and I were a team of two, but we weren't all of the team. Through Columbia Bible College and other friends, God raised up prayer warriors for us. For thirty-five years they prayed us through everything. They were part of the team, a praying part. But we needed a language inform-ant.

We enlisted a man named Gepi one day when we went to the village. He was the only man left in the vil-lage and he had a bad arm. "Gepi, what are you doing here?" we asked. "Why aren't you at the beer drink?"

"Oh, I couldn't drink beer," he replied. "I have an evil eye because of my arm. I can't dance with the group. I can't play stones with the men." (This was a game called "eating stones.") "I can't do that."

"Why, Gepi, you're so lonely all by yourself. Come on up to our place."

"You want me there?"

"Yes, yes, we'd like to have you. Gepi, you know, we need you. If you would come up to our place in the morning when the sun springs its eye out of its hole, and stay until it burns us with fire on top of our heads (noon), we'll give you a coin (ten cents)." We were trying to carry out government instructions to teach them to use money.

"You will? I can buy beer myself then and I won't have to drink from the communal pot."

The next day we really prayed that Gepi would come. We sat in our kitchen, which was separate from our sleeping hut. The kitchen, of course, had a fire going most of the time, and we didn't want to set fire to our grass-thatched roof. We sat looking from our window, and here came Gepi. He stuck his spear in the ground right by the tree full of white ants next to our house. Those white ants nearly ate up our house; they ate all the labels off the records we had of symphony orchestras! We never knew what we were going to play next! Every day we would go out and knock down the tunnels the ants built two and a half inches from the wall. That was the routine: knocking down all of the termite trenches.

Anyway, Gepi was there. How thrilling! He was covered with that red, oily mixture; but it washed off in water. He sat down in our living room and we knew it was a breakthrough—we had an informant. What strides in the language we made then.

"Where are the people?" I tried saying for the tenth time.

"Say it again," he said. "Oh, you just don't have any inner ear. You'll never be able to learn this language," said Gepi. We heard that all the time.

But, God worked. Soon we had a school for boys. Then we found that we were raising misfits since the boys were learning about the Lord, but not the girls. So for two years we prayed for a co-ed school. The mission, in holy horror, said, "What on earth do you mean? A co-ed school in that culture?" We knew it would mean that we get up at certain times all night long, policing the station, going around to make sure the girls were safe in their houses. But we were willing to do twenty-four-hour duty. Finally, after two years, the government and then the mission gave us permission. It was the foundation of our work—girls and boys becoming Christians, later getting married, becoming the foundation of the church.

We had a terrible time with competition among the students. But, we could never give an award to somebody who did better than the others. That was against the evil spirits. One girl was absolutely brilliant. We wanted to encourage her by giving her an award. We thought a lantern would be a nice gift. The students didn't have any lights. So Mary and I went to a local "store," where the post office was and bought her a tiny lantern. But she wouldn't even come forward to receive it. We could never get her to come and take her award because of fear of the evil spirit. God had to show us how to drive out the "sons of Anak." Only He knew what was the best way.

One of the government conditions for our school was that we clothe the students. Mary and I had to become seamstresses. She drew a pattern of the garment we would make for the boys. We cut them out and sewed them up on an old sewing machine that had been given to us. What a time we had teaching them to wear clothes. One man, Paul, who came to the school also accepted Christ. But when his four years of schooling were over, he ripped off his clothes.

When we started the girls school we mentioned in our prayer letter that we were going to need twelve dresses. The people responded and our twelve dresses were brought to us by one of the missionaries when she returned from furlough in America. Now, how were we going to get twelve girls to wear those dresses? We had to be innovative. One day I stayed down with the boys while Mary dressed the girls. I explained to the boys, "We're going to have a new thing, a brand new thing! We're not going to tell you what it is, but we just want you to look straight toward the blackboard. Don't look out the windows, just straight toward the blackboard and, when we tell you, clap your hands and don't stop clapping, just keep clapping your hands." So as the girls came down, draped in their new clothes, the boys clapped, looking at the girls in those dresses. When the girls sat down in their seats we told the boys they could stop clapping. If we hadn't done that the boys would have chased the girls away from school, laughing at them. We had to prepare them. That's the way it was all along: preparing the people for every new thing.

Paul, the young man who ripped off his clothes, had made one leap from the compound into the tall grass to go back and be an Uduk again. After doing the paper for four years he went back and picked up his spear. But God finally got hold of him. He learned in our school that children were a gift from God. Among these primitive people, part of the evil spirit influence was that they would bury their twins alive. But Paul prayed that his firstborn would be twins. And they were! He kept them in his own home, but, because the whole tribe mobbed the home to try to kill the mother and the twins, we had to help guard them. Paul was the first one to rear twins in his own home. He also began to help us with translation of the Bible. He became the first one with a heart for God and was willing to do anything.

The men of the village threatened Paul. While he was at the mission station helping us, the men would make sure that when going to their fields they would go right past our window. They would hold their throwing sticks in a threatening way, and call out, "You call yourself an Uduk man? You sit in the shade there and play with that white thing (the paper). Come on out and fight and show that you can really be a true Uduk man." I sat by Paul with books and magazines and dictionaries, looking for pictures to help in the translation work, trying to learn the right word to match a picture. I would see those muscles in Paul's neck swell up and I knew the anger was coming and he was ready to jump out the window and get into a fight. I'd say, "Lord, make him a man after your own heart. Lord, give him the power of your resurrection for that anger." Then I would see his muscles relax and I would know that we could go on with the next word. Paul learned to use all of those books himself.

The American Bible Society printed our New Testament through the influence of Dr. Eugene Nida. Oh, what a thrill it was when the first two arrived. By that time, Paul, with only the training we could give him, had been ordained as pastor. So, he said, "I want to do something for the dedication." He wanted to have one of the boys who was good at drawing draw a picture of Satan and put it on the baobab tree and have Satan's face the bull's-eye and call all the Christian men, from the oldest to the youngest, to come with their shining spears and spear that tree, the center of all the evil spirit worship in the tribe. Everybody was invited. What a thrill! The rainmaker with his spear ran forward and speared it—he didn't quite make Satan's eye then. But later on he hid his rain stones so that nobody else could make rain after he died. That was the result of prayers, because we had shown his picture to people at home during our furlough and they prayed for the rainmaker. The Bible dedication was a success. People came from everywhere.

Our frontier closed for us when all the foreigners were ordered out of the three southern provinces. Three hundred missionaries! Barbara Harper, Mary Beam, and I were among the last to leave. (Other missionaries were given only twenty-four hours' notice. Our district commissioner insisted that we have an extended time because of the orphanage, the church, the co-ed school and everything else. So they gave us a week longer.)

During that last week a truck came rumbling up the road. The Italian driver asked, "Is this the mission?" It was the rest of the New Testaments! We put them in the milk cans that we had saved from the powdered milk supplement for the orphanage, and the people took them off in all directions as we prayed, "Lord, you promised not to let your Word return unto you void." When armed police came to escort us from our station they used the butts of their guns to beat the people as they tried to follow us out of the area.

Three weeks later, after we left, the Christians were in the church we had built, having their Believers' Bible Study. This was the largest church in the whole area. People came from everywhere to see that great big thatched roof. It was burned twice by the Muslims. They tried to get rid of the church because, you see, we had invaded Satan's territory. But, we *had* driven out the "sons of Anak." Suddenly the people in the Bible study heard a great crash. It was frightening and everybody wanted to run out; they expected anything after we left. There were so many threats. Pastor Paul quieted the people and he and two deacons went to investigate the noise. It was the baobab tree that had crashed.

We still had not left the country; we were in Khartoum, the capital city, waiting to leave. Pastor Paul sent word and gave us the same message he had called to us as the butts of the guns were beating the people when we left the mission station: "God has built His Church. He has built His own stronghold here and the gates of hell shall not prevail against it."

The baobab tree had been the landmark we watched for as we trekked in deep mud through the tall grass. We'd see the baobab tree and say, "Not much farther to go through all this." Now that great tree had crashed! The people said, "The pastor told us the truth. The pastor told us the truth." He had told them that the true Spirit now indwelt them. No more did they need to fear the evil spirits. The church now possessed the stronghold of Satan. That was the frontier we went to take.

I told you we were in the land of the Nile. According to Ezekiel, "Every thing liveth . . . whithersoever the rivers shall come" (47:9). But the tributaries of the Nile didn't reach as far as we were.

One day Mary and I were going through the tall grass in our jeep. It was the dry season and the tall grass crackled as we made our own road. Suddenly I heard a faint voice, I said, "Mary, stop. I hear something." So we stopped. We followed a faint whisper, "Water, water!" Lying in the grass was a red-skinned Arab who had lost his way. He had come there with his herds for water and had gotten lost. The bees had sucked all of the water out of our water bags but we had some in tins for the jeep. We got some water and gave him a drop at a time with a medicine dropper to try to save him. We bundled him up lovingly into the little jeep. It wasn't a very soft bed for a dying man but we showed him all the love we could. We comforted him in Arabic because we had learned Arabic by ear, but it was too late. The river hadn't reached him.

Out of everyone that believes flows a river. That's what sharing is and that's what we're to be: rivers of water to all around us and to the frontier. "Everything liveth . . . whithersoever the rivers come." But it's going to take some who are willing for more than short-term service, who are willing for more than fringe benefits, who are willing to be totally committed: men and women after God's own heart, willing to strive and stamp out, by faith, the sons of Anak, the giants, Satan's stronghold in these frontiers made up of 2.7 billion people. But God knows where the seekers are who want to know His will. He's a safe and sure guide! Don't fail Him. Get going soon! Get into the last great push of getting the gospel to this new frontier of nearly two-thirds of the world's population.

11

GIVE AND GO: HOW TO MULTIPLY YOURSELF BEFORE PROCEEDING OVERSEAS

David Bryant

Basically, the world might be divided into *four major spheres:* (1) 1 billion people who, at least on a survey, would call themselves Christians; (2) 800 million people who are not believers but are easily reached with the gospel, accessible to normal evangelistic efforts by existing Christian fellowships without the witnesses crossing major human barriers; (3) 2.5 billion people who can only be reached through major new mission-ary-style evangelistic strategies by witnesses who penetrate formidable human barriers that have historically placed these people beyond the reach of the gospel; (4) 200 million active Christians out of which (as estimated by the World Evangelical Fellowship) approximately 70 million are evangelicals, committed to actively sharing their faith with non-Christians.

Can the challenge of reaching earth's unreached be met in our generation? Yes!—*if* those seventy million "evangelicals" have a vision not only for non-Christians like them (culturally, socially) and near them (geographically), but also for the very "ends of the earth," for peoples who have no one like them near them to tell them. We must recapture a vision of a Lord able to manifest His Kingdom within His Church sufficiently to break *through* those barriers, and to fulfill His purposes for the nations *through* His church in this generation.

Consequently, we actually face two challenges and must be committed on two levels: first, reaching the unreached (like the Muslim world as well as the Hindu, Tribal, Chinese, and Buddhist worlds—almost 2.5 billion people), *and* second, mobilizing the Church of Jesus Christ with a vision for missionary penetration of these major blocks of unreached peoples.

Included in this, of course, is helping people catch a vision for the unreached all around us (such as internationals on our college campuses and ethnic enclaves in our urban centers). But we must not stop here. The harder job is to spawn a heart commitment for those out of sight, out of range, and totally out of hope. I'm thinking of half the world's unreached peoples who reside inside a two-thousand-mile radius centered around Dakar, Bangladesh. For their sakes too, we must mobilize our fellow Christians with a vision for God's saving purposes among *all* these nations.

So much is at stake. We need to mobilize people with a world vision if we're ever to help fill the need for missionary manpower. Did you know that right now there are about eight thousand missionaries worldwide working among those 2.5 billion people to do full-fledged church planting evangelism? Look with me at the facts: worldwide we have about 950 thousand full-time Christian workers. More are needed. In addition there are 80 thousand Protestant missionaries concentrating their ministries on existing Christians, or on those who are reachable by existing Christians through normal evangelism. Of course, their work is also important. But, worldwide only eight thousand Protestant missionaries are concentrating their efforts on the 2.5 billion totally unreached peoples of earth. Do you see why we need to be actively involved in sharing a world vision? While it is a vision of who God is and where He's going, a vision full of purpose and promise, it is also a vision full of the *need*. It's in the context of a growing world vision within the corporate life of God's people that God will be able to speak and be clearly heard by those He is sending to close this tremendous gap.

There's another vital reason for giving a world vision: the tremendous worldwide opportunities currently begging for laborers. Opportunities listed in the Inter-Cristo computer matching service indicate approximately thirteen thousand openings overseas waiting to be filled right now. In light of the tremendous opportunities God has set before us, one of the greatest things any of us could do is to give God's people a vision not only of the need but of the tremendous opportunities which many of them could step into.

Finally, I suggest that we need to spread our world vision because the spiritual vitality of the church itself is at stake. At a meeting of the Student Volunteer Movement in 1901, John R. Mott, one of the movement's great leaders, observed:

> There is no subject, unless it be the study of the life of Christ, the study of which is more broadening, more deepening, more elevating, more inspiring than the subject of world-wide missions. No subject more broadening—it embraces all mankind, no subject more deepening—it takes us down to the very depths of the designs of God; surely no subject more elevating—I can think of nothing that so lifts a man out of himself; and can anything be more inspiring than the enterprise that commanded the life and death and resurrection of our Lord Jesus? I repeat it, therefore, that we do our fel-

low young men and young women a grave injustice to keep out of their lives this sublime enterprise as a special study.

Do you believe that? Do you believe that one of the greatest blessings we could give to any Christian is to give him or her a vision for the whole world the way God sees it? Do you believe that the vitality of their lives and of the church at large is at stake? As we've seen in the awakenings, as the church has been opened up with a new vision for Christ and His global cause, God has moved forward through spiritual renewal to carry out His purpose among the nations with renewed impact.

This brings us, then, to the basic question: are *you* a mission-minded person? If so, are you prepared to give your vision for the world to other Christians? Are you available to God's Spirit that He might use you to create an environment for faith in your Bible study group, your church, or your own family? Faith that opens them to Christ's global cause in such a way that God can be clearly heard and obeyed? Faith that opens up both those He is drawing forth to be penetrators and those He is assigning to stand behind them as senders?

"Give and go." It is a clear biblical principle. If anybody modeled this principle surely it was the Apostle Paul. Although he served as a missionary, he multiplied his heart for the world back at the congregational bases that sent him. For example, writing to the Corinthian church, Paul said: "For it seems to me that God has put us apostles [or missionaries, we might say] on display at the end of the procession, like men condemned to die in the arena. We have been made a spectacle to the whole universe, to angels as well as to men" (1 Cor. 4:9). A very sober description of those who "go." But then he adds, "We are fools for Christ, but you are so wise in Christ!" (v. 10). He becomes a mite facetious to shock the Corinthian church into a deeper concern for the purposes of God. So, he suggests: "Look, you see how we live for

the purposes of God. How about you? You see how weak we are and yet you claim strength. Have you ever shared our kinds of weaknesses in the mission of Christ? You feel so honored. Have you ever been dishonored the way we're dishonored in order to advance the gospel of Christ among the nations?"

Paul doesn't stop either; he really lays it on. "When we are cursed, we bless; when we are persecuted, we endure it; when we are slandered, we answer kindly. Up to this moment we have become the scum of the earth, the refuse of the world" (vv. 12-13). Why is he writing this? To brag? To gain their pity? No! He observes, "I am not writing this to shame you [neither is he writing to put them on a guilt trip], but to warn you, as my dear children. Even though you have ten thousand guardians in Christ, you do not have many fathers, for in Christ Jesus I became your father through the gospel. Therefore I urge you to *imitate* me" (vv. 14-16, italics added).

"Give and go."

Are you the "father" or "mother" for anyone right now? Is there anyone with whom you have that kind of relationship? If so, as you move out further in your work with Christ and His ministry in the world, you have a right to challenge them the way Paul does. Not just to consider missionary service. You can call them to something even deeper: to imitate a life committed 100 percent, at whatever cost, to serving the cause of Christ, even to the very ends of the earth. "Therefore I *urge* you to imitate me," Paul writes. "For this reason I am sending to you Timothy, my son whom I love, who is faithful in the Lord. He will *remind* you of my way of life in Christ Jesus, which agrees with what I teach everywhere in every church" (vv. 16,17 italics added).

To help us imitate Paul in this ministry of "giving and going," I would like to recommend we each establish three key objectives for the next twelve months (at least):

1. I will give my world vision to the core members of my Christian fellowship in such a way that within the next twelve months every person will have personally explored and prayed about their role in the world mission of the church.
2. From among those I influence, I will disciple a few within the next twenty-four months, into a sending base (or a team) to back missionaries overseas. (Here, you're looking for people who will stand with you, who have a vision for missions because they've caught it with you and are willing to own it as their own. They see you as "bone of their bone and flesh of their flesh" in that ministry, and embrace it with you in every way possible.)
3. From among those I influence (as a result of objectives #1 and #2) I will disciple at least one in the next twenty-four months to go into cross-cultural ministry. (This is similar to how Paul discipled Timothy, who not only traveled with him, but finally entered into his very own missionary ministry.)

Look at these three objectives for a moment. Do they seem manageable to you? Why would incorporating them into your life strategy be a crucial step for the impact of your life on world evangelization?

Who are the people right now that you influence in one of these three ways already? Who else might be added? Why do you want to help prayerfully explore their role in world missions? Of these, which four or five would you like to work with in-depth, discipling them as a sending base? And, who is that one person God has brought into your life who indicates a growing interest in cross-cultural ministry? May I suggest that some time this week you write down the names of those you will serve in this way during the next year.

My friend, Bruce Graham, directs the Institute of Hindu Studies at the U.S. Center for World Mission. When he was a little boy he intended to be an astronaut. As an eleven-year-old, he used to sit on the back porch of his home at night, looking at the moon and thinking of the day he would be able to walk on it. But while he was studying Aeronautical Engineering at MIT, a Christian international student from India won him to Christ and began to disciple him. Well, as you can imagine, being discipled by an international student can give you a world vision from the outset!

Finally, the time came when God redirected Bruce from a mission to the moon to a mission to the Hindu world, seeking new ways of reaching some of the 600 million Hindus in India. But Bruce didn't just "go," he also gave away the world vision his mentor had given him. While he was still a member of Park Street Church in Boston, he gathered around him a group of some thirty-five students. They formed what they called the Fellowship of World Christians. Bruce began to pour into their lives the growing world vision God was pouring into him. A number of them are overseas right now; many others are in significant roles of ministry, transferring their world vision to others.

Bruce moved to Southern California shortly before he set out for more extensive ministry in India. He and others formed a community called the Haggai Community. Based on the challenge God gave an ancient remnant through the prophet Haggai, they too assumed a responsibility to help rebuild a temple. Only in this case the temple was one of people, of "living stones" (1 Pet. 2). It too stands in ruins, because so many are totally unreached. The Haggai Community was made up of both those preparing to be "penetrators" and others who long to be "senders." One of the primary reasons for the community was to stimulate each other in their vision, to keep it alive and hold one another accountable to it.

When Bruce finally launched out for some months in India, he left behind him a whole community of people who shared his vision and burden. But he didn't stop there! Not only has Bruce gone to India several times to work there with a third-world missionary movement, but every time he goes he takes a group of students or young adults with him. For three or four months they observe the needs and opportunities firsthand. Through all he does, Bruce is giving them a *world* vision, while sticking to the three objectives we outlined earlier.

Now, on to more practicalities.

Over a number of years of trying to give a world vision to others, I've found some very helpful principles. I'd like to share some of these with you now.

The first principle is, *vision-giving is always a spiritual transaction.* It happens in an environment created by the Spirit of God Himself. Our mission is the world of unreached peoples, yes. The barriers we face are primarily cross-cultural. But the dynamic to move in that direction comes as God pours out His Spirit in answer to the prayers of His people. It's in this context—this dynamic of power and awakening—that a world vision most effectively spreads. It *is* a transaction between us and God.

Maybe one of the most important steps you could take, therefore, to share a world vision is to get a group of people around you to pray, not simply for the prayer targets of *Operation World* (as important as that is) but for the fulfillment of the world vision that *Scripture* already lays out before us.

Returning to the India scene for a moment: I've spent time there with leaders of the Friends Missionary Prayer Band, a movement of twenty thousand laypeople banded together in over five hundred prayer groups. They are committed to the evangelization of all of India in this generation, and to sending out many of their own to carry the gospel across caste, language, and tribal barriers. We're talking about literally thousands of castes and tribal groups where there is no church and no Christian to reach them at this hour. What a tremendous vision this prayer movement has embraced! Meeting every Wednesday to fast and pray all night with so little to work with, financially speaking; they willingly sacrifice what they have in order to send out the missionaries. And God is using the dynamic of their vision (for them it *is* like a vision for the ends of the earth) to bring revival in the churches of South India—renewal of faith in the Lord Jesus as well as a commitment to His purposes in India. The only explanation is that their vision-giving is a spiritual transaction initiated and completed in an environment of faith, springing from a movement of prayer.

Here's another principle to consider: *people are at all stages, at all points in their understanding of and their emotional or volitional commitment to world evangelization.* For some, it's an issue they've never thought about once in their lives. Do you know anybody like that? When they hear you, they panic. They think your very next statement will be, "Here, sign on the dotted line and take the next boat to China." It all seems so far beyond them, so irrelevant . . . almost "extra-terrestrial."

So the challenge we want people to face is the call to be *willing.* We must help them to be willing—not willing to go or willing to send first of all, but willing to be *open* to Christ and His global cause.

Let me illustrate. Dr. Robert B. Munger wrote a booklet called *My Heart, Christ's Home.* What an excellent way of looking at the Christian life! Here's the summary. I invite Christ into my heart (that is, my "home.") He roams through the various rooms—the many facets of my life—making the changes He has every right to make because He is Lord. Finally, I realize I should just sign over the deed, hand Him the key and make it all His home.

But from another perspective, my heart is Christ's *launching pad.* It's His base of operation. Let me rewrite Dr. Munger's parable to add this dimension.

You hear a knock at the door. You open the door. There's Jesus. But something's different. He's not like the paintings you've seen of Him. Instead He's standing there wearing a backpack! He says, "I'd like to come in for just a few minutes. I don't have long, I'm on the move, but we need to talk." So I invite Him in. He may roam through a few of the rooms, making observations about the dust of disarray. But you can tell there's something else on His mind.

He invites you to sit down with Him in the living room. Then He reaches in His backpack and pulls out a Bible and a map of the world. First He goes through the Bible, talking to you about the purposes of God that stretch back to the call of Abraham, and before, purposes that kept in view all the nations; redemptive purposes—to cover the earth with a knowledge of His glory as the waters cover the sea (see Isa. 11:9). He talks to you about what He has done to bring those purposes to victory and fulfillment, making peace by His blood, shed on His cross. He tells you that all things on earth will be summed up in Him. Then He unrolls His world map and talks to you about various places in the world where there are peoples who have not yet heard this wonderful message, who have not yet met Him. He shares His burden for the world situation as it currently stands, and for all He wants to do about it through His church.

Then, He closes His Bible, rolls up the map, and sticks them both back into His backpack. He looks at you. "Now, I'd like you to find your backpack, search the rooms of your house to pack up the things you're sure you'll need to follow me into this global cause, right to the ends of the earth. Then, come follow me."

So, you pick out the food, the reading material, the clothes—the things in your life that are absolutely essential to following Christ to the ends of the earth, wherever He wants to go. You want to be with Him in whatever He wants you to do, in light of what He has shown you in His Book and on His map.

Before you can fill your backpack, you notice He's already standing at the front door; He's on His way out. So, you load the bundle on your back and head out the front door. As you turn to shut the door you throw away the key because you're never going back again. Can you see yourself striking off with Him over the horizon with your backpacks bobbing behind you?

Now, that, to me, is an illustration of what it means to call people to be *willing* to go with Christ wherever He wants to go and to be whatever He wants them to be for the sake of His worldwide mission. Becoming a sender or penetrater isn't the first issue; being *open* to follow Christ without limits is.

In 1980 at the International Student Consultation of Frontier Missions in Edinburgh, delegates drew up a "Declaration of Intent." It had two sentences to it. It was composed by a special committee consisting of students from ten different nations. The delegation adopted it unanimously. That "Declaration of Intent" read this way:

> By the grace of God, and for His glory, I commit my entire life to obeying the commission of Matthew 28:18-20 wherever and however God leads me, giving priority to those peoples who are currently beyond the reach of the gospel. I will endeavor to share that vision with others.

There it is again: "I'm going, but I want to give my vision to others." What is that vision? According to the Edinburgh declaration, to be open to whatever the Great Commission has for me. Having nurtured an environment for response through a movement of prayer, you actually *start* giving a world vision to others by calling them to unqualified willingness and obedience.

Now let's look at additional principles to help you "give and go."

A third one is obvious: *stay close to Christ yourself.* Henry Martyn, a great missionary to India in the early 1800s, said, "The Spirit of Christ is the Spirit of missions and the nearer we get to Him, the more intensely missionary we must become." The more your life is saturated with Christ, the more you'll have a missionary vision to give to others.

A fourth principle: *keep it biblical.* Several years ago, after completing graduate courses on the theology of missions, I tried an unusual project. I worked through an inexpensive Bible with a pink highlighting pen, underlining every verse in the Bible that dealt with the global cause of Christ: with God's interest in, concern for, or action among the nations. I'd say that about 40 percent of my Bible turned pink. I was in shock! I had no idea that there was that much in Scripture on the subject. Of course, some of the passages dealt with God's judgment; others with redemption. But it's all His work with the nations. So, I suggest to you, whatever you do in giving a world vision, keep it biblical. You'll have no trouble doing it. Let's say you're in a weekly small group. One of the ways you could help that group catch a world vision is during its Bible study. Personally study the portion of Scripture beforehand looking for what's being said in context about God's purposes for the world. There will be a few times when you can't, in the study itself, help the group to see the implications of what they're discovering from Scriptures for God's purposes for the nations, especially through them.

Next principle I suggest: *bank on the premises.* The premises I bank on when I move into people's lives include: (1) the Church is on the verge of spiritual awakening; (2) God's Spirit is already at work in the lives of my friends, as He is in my own, to prepare us for what He's about to do; (3) God is more committed than I could ever be to world evangelization and to reviving all of us with a vision for Christ and His global cause. *He* wants to give them a world vision.

Over the years I've taken a survey in churches and on campuses prior to one of our World Christian Conferences. My findings indicate there are a great number of people out there whom God has made willing to look at the world, to move out with a vision for the world, if someone will just say to them: "I'm concerned about what you're concerned about. I'd like to explore that with you. Let's get together and do it!" I bank on such premises, on what I believe God is already doing to prepare the way before me.

Next principle: *expect a battle.* Satan's greatest concern, next to preventing people from coming to a saving knowledge of Christ, I'm convinced, is to prevent them from catching a world vision, from being committed to reaching those who have yet to come to Christ. As I've shared my vision, whether at large conferences or with single individuals, I've felt again and again that the experience has similar spiritual dynamics to sharing the gospel with a non-Christian. Spiritual warfare is going on. Satan seeks to prevent God's vision for the world from getting through. So be prepared.

Another principle is to *listen for the barriers.* There are at least three that I frequently find: (1) People struggle with the *cost* of being involved in world missions. (2) People resist based on *false images* they have about world missions. (3) People retreat into a current model of *discipleship* that leaves missions at the fringes of spiritual growth. There are other barriers. What have you found?

As you're seeking to give a world vision, do some listening. Find out whether their negative responses to what you say spring from blatant disobedience to the revealed will of God, or whether the person is in fact struggling with a legitimate concern that every one of us may have had, at one point or another, in our own growth as world Christians. We need to listen for those barriers and help our friends work through them.

Another key principle is: *build bridges of trust.* Have you heard about GMT? Anytime one goes through a rough experience in missionary preparation, we call it GMT: "Great Missionary Training." Well, giving a world vision is GMT! Here's one good example. You must learn to build bridges of trust in your host culture so that you can share the gospel with those who trust you as a friend. The same effort must be made if we are to get across our world vision to another Christian. People need to trust you first and believe you care for them as people. Learning how to do this is GMT!

Still another principle: *unveil the big picture.* In other words, be sure people see the whole scope of what God's up to. Don't give them just one little piece of the picture. Call them to explore the whole picture. From my experience it seems almost everything that's being said about world missions in Scripture or in the contemporary scene can be broken down into four areas (*In the Gap* takes a whole chapter for each of these areas):

1. God has a worldwide *purpose* in Christ that encompasses all creation, all history, and all people everywhere.
2. There is a world full of *possibilities* through Christ for fulfilling that purpose in our generation.
3. There is also a world full of *people* without Christ currently beyond the reach of the gospel for whom the purpose is also intended.
4. God has given every Christian a world-sized part with Christ that allows us to be strategically involved in His purpose for the whole earth.

Give them the whole picture, the big picture. It's so exciting!

Speak out for the enterprise called "missions." Don't be ashamed to actually talk about the process of strategically deploying cross-cultural workers across major human barriers to penetrate those people-groups blocked from the gospel by the barriers. Talk about the need for both *missionaries* and *"tent-makers."* Be sure, however, to keep the perspective of the overall picture of Christ's global cause and where "missions" fits in.

Another principle: *fire their imaginations!* Pentecost demonstrated that God wants to give young people new visions and old people new dreams. A group of some thirty students from five different campus movements at Penn State spent a semester exploring, week by week, the big picture of Christ's global cause. Often they were led by career missionaries. It was called the Institute of International Studies. In it God gave them a vision so thrilling, that fired them with such zeal, they couldn't let it go! So they banded together after the course into a "Caleb" project to send out four of their number to work in one of the most difficult to penetrate areas of the world. That part of their "project" ended with more triumphs, which fired them with more dreams. The whole group has fanned out in small teams to other campuses to challenge fellow students to believe God for the same things in their lives. How did it start? When students met together to share the big picture of world missions, and God fired their imaginations with *His* dreams.

Another principle: *glow with enthusiasm!* That's important in vision-giving. Simply put, you need to break through people's emotional barriers, through the fears and the reservations they often have, by letting them see *your* enthusiasm for Christ and His global cause. Sometimes that's all they need in order to be free in themselves to begin to follow after you—and Him.

Meet their felt needs is another principle. Often I try a little experiment with an audience. I ask the question, "What's in it for you if you become a world Christian? If

you take a world vision and put it at the heart and center of your life in Christ, and order your steps accord-
ingly, what's in it for *you*?" I have them brainstorm in
three major areas of concern: their own personal development, their growth as disciples of Christ, and their
on-going ministry for Christ right now. There are many
new and wonderful ways a life prospers, and our felt
needs are met as growing believers when we grow with a
world vision. As people see this, they want you to give
them more.

The next principle is: *infiltrate and integrate.* Get
your world vision into the mainstream of the life of the
people you're seeking to reach with it. Whether it's in
one-to-one relationships, small groups, or maybe a worship service in your church, get the world vision integrated into that experience on a regular basis so it's
constantly in the air they breathe, so that it feels like it
"belongs" to whatever they are doing.

Next: *stay flexible.* Start with people where they're
at. We talk about the Bible having progressive revelation: God's worldwide purposes move from what He
showed Abraham all the way up to its fuller dimensions
in the writings of Paul. Similarly, there's an experience
of "progressive revelation" for most of us as God brings
us along in our vision for the world. Stay flexible; work
with them where they're at. Don't push them too fast,
don't assume too much. Keep pace with the Spirit who
gives the vision.

Another principle: when you're discipling people,
disciple them in focus. What does that mean? Don't let
their growth in Christ become an end in itself. Always
keep the world before them as you disciple them to
pray, as you teach them to study Scripture, as you train
them to witness. I'm talking about brand new Christians. As a part of your strategy to give a world vision in
the next twelve months, ask God to give you someone to
win to Christ—a brand new Christian—so that right
from the beginning you can disciple him with a focus

that is not just on Christ and his personal life with Him but also on Christ's global cause and his place in it.

The next principle: *make it manageable.* As we help people take hold of a world vision, I believe every one can come to the place in his life where he can say, "I know this day my life has counted strategically for Christ's global cause, especially for those currently beyond the reach of the gospel." *In the Gap* suggests one model of how that would look. There are others. But make the vision manageable and practical, so they can say every day, "The vision you're giving me for the world has made a difference today in the impact my life has had on the cause of Christ." A commitment to faithful daily prayer for the world is certainly a great place to begin.

Get them into the action! The more you actually get people involved in your vision—not just by education, but also by practical action—the more it will become real to them. We do what we believe; we often believe what we do, too. That's where a *movement* of prayer for spiritual awakening and world evangelization can be so powerful. In it we can help people turn information into the action of intercession.

Then, *secure a second decision for Christ.* It was D.T. Niles who said, "Every Christian goes through two conversions. There's conversion out of the world to Christ but there's conversion with Christ back into the world." In a sense, there will come a point when you're sharing a world vision with an individual, or maybe even with a small group, where you'll need to take the initiative to say, "Now, on the basis of what you've found, are you ready and willing to open your life to follow Christ however He leads, giving priority to those peoples currently beyond the reach of the gospel?" We must press the "second" decision home when the time is right. It's as strategic as calling for a first-time commitment to Christ.

For those who respond, here's an additional princi-

ple: *get them together.* There are so many things in
society, in the church, even in our own natures that
want to pull us back from the world and even from
God's purposes for the world—back into ourselves and
our own selfish ambitions. One of the ways to defy this
spiritual law of gravity is to be banded with others who
want to move with us, and to keep one another accountable.

Link up with local churches. That's the ideal place
to get them together. Whoever you influence with a
world vision, especially toward overseas ministry, be
sure you link them up early with missions-minded people in local churches. And, help other people in that
church to stand with them in the same vision. ACMC—
the Association of Church Missions Committees—had
a conference with the theme: "The Local Church—
Seedbed for World Missions." How very true! How
important to remember in our vision-giving strategy.

Finally, *watch God work.* In an article from the most
recent *Evangelical Missions Quarterly,* Jim Reapsome
writes:

> In this research-minded age we also need to be
> wary of eliminating the mystery of God's sover-
> eignty in a person's life, in giving them a vision,
> in calling them to move with Christ to the ends
> of the earth. Certainly there's an important
> place for vocational counseling and testing.
> That's part of finding one's God-given strengths
> and interests. But no on likes to be pro-
> grammed. We must leave room for the wind of
> the Holy Spirit to be heard, even if we can't see
> it. Perhaps in the past the call was too mysteri-
> ous, but we believe the history of past student
> movements for missions reveals a strong ele-
> ment of the unexplained. No amount of
> research would have determined the conse-
> quence of the Haystack Prayer Meeting at Wil-

liams College one hundred and seventy-five years ago.

How did God give those five students a world vision anyhow? I don't know exactly. But it was clarified in a movement of prayer. It came on the crest of awakening. And it came to those who were serious about Christ and His Word.

One thing I *do* know, however: those five students committed themselves from the very outset to make the vision God had given them under that haystack something they would go on giving to others before they themselves ever went. In fact, they formed "Societies of Inquiry" that were eventually found in 70 of the 202 campuses in America before 1830.

May I encourage you to hear with Isaiah the statement, "Who will go?" and to say, "Here am I. Send me— send me first to multiply myself and my vision in my church or on my campus. Send me to give them the vision you've given me of Christ and of your purposes under Him for the nations. I'm ready to go overseas, yes. I'm also ready to *give* before I go."

12
THE HISTORY AND FUTURE OF INTERDENOMINATIONAL MISSIONS
Peter Stam

There is no mention that I know of in the Scriptures of interdenominational missions. As a matter of fact, there's no mention of *denominational* missions. I'll go one step further. There's no mention that I can find of *denominations,* except, perhaps, one little passage in one of Paul's letters where he makes some rather negative comments (1 Cor. 3:3-5). "Since there is jealousy and quarreling among you, are you not worldly? Are you not acting like mere men? For when one says, 'I follow Paul,' and another, 'I follow Apollos,' are you not mere men? What, after all, is Apollos? And what is Paul? Only servants, through whom you came to believe." So we conclude that in the eyes of Paul, as he wrote that passage, divisions within the Body were evidence of worldliness and lack of maturity. But the Scriptures are absolutely full of the subject of missions and missionary teams—in Old Testament, New Testament—and almost any page you turn to, there it is! The most obvious example is that of Paul and his first missionary team as they were commissioned by the church at Antioch to go forth. The implications of that team ministry for our present structure verifies that team work is biblical. Paul had a team. All through the book of Acts we read about Paul and his team: Timothy and Epaphras and Luke and Mark and Silas and Barnabas, different ones with whom he teamed from time to time.

Ideally, interdenominational missions come closer to the New Testament concept in that at least some of them represent the whole Church of Christ witnessing to the whole world. But we're still talking about human structures, not something that is divinely inspired and revealed in the Scriptures. I want to make clear that I'm using the term "interdenominational" to refer to all societies not directly related to a church denomination, whether they draw personnel and finances from the old-line denominations, from the newer denominations, or just from the independent churches. Certainly we are not talking about "anti-denominational" societies. Use whichever term you wish: interdenominational or non-denominational. We are basically discussing the phenomenon of mission societies not organizationally linked with church denominations.

Looking into church history in the past several centuries, we recognize that some denominations were established for historical and for doctrinal reasons and represent the efforts of godly and committed men to perpetuate and disseminate their spiritual and theological convictions, which were very deep and very real to them. Unfortunately we all are aware of the fact that some denominations have been founded on far less significant factors and have, at times, tended to major in minors. Some have been willing to establish a denomination on whether to have instrumental music in church or not. Some denominations have been founded on the basis of whether you should be baptized three times backwards or one time forward. Denominations have been founded on whether to lift up your hands when you sing praises to God or not. I'm being a bit facetious, of course. But, unfortunately, there have been some human structures set up in the name of the Church which have very little biblical or rational basis for their organization. Some reasons are cultural and some are personal, but that's the situation in which we live today.

However, we recognize that God has mightily used denominations. I mention this now because I want to make it very clear that we're not setting up an antithetical situation. Denominations provided the ecclesiastical support base for the first missionaries of the modern period, and they continue that function for many missionaries today. In 1732, Count von Zinzendorf, of the Moravian church, took a group of refugees into his estate, discipled them and sent them out to different parts of the world as missionaries. The Moravian church is, in a sense, a denomination and was used mightily of God to eventually reach out into every continent of the world. Then, of course, we know that William Carey was a Baptist. God used him to organize the Baptist Missionary Society. It was a denominational society. Carey, himself, went as the first western missionary to India back in 1792. The Church Missionary Society, founded in 1799, was within the Anglican or Episcopalian communion. Many other denominations on the European continent and in the U.K. were prominent early in the modern period of missions. The American Board of Commissioners for Foreign Missions developed out of the Haystack Prayer Meeting, primarily within the Congregational denomination. Adoniram Judson was one of their first missionaries going with the first party to the land of Burma.

If denominational mission societies were so active and so effective in getting our modern missionary period going, why the rise of interdenominational societies? Dr. E. L. Frizen, executive director of the IFMA, wrote a doctoral dissertation entitled, "A Historical Study of the Interdenominational Foreign Mission

Association in Relation to Evangelical Unity and Cooperation." In it he discussed this very question and stated four basic reasons for the formation of interdenominational societies in the 1800s and the early 1900s.

The first of these four basic reasons was *the desire to see that the missionary mandate was being fully pursued,* and the conviction that it was *not* being fully pursued by denominational boards. This included a concern that every available, appropriate method and resource be used in fulfilling the Great Commission. Did you know that concerned women organized the first interdenominational mission board in the United States? It was called the Women's Union Missionary Society and it was formed in 1860. A group of concerned women made repeated approaches to the denominational men's boards for the opportunity of going out to minister to women and children in Asia, and every time they were rebuffed. There was no vision whatsoever on the part of the denominational boards of those days to use single women in missionary work. The society existed under that name until just a few years ago when it merged with another society; so its ministry still continues.

Of course, today the prominent and effective place of women in foreign missions has been well documented and is very evident. Approximately one-third of our Africa Inland Mission missionaries are single women. We thank God for them. In no way would God have accomplished through us as a human structure what He has accomplished without the very strong, important, and effective place of women in missions.

The concern for the use of all available methods and resources has since then led to the formation of many other interdenominational societies with specialized ministries. Wycliffe Bible Translators is a notable example, while others include the World Radio Missionary Fellowship (HCJB—voice of the Andes); Gospel Recordings, and Mission Aviation Fellowship. Those and a lot of others were organized because they sensed that they were providing a specialized service which was not available up until that time.

The second major factor that Dr. Frizen referred to in his thesis as a reason for the establishing of interdenominational societies was *the existence of major unreached areas and people and the lack of any significant vision or plan for reaching them on the part of the denominational boards of that day.* God laid a burden on Hudson Taylor's heart to reach the vast multitudes in the interior of China. In his day there were societies at work in Shanghai and Canton and Hong Kong and various other port cities along the coast, but none had penetrated inland. So the China Inland Mission was born in 1865, just five years after the Women's Union Missionary Society. At the time Hudson Taylor began his work in China, there were only ninety-seven missionaries in all of China. Because of the evident unwillingness of the existing boards to move inland, Taylor believed the answer was an independent, interdenominational board with missionaries accepted from many different church backgrounds. So, the classic example, in many ways, of an interdenominational society, the China Inland Mission began its ministry. God's blessing on this approach was evident with rapid and steady growth. In 1929 the China Inland Mission had thirteen hundred missionaries in China, four hundred of them nationals and the other nine hundred expatriates. Total evacuation took place in the early 1950s because of the Communist takeover. Since then, of course, it's been renamed Overseas Missionary Fellowship and rejuvenated, and today it is working in many, many countries of the Orient with some eight hundred missionaries overseas at the present time.

A few years ago I had the opportunity of participating in the Thailand Consultation. On my way home, since I had never visited the Orient before, I made some brief stops in Hong Kong and a few other places, and I shall never forget the opportunity which that afforded me to see a different part of the world. During the several days I was in Hong Kong, I took a tour around the New Territories north of Hong Kong and got to within a few feet of the mainland China border. I saw the barricades and the barbed wire and the gates and I climbed a little hill where the Hong Kong New Territories government was a police post for the primary purpose of preventing mainland China refugees from escaping into Hong Kong.

I confess that as I stood on that hill and looked over the little river that formed the border, and the fences and the barbed wire in between, I thought back to those days when Hudson Taylor must have had something of a similar experience. But when *he* looked over into mainland China, there was no Church there. There were no believers there. Not one! Just those few along the coast. But when I looked over that border just last year, I did so with an awareness (because several of us had just had a briefing by old China hands in Hong Kong) that over there, amongst those one billion people in that great land of China, there are estimated to be somewhere between twenty-five and fifty million Christians, brothers and sisters of ours as part of the Body of Christ. Some estimates are even higher. Many of them have suffered a great deal. Many have been in prison because their faith in Jesus Christ became known. But they're there! Forty thousand house churches in China today!

In Hong Kong we heard about one large commune in the interior of China where there are thirty-five thousand professed believers in Jesus Christ! In one commune! The Christian faith in that area is so strong that the authorities have just thrown up their hands and given up. They couldn't cope with it without slaughtering the whole town. We heard that in that commune, and several others in that area, the favorite and the most sought out occupation by Christians has been that of barber. You can imagine why. They've got a captive audience and they use their profession for the glory of God. As they clip away at the hair, they share their faith in Jesus Christ. So, God has His people in the land of China. That's the way the China Inland Mission got started—because of a conviction and a burden that God put on the heart of Hudson Taylor to reach into the interior where nobody had gone with the message of salvation through Jesus Christ.

Peter Cameron Scott, the founder of Africa Inland Mission, is not very well-known in this country for a reason that I'll share with you in a moment. He was driven by a similar vision to reach the multitudes in the interior of Central and East Africa. At that time the only missionary work in East Africa was right along the coast. Peter Cameron Scott was burdened of God to reach *over* that area to the *inland* of Africa where nothing whatsoever had been done and where the slave trade was still carried on by the Arab slavers, who pitted one tribe against another and one clan against another. As a way of getting a little material wealth, they would sell their own brothers and sisters to the slavers. The slaughter and human suffering caused by the whole slavery movement is almost indescribable.

Scott went out in 1895 with a party of eight missionaries, landed at Mombasa on the coast and, after getting organized and securing porters to carry their goods, started inland. There were no roads in those days, just rough paths. The East African railway was being built but it hadn't progressed very far yet. It took the missionaries six weeks to cover two hundred miles. They finally came to a little place called Nzawe, near a pass in the mountains of that area, which was considered the gateway to the interior of East Africa. It was there that he established the first of our mission stations.

I had the opportunity of visiting Nzawe a few years

ago. It's not one of the strongest places in the Africa Inland Church today. At Nzawe, the very first mission station of Africa Inland Mission, there was not even one believer until thirty-five years after the missionaries first settled in there. Why? Because missionary work in the frontier area is a spiritual battle. That particular place was the domain of an unusually powerful witch doctor who was considered to have demonic powers and was so highly respected by the people of the Kamba tribe in that whole area that he was able to prevent any establishment of the church of the Lord Jesus Christ for a period of thirty-five years.

The missionaries moved into other areas of that same tribe, established stations, and very quickly the work took root. Today the church among the Kamba people alone numbers about 400 thousand people, many hundreds of congregations.

When Peter Cameron Scott first embarked on this venture, his vision was to establish a chain of mission stations, starting at the coast, at Mombasa on the Indian Ocean, and stretching more than halfway across the continent of Africa to Lake Chad. His thought was that this chain of mission stations, in each case, would be bases out from which the missionaries and ultimately the African Christians would spread in an attempt to permeate the whole of Central Africa. But Peter Cameron Scott never lived to see that vision fulfilled. One year and five months later he was in his grave. When I visited Nzawe I stood at the foot of Peter Cameron Scott's grave and gave my life in a new fresh way to Jesus Christ for the accomplishing of His burden.

The first party of missionaries who went out in 1895 numbered eight, with Scott as their leader. In five years, there was only one left. Four of them had died; three were invalid at home; only one left. Missionary work is a battle.

In the land of Congo, where my wife and I worked

and lived for eighteen years, and where we were involved in training leadership for an already established church, I am told that there were twenty missionary graves before there were twenty believers in Jesus Christ. Missionary work was tough in those early days.

But that was the vision! There were no denominational boards in those days that were willing to penetrate beyond the coast into the interior. So one young man got the vision and established the mission. Today there are seven hundred missionaries working in twelve countries including the U.S. which has "hidden people" area in Newark, New Jersey.

The Sudan Interior Mission, a sister mission of ours, has a very similar story. Roland V. Bingham was its founder. His vision was to evangelize the people of west Africa. Once again, the denominational boards at that time were just along the coast. Roland V. Bingham and two friends, a trio of men, went to Nigeria to explore the lay of the land and to investigate the possibility of establishing mission work there. Then they came home and approached a number of denominational boards. One denominational leader said to him, "Young man, you will never see the Sudan. Your son will never see the Sudan. Maybe your grandson, but that's not likely." So Bingham was used of God to establish the Sudan Interior Mission which today works in a dozen or so countries in Africa with about eight hundred or so missionaries, one of the largest and most effective of the inter-denominational boards. The church which has been brought into existence as a result of the ministry of that society is one of the most missionary-minded churches in Africa today. I believe the church in Nigeria has already sent out more Third World missionaries than any other country in Africa, or any other church in Africa.

We could go into more detail about some of the other societies that were organized about that time. In Latin

America there was the Central America Mission, now CAM International. There's also the South America Mission established in 1902 as well as other societies in Central and South America, and God has used them likewise to reach into the interior, into areas which were not yet being evangelized. Reaching them was not a part of the vision of the denominational leaders of that time.

A third factor for the establishing of interdenominational societies is that of *financial support for mission work.* This was a major issue. Denominational boards of those days were limited by church budgets. In many cases they were not able to accept new workers because of the budget limitations. Some of the men who were led of God to organize interdenominational societies, did so with a conviction that God was well able to provide the funds needed if He led His servants to go into that kind of a venture. So the interdenominational boards became known as "faith missions," not because they believed they had any monopoly on faith (that's obviously not the case), but simply because they had no direct links to denominational budgets or treasuries and therefore had to look to God alone, rather than to any human organization for the funding of their ventures.

Then the whole concept of personalized support, which came into vogue at that time, was used of God to tremendously increase the number of missionaries. Missionary candidates went around to various churches seeking to raise their support as a sign that God really wanted them to go, that it was really God's will for them as individuals, and a very large number went out through the years as a result. God used it. You may not like the idea of having to raise support. I know it is a barrier in the minds of many young people today, and I can understand that. But I can also look back on our own experience and on the experience of many of our missionaries through the years. We have seven hundred now. We watch the financial records and see how God works miracles in meeting the needs of those He desires to serve Him out there. It's not that faith is so great but it is a long succession of miracles and a demonstration that we live and serve and trust a faithful God. It works! When God is in it, it works. The financial factor was a very significant one in the organization of interdenominational boards.

There is a fourth factor that Dr. Frizen mentioned and that is *the theological issue.* The theological issue was becoming increasingly important as the leadership in the old-line denominational boards was gradually assumed by men who were theological liberals, with a growing emphasis on what was at that time called the "social gospel." Many churches and individuals, both inside and outside the denominations, wanted to be sure that their missionary funds were used by societies and by individuals who held firmly to the authority of the Scriptures and evangelism based on the uniqueness of Jesus Christ as the only way of salvation. Because, in many cases they could no longer count on a theologically conservative stance on the part of the denominational boards, they began to increasingly put their missionary funds into the interdenominational missionary boards.

The World Missionary Conference at Edinburgh, Scotland, in 1910 was a turning point in this regard. Kenneth Scott Latourette, a well-known church historian, had this to say about Edinburgh, 1910: "Largely because of the influence which issues from Edinburgh, 1910, the ecumenical movement became widely inclusive," meaning that denominations and their mission boards increasingly were cooperating on as broad a scale as possible, *regardless of doctrinal beliefs.* That's what we mean by the term *inclusive,* and that was the meaning of Kenneth Scott Latourette's comment in this particular situation. In the ensuing years the denial of the deity, the virgin birth, and the resurrection of Jesus

Christ, of the lostness of those without a knowledge of Jesus Christ, and of the need for any verbal witness, became commonplace.

In many ways, the distinction between denominational and interdenominational is unfortunate and invalid. Interdenominational missions could not exist today without denominations. The denominations are a major source of both personnel and funds. Many of the younger denominations, with which you are well acquainted, such as the Conservative Baptists, the Christian Missionary Alliance, the Evangelical Free Church, the Presbyterian Church of America and others, are evangelical groups—one in heart and spirit with the interdenominational missions—and they cooperate effectively and in-depth on various fields throughout the world.

I've been at mission conferences where a lot of societies have their booths and their displays, their literature, and their representatives. Urbana is a prime example, with 160 mission boards represented. And I'm sure that many people, perhaps many of you, get the impression that all of these boards are competing with one another. That is a tragically false impression. If you could see the extent to which mission boards actually cooperate when they're on the job overseas, it would thrill your heart. All over the world today evangelical societies are pulling together in cooperative ventures to finish a job that none of them could do if they had to do it alone. A couple of examples: Out in Eastern Zaire there is a place called Nyankunde where there is an organization called the Evangelical Medical Center. It consists of six different mission groups, organized into one consortium, and came into existence after the Simba Revolution.

The six societies working in Northeastern Congo (Zaire as it is now called), were all evangelical groups preaching the one way of salvation through Jesus Christ. All had to evacuate when the Simbas moved in.

Some of the missionaries lost their lives, some were not able to tolerate that kind of tension and left the work. But all of the societies lost personnel. So, when the societies were able to resume their work in Congo, it was very evident that the half a dozen or more hospitals, which had operated until that time, could no longer function in the same way. There was no longer adequate personnel to man them.

The six missions therefore got together and agreed that one strong medical base should be established where there would always be doctors present; where there would be a training school for African medical assistants, midwives, and nurses. They planned to cover the other hospitals by air safaris on a regular basis. The various societies would continue to operate their hospitals with nurses in residence and with the doctors rotating on a monthly basis by Missionary Aviation Fellowship planes.

The societies which set that up back in 1966, in addition to AIM, were the Plymouth Brethren, the Conservative Baptists, the Unevangelized Fields Mission, the Heart of Africa Mission, (WEC), and the Missionary Aviation Fellowship. That medical center has continued since 1966 until the present time, and has been a tremendous example of mission societies pulling together to do a job that no one of them could have done alone.

Government medicine in that part of the world is practically non-existent. There are a fair number of Zairian doctors, but what can they do when the hospitals are bare of any equipment or drugs? Any drugs that reach that part of the world through government circles quickly get into the black market. The result is that Nyankunde Medical Center is the only major medical facility in northeast Zaire, where the population is five to six million people. God has used that medical witness to bring multitudes to a knowledge of Jesus Christ. Theirs is a holistic approach: they minister physically and spiritually. Every one of the medical staff in that hospital are men and women who know the Lord Jesus Christ. All around the world there are examples of societies, interdenominational/denominational, who are one in Jesus Christ, standing on the Word of God, and doing a job together in cooperation.

Enough of the past. To look into the future, we've got to go through the present. Very briefly, I believe that today interdenominational missions are on the cutting edge of world evangelization. They've continued to grow during the past century. By 1979 there were 462 societies with 27,497 missionaries, including both career missionaries and short-termers. The denominational boards number 170 with a total of 23,662. The old line denominations, by and large, have continued to shrink in terms of their missionary outreach, with the exception of the Southern Baptists. The Southern Baptists have 3,000 career people and about 2,800 short-termers, nearly six thousand of the total of denominational missionaries.

In contrast, the denominational agencies related to the Division of Overseas Ministries of the National Council of Churches, and thus the World Council, have shrunk in terms of personnel by 22 percent by 1979. Their missionaries number only thirty-eight hundred, including short-termers. Why? There are various reasons. In some cases there were truly evangelical missionaries who set out to do a job, finished the job, and went home. But that's not the whole picture. For one thing, they have taken seriously their own call for a moratorium on sending missionaries to Third World nations. There's been a lot of talk in the last few years about moratorium. Some of it grew out of a conference held in Africa, sponsored by the All Africa Church Conference, where some of the leaders called for a moratorium on the sending of all missionaries and of foreign funding for the churches in Africa. The cry was taken up by many of the ecumenicals; it fitted in beautifully with their concept of universalism and syncretism.

After all, if everybody's going to get saved eventually anyway, what's the point of spending time, money, and personnel in sending missionaries? It's a waste of time! I'm sure that that is part of the reason for the shrinkage.

D. T. Niles once said: "I keep always in the foreground of my thought the fact that all those to whom I am privileged to speak about my Lord are already one with me in His saving ministry." If I believed that, I wouldn't have given my life for foreign missions. If that is true, Jesus Christ would not have given His life for the world.

Bishop Pike wrote in *The Christian Century*, shortly before he died: "The kind of God I first believed in who would limit salvation to a select group of people is an impossible God. As to this God, I am now an atheist." Paul Tillich wrote: "Ultimately all existing humanity will be absorbed, like Christ, into the eternal ground of all being." What a tragic departure from the inspired scriptural record which tells us there is only one way—and that is through Jesus Christ our Lord. That's the reason He gave Himself. That's the reason He came. I believe that with all my heart. God asks us to present to a needy world, a lost world, the fact that Jesus Christ is His way—and He's the only way. When someone has no message, it's better that they stay home!

But there are many within the denominational boards who preach the same truth we do. We thank God for them and we hope they stay on the job; many of them are! I repeat that because it is not possible to clearly dichotomize between the denominational and the interdenominational boards.

By and large, evangelicals have repudiated the moratorium concept. The Lausanne Congress had a declaration to make on that subject. They recognized in the Lausanne covenant that there are areas where the church is now established and strong and no longer needs missionaries and, therefore, should be allowed to develop their own sense of national independence. In that sense, the concept of moratorium is applicable in local situations. Aside from that, as long as we accept the Great Commission as God's mandate, the mandate of Jesus Christ to us to share the Good News, we cannot accept the concept of moratorium as being a biblical concept.

A few years ago my wife and I were in Kenya, and one day we had the very unusual privilege of having diner with the president of Kenya. He was present at one of our stations for the opening of a new hospital and we were invited to sit at his table. His name is Daniel Arap Moi and he is a true believer in Jesus Christ, and a member of the Africa Inland Church. He was led to Jesus Christ as a young lad by an African evangelist who in turn was led to Christ by a missionary. President Moi himself was discipled by a missionary and has grown up as a true, consistent believer in Jesus Christ. During our conversation at the table that day, he said to us, among other things, "Forget about moratorium. We don't believe in it here. We want you to go home and recruit as many missionaries as you can: doctors and nurses and teachers; especially teachers, because our African young people here need to have Christian teachers with Christian moral standards." He was reflecting the fact that Africanization of those schools had progressed so fast that a lot of corrupt and immoral influences had entered into the schools, and the president himself was decrying that fact.

This is one example of a man in a prominent place who is speaking out fearlessly for Jesus Christ. Pray for President Moi. He is under constant pressure, as you can imagine. But we thank God for him. Kenya is one of the most stable lands in Africa today and, because of that, it provides a base for many of the other countries where we, together with Africa Christians, are reaching out with the gospel of Jesus Christ.

If moratorium is not for us, what of the future?

I would like to conclude by making a number of suggestions—not predictions—as to where I think interdenominational missions ought to go in the days to come. We can extrapolate on present growth patterns. We can set goals and objectives and get on with our strategic planning. But I don't think we can make predictions. That's too risky.

I believe that, as we look into the future, Jesus Christ has given us a *possible* task. When He told us to take the gospel to all the world and share it with every person, He was not asking us to do the impossible. He wouldn't have done that. The Haystack Prayer Meeting group said, "We can, if we will." I believe, with all my heart, that Jesus Christ has commanded us to do something that, with His help and with His power, it is possible to do. But if we're going to do that, then I believe that we could give another name to Ralph Winter's third era and call it "The Last Great Push"—the last great push before the return of Jesus Christ, regardless of the details of your eschatology. The Word of God says that Jesus Christ is going to come back again. I believe that with all my heart. I believe there are indications in Peter's epistles (2 Pet. 3:8-9) and other Scriptures that He has delayed His coming because we haven't finished the job that He has given us to do. We're in the last great push right now. God has given us a job to do that is possible with His help. In fact, He is the One who's doing it, but He has chosen to work through men and women like you and me. Isn't that exciting?

There are some factors, though, that will need to change if this last great push is really going to get rolling and finish the task. First of all, I would like to call (and, of course, I'm not alone in this) for cooperation to the fullest possible extent between all evangelicals, denominational or interdenominational, regardless of what the structure is in evangelism, in leadership training institutions, in medical and relief work, and generally, in all aspects of missionary activity. There is no place for competition between fellow-believers in getting the job done. Competition may have a place in business and finance, but it doesn't have any place as we try to reach men and women for Jesus Christ. Both denominational and interdenominational agencies have been, and at times still are, guilty of sectarianism and competition. That's tragic, whether it's a denominational or an interdenominational organization, and we ought to be done with it and recognize what the Scriptures are talking about when we read about the Body of Jesus Christ. We must work toward a worldwide demonstration of the reality of the Body of Jesus Christ. In the body, one hand doesn't compete with the other hand; they pull together.

Secondly, we'd like to call for a merger of mission societies to a far greater extent than has taken place so far. In 1979 there were about 714 protestant mission agencies in North America, not counting the U.K., Europe, South Africa, and Australia. That's just here in our land—714! The vast majority of them are very, very small. In fact, of all of the agencies with overseas personnel, and there are 476 of those, the median size is 33.8 missionaries. Fifty percent of protestant missionaries working overseas in 1979 were members of fifteen societies. The rest of the societies are quite small. The vast majority of them have two, three, five, one, zero listed as the number of overseas workers in organizations which call themselves Mission Societies. Why did they ever get started? They put out their publications. They hire clerical staff. They go into all of the cost of administrative work today for what? Two, three, or five missionaries—or none? Now, there are exceptions to that, thank God. There are reasons why God lays it on the hearts of individuals, even in our day and age, to set up new organizations; but they ought to be very few and far between, and with special ministries not already being performed by others.

Many of the organizations which have been operating for years are carrying on ineffectively today because they are so small that it's impossible for them to be efficient. Therefore we call for more mergers and for a study of possible mergers wherever that can do away with overlap, competition, waste, or inefficiency. It won't work everywhere. In the last few years there have been twenty-two interdenominational mission societies which have merged into eleven. That's a good start. Some years ago, the IFMA had a committee which we called our "Merger's Committee" which specifically set out to encourage societies to pull their operations together wherever possible. That has just been reestablished, and we trust will be effective.

Thirdly, I'd like to call for a moratorium on the establishing of new agencies—not total, of course—I'm not God. But may I suggest that with 714 protestant mission organizations in this country, we don't need any more new teams. All we need is to strengthen the hands of those who are already in the business, who have established a record of reaching out, and to help them get on with the job. If you try to set up your own team without any expertise or background, you're asking for a lot of trouble and a lot of wasted dollars and a lot of wasted man hours and lost opportunities—because it takes about thirty years for most organizations to minister effectively.

We call for consultation and teamwork in entering new fields. Our mission recently began a new work in Namibia of South West Africa, but only after close consultation with African Evangelical Fellowship, which already had a couple there. The decision was then made to move into Namibia in close cooperation with them, and actually under their administrative control since they were there first.

Unfortunately, there have been cases where a mission society has moved into a country new to them and right alongside another society already at work, seeking to establish churches which, to all intents and purposes, are competitive. I don't think that's a good use of God's people and God's money. My call then, is not only for a moratorium on the setting up of new organizations, but for cooperation between societies as we enter new fields and seek to reach hidden peoples.

We call for the setting up of mobile strike forces by various societies in different parts of the world which would be ready to move into a newly opened door on very short notice. This is a fairly new concept. Let me give you an example or two.

A few years ago, Mozambique (Portuguese East Africa) became independent. Prior to its independence, it was a Portuguese colony. The Roman Catholics were very strong there and missionary work was hindered greatly. For nine months, Mozambique was wide open to missionary endeavor. Then the new Communist Marxist government took over, threw scores of pastors into prison and expelled all missionaries, and the door has been closed ever since. We're praying that God will open it. We'd like to go into Mozambique as soon as the doors open—perhaps only to African missionaries.

But, if at the time of the communist takeover we had been aware of the opportunity and had such a mobile strike force ready to move in, can you imagine what nine months of concentrated evangelism might have meant to Mozambique? We might have even had a totally new story. Today it's a closed land, and I understand that in the northern part of Mozambique there are at least six million that are totally unreached by the gospel of Jesus Christ.

We had a happier experience in our work in the Comoro Islands. The French left there after unilateral declaration of independence. We were invited to send medical and educational teams in and in four months' time we had twenty-two people in the islands. God gave us two years there. At the end of two years, working among a totally Muslim population of about 400 thousand people, God miraculously brought about a break-through, with some two dozen converts. Half of them have already spent time in prison because of their confession of faith in Jesus Christ. Then, after two years, because there were converts as a result, the government expelled us—the whole team! We have to be ready for that kind of thing today. We have to be ready to cope with political uncertainty, with dangers and uncertain the future. We don't know how long we're going to be in any of these fields today. God is calling us to a life as *pilgrims*, just as He did Abraham. Are you ready to be a pilgrim? Are you ready to go into a land where you know you might not have very long to work?

Right after we were expelled the government of Comoros was overthrown by a military coup. The Marxist Muslim president was assassinated and another traditional Muslim government took over. Now, a couple of years later, because of the record we'd already established there in terms of helping them with medical and educational needs, we've been invited back and are recruiting another team to minister there. We have eight in the islands now. Pray with us.

This is the pattern I believe God would have us follow: the organization of mobile strike teams, experienced missionaries together with younger missionaries who will be carrying on their usual work in other lands, but with a prearranged understanding that if a door opens into a new area, they'll be ready to move on short notice and get on with the job.

Dr. George Peters, professor of missions at Dallas Seminary for a number of years, authored a book called *The Biblical Theology of Missions.* He states: "The idea that we are living in the post-mission era is not borne out by the Scriptures, by the need of the world, the expectation of the younger churches or Christians. The fact remains that the needs are staggering, the demands are pressing, the possibilities are overwhelming, and the response is unprecedented. God is at work as never before. This is not the time to doubt or question or to be bewildered, confused, and hesitant. This is the time to be brave and daring; to undertake greater things for God than ever; to be out in the harvest and the battlefield. We are living in dangerous times where opportunities unredeemed may become our fiercest tragedies; where needs unmet may become our future opposition; where sin-bound slaves unloosened may become our future masters. Our times demand absolute loyalty to the Word; complete devotion to our God; unreserved obedience to and reliance upon the Holy Spirit; unflinching determination to complete the evangelization of the world according to the purpose of God and the command of our Lord; and radical thinking and drastic revamping to bring missions up-to-date and to accomplish our task."

Denominational or interdenominational, let us ask the Holy Spirit of God to give us the wisdom and the insight to use structures, human though they be, and therefore imperfect, as instruments to glorify Him through the building of the Church worldwide.

13
THE IMPORTANCE OF WORKING AS A TEAM
Robert B. Munger

I believe my directions and guidance have nearly always come out of a team association. During my senior year in seminary, when we had to make some big decisions about where we were going to serve, three of us met four mornings a week for about twenty minutes. We had a map of the world posted on the wall and the burden of our concern was, "God, where do you want to place us? We offer to you our vocation and our location. Now help us get placed." I know that He really guided us.

I never landed on the field; I'm what you would call a frustrated missionary. No board would send me for health reasons, but I've always had a world concern. God knows mine is a bona-fide commitment: I've always felt the world is my field. My joy is in forwarding the cause of the gospel for the whole world.

The importance of working as a team is graphically pictured for us in Ecclesiastes 4; beginning with the ninth verse. In biblical times travel was difficult. The wise traveler on a long journey always sought companions. So, the wise man in Ecclesiastes writes as follows: "Two are better than one because they have a good return for their work: If one falls down, his friend can help him up. But pity the man who falls and has no one to help him up!" The roads were often wet and muddy. In that part of the world, mud might be a foot deep. If you fell in that kind of mud and didn't have somebody to help you up on your feet, it was just too bad. "If two lie down together, they will keep warm. But how can one keep warm alone?" How can you keep your heart warm by yourself? Have you figured out a way? "Though one may be overpowered, two can defend themselves. A cord made of three strands is not quickly broken" (vv. 9-12).

Now the preacher contrasts these two ways to travel in life. You can go it alone or you can travel with a company. You can say, "I will go by myself and do it my way and I'll get there all by myself." Or you can say, "I understand this is a long, difficult, dangerous journey so I will go with a companion and we'll share the trip together, supporting each other and helping each other in order that we arrive at our common destination." The preacher says, of course, that the latter is the better way to travel. *The Living Bible* translates the same verse: "Two can accomplish more than twice as much as one, for the results can be much better." You not only arrive where you want to go, but you arrive in better shape.

Reflecting upon this, we see a solid theological ground for teaming in mission. God Himself is a Trinity: Father, Son, and Holy Spirit. The Persons of the Trinity do not function separately or independently, but they are mutually together in honor, love, and service. They're almost indistinguishable and, yet, they are distinct. They're not jealous of one another. They're not working contrary to one another. They're not independent of one another. They work together and model for us what the Christian life is to be.

The New Testament emphasizes the importance of

teaming together for maturity and for mission. God moves to unite believers as one with Himself, that the world may believe. The very way in which we relate in unity gives a witness to the world, enabling them to believe in the Father, Son, and Holy Spirit.

Christ commands us to serve and love one another. We are to do this so that the world may know that we are His disciples. The very context in which that command is given (John 13) is interesting. Jesus, having loved His own who are in the world, loved them to the uttermost. He demonstated the quality of His love and what He was about to do in love for them. When the disciples refused to wash one another's feet (that was the common job of the servant or the slave), Jesus did it. There weren't any people with them who carried the role of a servant. The disciples had just been debating who was to be greatest in the Kingdom of God and no one was about to wash his brother's feet. James and John wanted to sit one at the right hand and one at the left. Do you think that Peter would wash their feet? Or that James and John would wash anybody else's feet? Not on your life!

After a prolonged and rather embarrassed silence, wondering who would do the task that had to be done before they ate, Jesus rose and put aside His robe. Girding Himself with the towel, He took the basin and water and washed the disciples' feet. After He'd done that, He said: "Do you understand what I have done for you? . . . You call me 'Teacher' and 'Lord,' and rightly so, for that is what I am. Now that I, your Lord and Teacher, have washed your feet, you also should wash one another's feet. I have set you an example that you should do as I have done for you. I tell you the truth, no servant is greater than his master, or is a messenger greater than the one who sent him. Now that you know these things, you will be blessed if you do them" (John 13:12-17). Then, in that context, "A new commandment I give you: Love one another. As I have loved you, so you must love one another. All men will know that you are my disciples if you love one another" (vv. 34-35).

It's very difficult for one Christian to model complete Christian love. How do you do that? You can love the non-Christian in many self-giving ways and serving ways. Thank God for that. But there's something about the mutuality of the contextualization of Christian love in the Body, visible and real, that authenticates the truth.

We had faith renewal teams in seminary that went out once a month during each school year. We sent out about thirty teams during the school year. Usually the teams consisted of six people—men, women and couples. It was a practically demonstrable fact that if these six students loved one another as brothers and sisters during the week, when they went out on weekend missions as a team, they had a telling impact for God. But, sometimes there was tension and jealousy due to frustration because they did not get a major speaking role. If this inner conflict was present, it didn't matter how good the different individuals were, the mission did not seem to be one with the Spirit of Christ. This is tremendously important. Unity of the Body has to do with the very life blood of your mission.

"Love one another. As I have loved you, so you must love one another. All men will know that you are my disciples if you love one another." I took that in three ways during different periods of my life. The first period I saw this largely in being encouraged to commit myself to Christ through a group of young people whose life together was one of love and joy. I thought of it like this: If the outside world looks in and sees a group of Christians who really love one another, they will say, "They must be Christ's followers. It's great to see love and joy in their midst." That's true.

Then another truth broke upon me in later life. If I am to be a faithful servant of Jesus Christ, a disciple people recognize as a follower of Jesus Christ, I need to be loved by others around me as Christ loves me. I need some demonstration of His love by a brother and a sister and I need to be loving that way myself towards a brother and a sister. I need to be growing in the laboratory of love so I know how to love the non-Christian. It's extremely difficult to love a non-believer if you don't have a believer around you to love. Anyone who is out in the field alone will tell you that. So, it's important that we love one another that we may be followers of Jesus Christ.

Even more recently I am seeing something else. I think that to love one another even as Christ has loved us is an end and not merely a means. The great end in glory is to be like Jesus for we shall see Him as He is. To be fulfilled in Christ is to be like Him. We are to be in process now. If that's the way we're going to be in glory, then let's begin to love one another now, even as Christ has loved us, because that's the quality of life we're going to have in glory. So let's learn in that laboratory. This is His new commandment; His last word. Yes, the Great Commission was given after His resurrection, but I think the Great Commission rests upon the previous two commandments: to love the Lord our God with all our heart; to love our neighbor as ourself and one another as Christ has loved us. Then the gospel witness becomes an extension of that love. Don't short-circuit it. The Great Commission is not a substitute for the Great Commandment. It's an extension of it.

Teaming was modeled by Christ and the disciples. Jesus called twelve to be with Him. He did not go into a synagogue or a corner of the Temple and set up a shop on discipling or "how to engage in mission." He took the twelve with Him, that in their relationship they might catch from Him how it was done. He always sent them out at least two at a time. The twelve went out and then the seventy. They were in association with Jesus in a close-knit fellowship: walking, eating, sharing, serving, and struggling with each other as fellow followers. With our Lord's example, encouragement, and presence, they were being trained in how to live together as brothers. When they were filled with the Holy Spirit, He enabled them to fulfill the life-style in which they already had been trained. To me that's very significant. The Spirit of God came upon the company who already understood the basics and the Spirit enabled it to happen.

Even Jesus seemed to reach out for Himself. Even the Son of God wanted companions in the work. As He went into His final crisis before crucifixion in the garden at Gethsemane, He took Peter, James, and John. Why these three? Because, it seems, they understood Him best. He thought they would understand more than the others. They seemed to be the inner three and certainly John, who leaned upon the Saviour's breast, knew the heartbeat of his Lord. So Jesus took those closest to Him and went into the garden and made His prayer: "Father, if you are willing, take this cup from me." He wanted them there in that agony. He needed them. If Jesus wanted companions that He might wrestle through, in prayer, the will of the Father, then, boy, do I need companions when I meet my crises and my needs and my confusions!

It's sort of a relief to me to know that Jesus had His times when all was not sweetness and light. He said, as He went into the Garden of Gethsemane, "My soul is overwhelmed with sorrow to the point of death." I don't even know if I'm going to live through this agony. Come pray with me. The one great difference about the Lord Jesus is that He knew what to do with His struggles, His issues, and His conflicts. He took them to the Father and He came out at peace. He knew the Father was with Him. He said to Pilate, "You have no power over me if it were not given to you from above." Earlier He had said to Peter, I have "twelve legions of angels" that would come running at my command, but I know the will of the Father and I'm going. He goes into the garden one way; He comes out confident.

It's okay to have struggles, but, what do you do with them? If you say, "I'm going to sweat this out alone and pray it through alone," you don't follow Christ's example. He shared with the inner core. That's why it's so important to have a team you trust who knows you well enough to sense what's happening on the inside. I trust and pray that you have something like that.

At Pentecost the Holy Spirit formed the early Church into a sharing, caring, supporting fellowship. They were not briefed on their mission, anointed with the Spirit, and sent out separately. First of all, they were fused together by the Spirit into a living organism of love and mutuality. It was out of that, in due course, that the Word emerged.

Look at Acts 4:32: "All the believers were one in heart and soul. No one claimed that any of his possessions was his own, but they shared everything they had." Where did they get that idea? Well, they just had one purse for the twelve, right? That was the life-style of Jesus and they carried it out. Now they had the love that enabled them to do it. "With great power the apostles continued to testify to the resurrection of the Lord Jesus, and much grace was upon them all" (v. 33). Corporately the Holy Spirit was given. Corporately they bore their witness. When Peter stood before the multitude at Pentecost with the eleven, as he would make a point, the eleven would say, "Amen, Peter, we know what you're talking about and that's true." The crowd seeing and hearing Peter saw the eleven with their faces aglow and they knew that all twelve knew the same Lord and had the same faith.

Paul's exalted letter to the church in Ephesus speaks again and again of the Body of Christ. In Ephesians 4:1-16, reference is made five times to the Body of Christ, a living organism. Verses 15 and 16: "Instead, speaking the truth in love, we will in all things to grow up into him who is the Head, that is, Christ. From him the whole body, joined and held together by every supporting ligament, grows and builds itself up in love, as each part does its work." Each part working properly, making bodily growth, upbuilds itself. Each part is needed; each part functioning, each part contributing so that the whole organism flows.

Just one joint out of joint not only hurts the whole Body, but something ceases to function effectively. I fell on my right elbow about three months ago. It was a stupid fall on the hard concrete. I couldn't do much with that arm for a period of time. I felt it. The injury hindered my elbow's function. So, if we are not properly fitted together and functioning smoothly in love and cooperation under the Head, Jesus Christ, we have difficulties. It's a very simple analogy.

In 1 Corinthians 12, Paul writes that the eye cannot say to the hand, "I don't need you"—I can get along without you, brother. I can get along without you, sister. I'll do my thing. Nor does the head say to the foot, "I don't need you." No, every member of the Body is needed and we need each other.

Thank God for the growing awareness of the nature of the Church. The emphasis upon body life is one of the great recoveries of these last years. Paul Tournier said, "Two things one cannot do alone: marry and be a Christian." You need your brother.

The first-century Church, beginning at Jerusalem, was composed of close-knit bands of people who were sharing life together. They could not think easily of life apart from one another and when differences arose in the Corinthian church, Paul hits it head on. To him it was heresy that there should be sects and divisions in the Body of Christ. He really dealt with it. He said, "Brothers and sisters, if you don't shape up, I'm coming."

The first missionaries sent out were commissioned as a company: Barnabas, Saul, John Mark. They traveled together with a common purpose, common fellowship, and common support and they were responsible for one another, as well as helping and enabling one another. Apparently the Antioch church was well enough aware of biblical principles so that they made sure they took their most gifted leaders. They didn't say, "Well, Barnabas, you're the older Christian. You go first and then you come back and report, then we'll send Saul." They sent their best men because they wanted a first-class, effective team out there. That's a great lesson for the Church, isn't it? Certainly, we should travel together.

I know that in missionary history there are exceptions to this. I know there are certain individuals that would have a very difficult time teaming, and I wouldn't want to hinder them. I know some godly men who are marvelously gifted to make their way with Christ, and the Word, and the power of the Spirit of God, and can do tremendous things alone. But, I think these individuals are the exception and not the rule.

Let me give you some reasons, in addition to these biblical principles, why I think it's important for us to team it.

I think we need one another in Christ *to maintain our clear sense of identity.* If you're in a cross-cultural situation where everybody else around you is a nonbeliever, you have to really struggle, if you are alone, with who you are and why in the world you're there.

I remember sitting in a football stadium waiting for a friend to come and take the seat next to me. He was delayed and I was sitting in the stadium all alone. There were about sixty or seventy thousand people there. I could not see a person around me that I knew. As far as I could see, I was the only believer. Since it was Saturday afternoon I was thinking about the sermon I was going to preach the next morning. As I turned over in my mind those major points and looked out at this completely secular crowd, that outline looked absolutely ridiculous. "What am I doing?" I thought. Then the friend came. During half-time when we could talk, I said, "Hey, this is what I'm thinking about for tomorrow morning's sermon," and I shared one or two points. He gave me his feedback and, all of a sudden, it seemed great! All of a sudden I found my identity again!

I like Keith Miller's story. Several years ago, when his girls were small, the family was living in Norman, Oklahoma. During a summer thundershower in the middle of the night, he and his wife got up to close the windows and shut the door. When they got back upstairs to the bedroom, they found their six-year-old daughter standing there, just sobbing her little heart out. She was frightened so she leaped up into Daddy's arms. He was trying to comfort her and asked, "What's the matter, honey?" She said, "I woke up and I heard the thunder and saw the lightning and the wind was blowing and I was frightened. I came in here and looked in your bed, Mommy, and you were gone. I looked in your bed, Daddy, and you were gone, and I went back and looked in my bed and I was gone!"

You need a loving person around you, in Christ, to let you know who you are, to keep your faith alive and bright and sharp. Alone is hard.

Wayne Oates, who is now at the University of Louisville School of Medicine and also teaches at Southern Baptist Seminary says,

> A group of our students and I asked . . . a neurologist to give us a lecture on the brain syndromes and human behavior. He took us to his laboratory and showed us a large sequence of brains that he had in his pathology work taken from people how had died. There were brains of persons who had died of trauma to the brain; there were those who had died of infection; others who had died of growths like cancer; others who had suffered from chronic alcoholism, or the effect of lead poisoning and other types of

pathogens. And then he showed us those who had suffered from arteriosclerosis, some of them very young people, as compared to our usual thought that this is a symptom of advanced age. Then in the midst of his lecture he said, "The brain is nourished by stimulation from meaningful relationships to other people. And in the absence of this the brain starves. We need to find the secret of adequate and proper stimulation of the brain by a meaningful and enriching community." Which was like a bolt out of the blue to us—to hear this from a neurologist in a pathology lab.

And I came to the conclusion from this that [for] my colleagues and me in the department of psychiatry and behavioral science, . . . the first line of care for either the well or the sick is an adequate life support system in a meaningful community of face-to-face relationships.[1]

How do you think you're going to maintain warm love if you're not loving and being loved; if you are not in a meaningful face-to-face relationship with brothers and sisters who care about you? Your whole brain is going to starve. That would frighten me to death. I haven't got very much to work on and the cells need all the help they can get!

We need each other not only for our identity and health of spirit, but for guidance and effective strategy. Let's go back to that passage in Acts 13:1-3 where we find the believers waiting upon the Lord, fasting and worshiping. It was then that the Holy Spirit said, "Set apart for me Barnabas and Saul for the work to which I have called them" (v. 2). After further prayer, they sent them off in the power of the Holy Spirit.

Then, in the Council of Jerusalem (Acts 15), concerning what to do with the new believers, they didn't let Peter make the decision by himself. No, they gathered together. They prayed about it. Corporately they came to a conclusion. We see these little patterns early: for guidance and for effective strategy, Christians came together that they might better know the mind of Christ.

Think of the creative leading of the Haystack Prayer Meeting. Where do you think that idea of world evangelization and working as a team came from? It came from God and it came from God through five young men who were together in purpose and heart, waiting—and God spoke to them.

One of the great demonstrations of the power of teaming today is Billy Graham's evangelistic team. These men have been in close relationship as a team for nearly thirty years. Not only have they maintained a quality of life in Christ teaming together, each person contributing his role, but their families have held together and that's a greater miracle. You know how that happened? When Billy and most of the team were with Youth for Christ, they were praying about their future and decided to have an all-night prayer meeting. I don't know the exact composition of that prayer meeting but I know that some of his current team were there. In that meeting, almost as if it were a class from God, came this message to Billy, "Multitudes, multitudes in the valley of decision. I sent you to reap." They were given a vision and faith and they went. But it happened while they were together.

Early in my ministry an occasion like this occurred at Forest Home in 1948. There was a college briefing conference. About 500 students were coming on Labor Day weekend. Three weeks before that there was a Sunday School convention. Henrietta Mears had a group of young men and women there to assist her in the ministry of the week. It was an adult conference and she was using some of her own interns and temporary summer workers to minister with her. It was her practice, from time to time, after a meeting to go to her cabin and pray. She had just come back from a world tour and had seen war-torn Europe in shambles. She had observed the hunger, the destitution, the misery of the Orient, and when she returned home she was stirred to the depths. This night, in front of those four or five hundred adult teachers, she poured out her soul for a hurting, lost world.

Then she invited some of the young men and women to her cabin. I guess about a dozen of them were there and they began to pray. They were not particularly praying for an anointing of the Spirit. They were praying for the multitudes out there without God, without hope, and in absolute misery. As they prayed the Spirit of God came upon them and gave them a vision of the university and college campuses of American being penetrated with the gospel and, out from that, came an army of volunteers that would penetrate to the ends of the earth! A great vision! Now, think of who was there: Dick Halverson, Bill Bright of Campus Crusade, and Louis Evans, Jr., Jack Frank . . . You see what I mean? It was together, before God, that they got their vision and their power. It wasn't alone, though often that can be the case.

For effective strategy and guidance, for personal support and accountability, we need one another. In 1 Corinthians 4:14-21, Paul writes to the Corinthians: "I am not writing this to shame you, but to warn you, as my dear children. Even though you have ten thousand guardians in Christ, you do not have many fathers, for in Christ Jesus I became your father through the gospel. Therefore I urge you to imitate me. For this reason I am sending to you Timothy, my son whom I love, who is faithful in the Lord. He will remind you of my way of life in Christ Jesus, which agrees with what I teach everywhere in every church. Some of you have become arrogant, as if I were not coming to you. But I will come to you very soon, if the Lord is willing, and then I will find out not only how these arrogant people are talking, but what power they have. For the kingdom of God is not a matter of talk but of power. What do you prefer? Shall I come to you with a whip, or in love and with a gentle spirit?" How's that for admonition? Accountability? "I sent Timothy to you to model. Timothy's a good model. He fulfills everything that I have learned from the Lord. Has that not been enough or are you going to have to have my personal presence?"

One reason we're so half-hearted in our discipline and so weak in our follow-through is that we do not have oversight or accountability. The army doesn't get a lot of recruits together and say, "Here's your rifle. Now try it out and learn how to fight. You're intelligent people; here's a handbook, do it." Not on your life! Those recruits are under discipline. Today's Christians are the most undisciplined crowd in centuries. We hate authority or discipline. We run a mile from it. Helmut Thieleke said, "American Christians have not learned a theology of suffering. We're so afraid of pain, we run from it."

Growth means discipline. I don't mean somebody hitting you over the head with a club, shaping you up with duty, duty, duty. I'm talking about someone who enables you and encourages you to be the person God wants you to be. There's an illustration of this that I use again and again because it is something that literally saved my life. In 1956 I came back from a mission assignment in the Middle East. We had visited some mission stations; I'm diabetic so my whole program was impossible to maintain. When I got back I was in very poor shape. There was a man whose daughters had come to faith in our church who was an international figure in endocrinology. He was one of the co-discoverers of cholesterol. After meeting and talking with him, I asked him if he would take my case. He agreed. I took all of the tests and he examined me and after a week or so he sat me down and said, "Now, Munger, I'm going to lay out a program for you. I think I can put you on your feet but you're going to have to follow a program that you're not going to like. I want you to listen carefully because, at the end, I'm going to ask you, 'Are you going to do it or not?' If you're not going to do it, say so. You'll save my time and you'll save your own.' I said, "Oh, I'll try to do it."

So he laid out the program. It was miserable! He put me on a formula and took all food away from me. I could only eat this formula for a period of three weeks or a month. I was walking around with a Thermos bottle all of the time because I had to be continually drinking this stuff. You take a Thermos bottle to a football game and you can be misunderstood! He said, "I want you to get exercise every day, not just a little walk around the block, but a real workout every day." He got through the program and then said, "Are you going to do it or not?" I said, "I'll do it. I'll do my dead-level best." He said, "Okay, I want you to telephone me every morning at seven o'clock, except Saturday and Sunday, and tell me what you did the day before." So I called him at seven o'clock and told him what I ate and then he'd say, "What did you do for exercise?" This was difficult to fit into my schedule.

I remember one time coming home from San Francisco. I had been moderating a meeting all day, and didn't get home until eleven o'clock. I was tired so I went to bed. I called him the next morning and he said, "What did you do for exercise?" I told him what my day was like: busy in San Francisco from morning until night. I wasn't shopping; I was working, doing important things. Then there was a long pause and he said, "Tell me, do you think your work is important?" I said, "Yes, I do." "Well," he said, "then you have no choice. If you want to stay on your feet and do your work, you've got to keep your program." I said, "What in the world was I to do in San Francisco about a responsibility that kept me from eight in the morning until I got home at eleven at night?" He said, "I don't know. That's your business. I don't want your excuses. I want you to do it!"

I would never have done that program unless he had really dealt with me. He taught me the power of accountability to a significant person—himself. You don't need a whole group of people in a team. Perhaps it's best for you to have one significant person with whom you can share the inner life without reservation. Where you need strength and support and obedience and love, let that person hold you accountable. I need that and the affirmation and absolute support of caring love.

You see, we can get the love of God through the Scripture and by the Spirit of God, but when that love is made visible and tangible and objectified by a brother or a sister, it's a powerful affirmation of the love of Christ. That's one reason why He said, "A new commandment I give you: love one another. As I have loved you, so you must love one another," John 13:34. He said, "You will remember that I'm with you and that I'm loving you still." That's a powerful affirmation. You're not forgotten, you're loved. You're not alone; there's a companion with you and He's the King of kings and the Lord of lords and He's not going to turn away from you. How do we love each other? As Christ loved us. That's a model.

Louis Evans has a little book for groups called *Creative Love*. It's a very helpful little book on loving one another as Christ has loved us. Dietrich Bonhoeffer's little book, *Life Together*, has two chapters on how to minister to each other in the Body of Christ.

Charles Mellis, in his book on *Committed Communities*, written to show the power of a committed team, writes: "Ministry and mission are most effectively done through a company of those committed to Christ and to one another." I believe he means commitment to Christ, commitment to each other in the Body of Christ, and then commitment together to do the work of Christ, to function as a self-giving body that Christ may be known and loved and served. In this book he also writes about the missionary (Celtic) monks who evangelized Germany and North Europe and the terrific sacrifices and disciplines and heroism of that group. It's incredible! They went as a company, sealed together in the Spirit of God.

The Moravian Brethren always went as companies, teams. They still do. There was the Serampore Trio— William Carey, William Ward, and Joshua Marshman. The first thing William Carey did when another missionary couple joined him was to ask them to sign the Serampore Covenant. Read it some time. It was a solemn covenant saying that they were sharing all things in common; they were going to pray together; they were going to be as Christ to each other, God helping them. You cannot explain the productivity of that early missionary band unless you see the fact that they were not merely alone, but were giving their gifts to each other to forward the witness of Jesus Christ.

When I came to my last assignment, taking a new role I'd never played before in a new church, I didn't know exactly how to do it. But I knew, as I went to the church in Menlo Park, that if I was going to be most effective for God, up to my capacity, that I needed to have some brothers around me. I needed men with whom I could share myself and who would give me loving, straight feedback so that I could get an understanding of how to best serve Christ in that situation. Before I arrived at the church to begin my duties, an elder from the church wrote to me and said, "I'm not going to be serving on the session this next year. I would like very much to be available to you in any way that I can be of help." It was a godsend! I told him what I wanted was a prayer partner and, "If you can find two or three other brothers who would just like to pray for me and with me, let's get together when I arrive."

So, when I got there we met together and talked over what I had in mind. I didn't go to them and say, "Brothers, you lucky guys, I'm going to disciple you!" I said, "I need you. I need your prayer. I need your honest evaluation of my ministry. Will you meet with me regularly as prayer partners and colleagues in the ministry?"

If you find it difficult to get people to help you in ministry, maybe you're going there as the one who's going to show them how to do the work. But, the moment you indicate that you need them and that together you will find the will of God, they'll get on board with you.

These men met with me for several years. It was marvelous. I tried to keep faith with them where I was, the decisions ahead of me, my needs, what my program was, what was happening in my personal life, and so forth. We would pray for our loved ones and all of that. By the second meeting, it was a mutual thing and all of us were sharing, with each other, our needs and our vision and our hope and our prayers.

Of those seven men, five have had significant vocational changes. That's really phenomenal for they are young men from 45 to 55. I really believe in each one of these instances they were given courage and faith to be obedient to God. They stayed in secular work but they made significant changes for Christ that they might be more effective for the Lord Jesus and their work.

You can team it wherever you are. This is the time to build a team. Get two or three like-minded people who have the same vision and heart and begin to pray together and plan together and think together and open yourself up so that God can guide you. Of the little team I was in with two other men while we were in seminary one served forty years in Africa; one spent forty years in Korea; and my role has been here. I think that team was a significant factor in sending us where God wanted us to be.

How long will it take you to get together with a brother or sister and start teaming: praying, caring, loving, thinking about somebody else besides yourself, being as interested in their future as you are in your future? Pray about it and you will be astonished at what God will do.

Note

1. Wayne Oates, Professor of Psychiatry and Behavioral Sciences at the University of Louisville School of Medicine. He is also Professor of Pastoral Care and Training at Southern Seminary in Louisville.

14

PACESETTERS: STUDENTS IN PRAYER FOR SPIRITUAL AWAKENING AND WORLD EVANGELISM

David Bryant

Awakenings, prayer, missions, and students. How does it all fit together? That's a very significant question. Frequently, this four-fold mix has formed the *stuff* of Christ's global cause. Biblically and historically God has woven a fascinating fabric: He sends spiritual revival in the life of His Church which brings an accompanying impact for world evangelization. People of prayer have been His shuttle in this global tapestry. And, often the pray-ers have been young people.

Many years ago the world Christian, John R. Mott, leader of the Student Volunteer Movement that sent out of a renewed Church some twenty thousand new missionaries from 1886-1935, profiled the kind of praying students he saw in his generation:

> An enterprise (including a ministry of intercession) which aims at the evangelization of a whole world in a generation, and contemplates the ultimate establishment of the Kingdom of Christ, requires that its leaders (including the

pacesetters in prayer) be men with farseeing
views, with comprehensive plans, with power of
initiative, and with victorious faith.

Such pray-ers are to be found over the past three
hundred years as the Church worldwide has experienced a number of "Great Awakenings." Every one of
these awakenings involved Christians banded together
in a movement of prayer. Often these movements were
called "Concerts of Prayer" or "Unions of Prayer." And
out of these concerts came not only renewal in the
Church but major advances in the global cause of
Christ. Dr. A.T. Pierson has noted, "There has never
been a spiritual awakening in any country or locality
that did not begin in united prayer." Dr. J. Edwin Orr
concurs, "History is full of exciting results as God has
worked through concerted, united, sustained prayer."
By whatever term you would call it (Concerts of Prayer is
a term that fascinates me) such a movement is desperately needed in our generation. Again, I believe today's
students are ready to set the pace, as they have so often
before.

Recently I attended the Oxford Conference on
Research in Revival at Oxford University in England.
Lectures were given on awakenings past and present,
including reports about awakenings in eastern European nations today. One country in particular was
highlighted. For obvious reasons I should not be too
specific: it is best not even to name the country. However, tremendous revival is in progress there! Stirrings
of this began in the early 1960s. Now God is reviving literally tens of thousands. Thousands more are coming
to Christ. At least fifty thousand laypeople are in training to lead Bible study groups and to do evangelism. In
the past few years, seventy tons of Christian literature
have been disseminated. Christians in other Eastern
European nations are inspired to new faith by the
reports. The challenge of this revival is even penetrating

beyond eastern Europe right into the heartland of Russia.

Those involved in serving the revival estimate that, in the next few years, some twenty million citizens of their country will hear the gospel personally, most of them for the first time clearly. God has opened this door. His Spirit has been poured out.

And, one exciting dimension of this drama is that students-in-prayer are in the vanguard of the revival. From the very beginning it has been so. In the early 1960s students banded together to study the Scriptures and to pray for themselves and for their nation; in turn, they became a stream of living water that has now grown to a mighty river. By their praying, coupled with their evangelistic zeal, young people have been the pacesetters not only of the awakening itself, but of its fruits.

At Oxford I asked a representative from eastern Europe, "By any chance, is the revival there also creating concern for *world* evangelization?" He answered, "Most definitely! The Christians whom God is reviving and mobilizing in that country have a sense of destiny, they believe God is calling and preparing them to eventually minister to many nations."

That's the explosive potential in the mix of awakening, missions, and prayer. God sends awakening, God mobilizes awakened people for the very ends of the earth, and God often uses students-in-prayer as the pacesetters of what He means to do through the broader impacts of awakening.

What do historians mean by "awakening"?

When the Spirit of God moves in the Church to quicken a new vision so that, in its generation, the Church cannot turn over and go back to sleep on what He is doing in the earth but must rise and get going with Him, that's *awakening*.

Awakening comes as God gives new eyes to His people to see all over again the gospel of His grace, or to see

238 *The Unfinished Task*

aspects and dimensions of that gospel that have grown fuzzy for them. They wake up to the good news of Christ: not only what He's done *for* them, but what He wants to do *in* them, and beyond that what He wants to do *through* them. A true awakening brings God's people to integrate all three dimensions more clearly. Interestingly, though, a key sign of His reviving work is the revitalization of the *third* dimension of the gospel: the good news of what Jesus Christ wants to do *through* us. That's why, again and again, as God has poured out His Spirit on the Church it has resulted in major new missions mobilization.

Awakening is God reintroducing us to Jesus. And as God wakes us up to see Jesus in new ways, this leads us to trust Him in new ways so that we begin to love and obey Him in new ways, so that we ultimately move with Him in new ways for the fulfillment of His purposes for our generation, right to the very ends of the earth.

God-given awakening alerts us to fuller dimensions of Christ's lordship. We engage fundamental questions: Is He Lord of heaven and earth? Is He Lord of history at whose feet the nations will come declaring, "You are Lord!"? Is He Lord of this particular generation, able to overcome the challenges raised up against His worldwide purposes? Is He Lord of His Church with the right to call her to the task before us? Is He Lord *through* His Church, able to empower her and work through her to fulfill His global cause? Aroused with renewed vision that says, "Yes, He is!" awakened Christians again boldly confess, "He is the Lord of *my* life and through *my* life as well—without limits, even to the ends of the earth!"

Awakening comes when God does what Paul prayed for so often. God answers Ephesians 1:17-23—He gives His people new eyes in their hearts to see the hope of their calling and His resources in the saints. The power that is at work in them becomes increasingly tangible as the power that raised Jesus from the dead and seated Him above all rule and authority in this age and the age to come. Similarly, it is when God answers the prayer of Ephesians 3:14-19—He inwardly strengthens His people with might by His Spirit so that Christ is at home in their hearts by faith, so that rooted and grounded in love they understand all dimensions of Christ's love. In fact, they force on into a love that knows no bounds, that fills them with the fullness of God.

All of this is awakening! And, it has to lead, ulti-mately, to renewed mobilization of God's people toward the unreached of the earth. When we are filled with the fullness of God's *love*, can anything less than worldwide evangelization be on our hearts? Christ becomes our highest *passion* that, in all things and among all peo-ples, He might have preeminence. The gospel becomes our highest *profession*, for we want to lose our lives for Christ's sake and the gospel. And earth's unreached peoples and nations become our highest *priority*. We seek to preach Christ where He is not yet named, so that those who have not seen and heard may do so (Rom. 15:20-21).

Christ, our highest passion! The gospel, our highest profession! Unreached people, our highest priority! That's awakening! It has been in that kind of spiritual atmosphere, particularly as we've been able to chart the record over the last three hundred years, that God has ignited major movements of prayer—often called Con-certs of Prayer and often with young people in the fore-front—that have undergirded grand strides in His mis-sionary purpose.

Not long ago I stood in the courtyard of the oldest section of Pembrook College, one of the thirty-five col-leges that make up Oxford University. Within those aged walls George Whitefield studied in the early 1700s. George Whitefield (whom some describe as the "Billy Graham" of the 1700s) was mightily used during the Great Awakenings that began around 1730. He preached without any of our modern address systems; yet his words could be heard a mile away. He crossed the Atlantic Ocean by ship seven times to proclaim Christ not only in Great Britain, but in the colonies as well. "The world is my parish," he said.

While he studied at Oxford, he joined a small group there called (by its detractors) "The Holy Club." The group began under the Wesleys, particularly John Wesley, a professor at Lincoln College in Oxford. They met in Wesley's office to search together into all that the gospel meant. They lacked full assurance of their salvation, but they had a zeal for God. They wanted to know Christ and to serve in love those poor and forgotten people that most contemporary Christians were ignoring.

Walking one day in the quiet gardens across from Pembrook College, George Whitefield, pondering the radical search of the Holy Club, had his heart opened by God to see finally what he could not uncover by his own efforts. He awakened to all Christ had done for him, in him, and all He was ready to do through him. One passage in particular struck home: You must be born again (John 3:3).

Awakened, he first became a man of constant prayer. It would be said that he would rather pray than eat or sleep. Out of prayer came over eighteen thousand sermons preached before millions until he literally burned himself out, dying at the age of fifty-four. Every sermon trumpeted glorious salvation in Jesus Christ, proclaiming to one and all, "You must be born again."

God used this young man of prayer, with his simple message about Christ, to tear away the blinders from the hearts of His people. They too found what Whitefield and the Wesleys discovered. Increasingly the Church embraced Christ in a new way, so that people came to trust Him in new ways that led them to love Him then obey Him in new ways. As a result, the gospel expanded in the English speaking world and beyond. Both the Wesleys and Whitefield, who themselves had served in their early twenties as missionaries to the Indians in Georgia, mobilized awakened Christians into prayer bands, called "societies," for the purpose of significant action. Their concerted prayer efforts focused on Christ and the Scriptures, kept each other accountable in spiritual growth, spread the reviving work of God to their fellow Christians, and focused outward on those within their own society who, because of economic and cultural differences, were basically untouched by existing Christians with the gospel.

Here's why I'm relating to you this little case study on awakenings: many believe we are on the verge of a similar "Great Awakening." At that Oxford Conference on Research into Revival, I gathered with historical scholars, missionaries, and others from various parts of the world who had studied awakenings of the past and present (such as in eastern Europe today and during the days of the Wesleys). We were like a consultation of "seismologists," come to measure "tremors" in the Church in order to determine, if possible, whether or not another major "shaking" might be just ahead. We asked ourselves the question: "Are we on the verge of another Great Awakening?" The opinion seemed to be unanimous, "Yes we are!" And, if we are, this has direct implication on our immediate need to form Concerts of Prayer in our churches and on our campuses.

These revival seismologists cited at least three reasons we might expect awakening:

1. It is the *divine pattern* in Scripture and throughout history: God revives new generations of His people to carry forward in the earth. He has done it before. Is there any reason we should not expect Him to do it again in our lifetime? Is there any reason not to seek Him for this earnestly?

2. There are also signs of *dramatic preparations*. It seems that God is preparing the way for another great awakening. Consider some of the evidence: the strength of the evangelistic movement worldwide; world

level consultations to lay strategies for total world evangelization; the rise of missionaries from the third world church (over fifteen thousand); the upswing of interest in world outreach among American and European collegians, etc. If God is building this "fireplace" to project the heat of the gospel out to the ends of the earth, can the fire of revival be very far behind?

3. We face the *desperate necessity* for a great awakening: the world rests on the brink of a moral bankruptcy and international holocaust; many predict severe global famine this decade; and there are still 2.5 billion people currently beyond the reach of the gospel, with no witnessing churches among over seventeen thousand people groups within that 2.5 billion. The Church stands helpless before the challenge unless there is an unprecedented outpouring of God's love and power on His people everywhere.

Dr. J. Edwin Orr, who chaired the Oxford Conference, is probably the world's leading authority on the whole phenomenon of awakening and revival. In fact, he has received three earned doctorates from three different universities, including UCLA, in the studies of awakenings. In his many volumes he has documented the impact of awakenings in the last three hundred years, with special focus on the resulting missionary advances particularly through students. (Sometime you ought to read his *Campus Aflame.* Do so in tandem with David Howard's book, *Student Power in World Missions.*) Here is what Dr. Orr observes, gleaned from three of his books:

> The Concerts of Prayer for revival in the 1780s in Great Britain and in the 1790s in the U.S., and the renewed Concert of Prayer in both countries in 1815, and in several European realms besides, was clearly demonstrated to be the prime factor in motivating and equipping Christians for service in a worldwide movement

which totally eclipsed the military might of the
nations in the battle of Waterloo. A century of
comparative peace among nations made the
1800s the great century of pioneer evangelization . . . .

When at the height of the 1798 revival in the
eastern states of the United States, the New
York Missionary Society was formed by the ministers of four denominations, the work was
launched by redirecting the Concerts of Prayer
into missionary prayer sessions every second
Wednesday of the month at candlelight. Sometimes they would pray all night to entreat the
outpouring of the Spirit for the proclamation of
the gospel to all nations.[1]

As in the first half of the 1800s, practically
every missionary vision, from the Great Awakening of 1858 onward, was launched by men
who were revived or converted in the awakenings of the sending countries.[2]

As Dr. Orr narrows the focus of the awakenings
down to the impact of students in prayer, he writes:

The college revivals of the early nineteenth century provided volunteers for the missionary
societies that they, themselves, provoked into
action. Continuing revivals supplied the steady
stream of missionaries to India, South Africa,
and the islands of the Pacific. The awakenings
then, of the mid 1800s (1858 and onward) provided volunteers for the existing missions and
for the new interdenominational faith missions
that carried the good news and good works into
east Asia and other parts of Africa and Latin
America, as well as the earlier opened fields.
Subsequent awakenings on campus and in
quadrangle supplied a veritable torrent of thou-

sands of missionaries for overseas service. It is not surprising that the student awakenings of 1905 accelerated this movement, providing volunteers by the hundreds annually for all the mission fields of the world—a recruitment more remarkable in the retrospect of history just before the onset of war and revolution that kept the world in turmoil for three-score years.

No single evangelist was responsible, nor did visiting clergy initiate the campus movement. *The biggest single factor was the services of intercession going on all around* [quoting Charles J.H. Fahs, a leader of the Layman's Missionary movement in the early 1900s]. Student missionary uprisings, like college revivals, when traced to their sources, are shown to have started invariably in a group of students associated for prayer. The missionary impulse was felt on campuses far apart, north and south, east and west, in the United States, Canada, Britain, Scandinavia, and other parts of Europe, South America, Australia, New Zealand, and on the mission fields themselves.[3]

What does all of this mean for us? For one thing, it should fill us with holy fear and trembling as we anticipate similar spiritual accelerations through God's intervention in the life of His Church today, giving us new vision for Christ and His global cause.

For another thing, it tells us that the plans that we do lay for our own particular involvement in Christ's global cause, must begin and end in the work of God. The mix of prayer with awakenings and missions clearly demonstrates that world evangelization is God's business, to be accomplished by God's resources, for God's glory.

And another thing: it teaches us that as we seek to mobilize fellow Christians for Christ's global cause, in the end we're really calling them to see *Christ* in a new way. That can only happen as God gives this vision to them even as He has first given it to us. We *all* stand in need of an awakening if the Great Commission is to capture our hearts and take new strides with our feet.

But one final lesson is important to learn: the history of awakenings substantiates how often God lays His hands on young people and students who just pray and then emerge from the awakenings to strongly impact the resulting missionary advance. Usually it has been young adults who became the "pacesetters" of prayer for the awakenings; then, they assumed a similar role in extending blessings out of the awakenings to the nations. God revives His Church in general, giving new vision for Christ and new commitment to His cause, while at the same time raising up students to be pacesetters in intercession and outreach. Young people take the vision solemnly and seriously, then move with it in prayer. In the process, they become key to revitalizing the Church-at-large, releasing its energy and power to send the gospel worldwide.

The roots of Inter-Varsity Christian Fellowship demonstrate this pattern. Many trace IVCF back to prayer meetings that began in the late 1840s at Cambridge University. Awakenings preceded these meetings throughout Great Britain and in other parts of the world. So, prayer was a logical and normal response among students in that day. These "Prayer Unions" persisted beyond 1858.

But as 1858 brought the tremors of the third Great Awakening, the Cambridge Missionary Union was formed. Finally in the 1860s, riding the crest of the 1858-59 awakening, the Daily Prayer Meeting was created at Cambridge, bringing together the fervor of the student Prayer Unions and Missionary Unions.

The Daily Prayer Meetings (DPMs) met in Henry Martyn Hall, named after a great Cambridge missionary to India. Within its walls hang pictures of Cambridge graduates who have died on the mission field. Daily Prayer Meetings have continued there for over a hundred years, almost without fail. And, literally hundreds of students have gone forth from them to be missionaries to the ends of the earth. Thousands more have been awakened to Christ and His global cause in such a way as to play a major role at the sending base behind those who have gone.

And it's in this mix of awakenings, missions, and prayer that Inter-Varsity marks its beginnings!

The Student Foreign Missions Fellowship, the arm of Inter-Varsity ministering primarily to Christian colleges and seminaries, looks back to revivals in 1936 at two Christian Colleges (Wheaton College in Wheaton, Illinois, and Columbia Bible College in Columbia, South Carolina) where students were so touched by the Spirit of God in that school year that classes ceased for days to allow prayer all day and all night. The following summer, student leaders from both campuses, revitalized by these local awakenings, met together to say: "Listen, the vision of the Student Volunteer Movement is dying! It must be reestablished in our generation! Why don't we do it?" Students of prayer, revived with a new heart for Jesus Christ, took the implications of their experience seriously and formed the Student Foreign Missions Fellowship.

Or study the event we could call the "Williams College Connection." What a case study it provides of how students in prayer become pacesetters of the missionary impact of awakenings. The story begins with the Great Awakenings in the late 1700s, when an English pastor circulated a little book written by Jonathan Edwards and first published during the Great Awakenings in the mid-1700s. The title: *A Humble Attempt to Promote Explicit Agreement and Visible Union Among All of God's People in Extraordinary Prayer for the Revival of Religion and the Expansion of Christ's Kingdom.* That's the title, not the table of contents!

And, the title says it all!

Edwards's call to prayer for reviving the Church for the worldwide purposes of God stirred up many in his day to form "Concerts of Prayer" (as they called their monthly prayer meetings). It had the same impact when reissued decades later by a small prayer band of five men in England. Again it revitalized a vision for awakening as Concerts of Prayer began to reemerge. One of those five leaders was William Carey, who later moved from being a young school teacher and cobbler to becoming the "father" of the modern missionary movement and a missionary himself to India.

These prayer concerts spread to the United States, sustaining a significant spiritual crest that eventually hit college campuses on the Eastern seaboard in the early 1800s. Prayer gatherings, even daily prayer meetings, were a normal occurrence in many schools, including Williams College; then in 1806, in the full strength of that awakening, we find a student prayer meeting under a haystack. God was working in the lives of students already revived. In fact Samuel Mills, one of the "Haystack Five," came to Christ at the age of eighteen as a result of awakenings that touched his father's church.

Awakenings and students in prayer converged and the results had international repercussions. After their haystack experience, the students banded together as the Society of the Brethren. This society had two purposes: to encourage those committed to world evangelization, particularly through a movement of prayer; and to help spread a mission vision to others. The Williams College five went on to seminary. There others banded with them to petition the Congregational churches of Massachusetts to create a missionary-sending society which eventually initiated the formation of the American Board of Commissioners for Foreign Missions, the first American overseas missionary society.

God wasn't through back at Williams College either.

Following the revivals that led into the Haystack Prayer Meeting in 1806, there were at least six subsequent revivals on that campus before 1830. Every one of them sprang from prayer and produced additional missionaries for the field.

Meanwhile, at Andover Seminary in 1807, Samuel Mills and others formed the Society of Inquiry, gathering students together to study about the needs in world evangelization and to pray for its fulfillment. A new student missions movement was underway. By 1856 these Societies of Inquiry were widely placed. Of the 202 colleges and universities in this country, 70 had Christian societies (similar to an Inter-Varsity chapter) and 49 of those 70 had Societies of Inquiry. Students of prayer banded around world missions concerns. This study-and-prayer movement spanned the years between the earlier awakenings and those that God gave at mid-century point on campuses and in the Church at large.

Imagine what could happen if we had those percentages today, forty-nine out of seventy! Within Christian campus ministries on a thousand campuses in this country, we'd find eight hundred fostering student missionary movements—groups studying about and praying faithfully for revival and the fulfillment of the Great Commission.

Back to the "Williams College Connection." In 1858 the next great awakening came, distinctly marked as a "movement of prayer" in the Church worldwide. There were no George Whitefields or William Careys as such. But in September of 1857 a man of prayer, Jeremiah Lamphier, started a prayer meeting in the upper room of the Dutch Reformed Church Consistory building in downtown Manhattan. He sensed the need for revival in the Church if she was to fulfill her destiny in his generation. In response to his advertisement in the daily newspaper, six people from a population of one million showed up. But the following week there were fourteen, the next twenty-three, and in a few months there were thousands! This was the beginning of the awakening. It resulted not only in tremendous revival at home, but also in one of the great missionary advances in the Church's history, climaxing in the Student Volunteer Movement. That trail from 1857 to the SVM is quite intriguing.

First came a vision for the college work of the YMCA in the early 1860s, which in its day was very evangelistic and missionary minded. One of the leaders of this collegiate thrust was a young fellow fresh out of Princeton University named Luther Wishard. As the newly appointed corresponding secretary for the YMCA, Wishard knelt one day in the snow at the Haystack Prayer Meeting monument at Williams College. There in the cold winter of 1878 he surrendered himself to the Lord for the express purpose of completing the vision those first students received in 1806 while praying. In his book, *Student Power in World Missions*, David Howard notes,

> While Wishard keenly wanted to go overseas himself, he became convinced for the present time he could make more impact by remaining in the United States to bring about a missionary uprising and thus reproduce himself many times over through out the world. The missionary cause became the center of his work in which all his other activities converged.[4]

It was Wishard who prevailed upon D.L. Moody to hold a summer Bible study and prayer conference in 1886 at Mount Hermon, Massachusetts. In his travels, Wishard had met a student, Robert Wilder, founder of the Princeton Foreign Missionary Society on his campus. He prevailed upon Wilder as well to attend Mount Hermon to give missionary vision to the students who came. Believe it or not, Wilder's father, a recently retired missionary to India, was one of the original Williams

College missionaries in the early 1800s. The entire Wilder family had been praying lately for God to raise up one thousand new missionaries from the universities. Robert and his sister, Grace, covenanted to pray together for this until it was answered. Their prayers were answered! Awakening came.

At the 1886 conference, students were so captivated by the world vision shared there that they began to band together to pray right then. Over a hundred of the two hundred who attended committed themselves to foreign missions before the month was through. By 1888 the Student Volunteer Movement had taken clear shape. Wilder himself traveled to campuses during the first year of the SVM, enlisting two thousand students as volunteers for world missions service. Thousands more were summoned to new commitments to Christ and His global cause as a result of the efforts of this one man.

In turn, the Student Volunteer Movement became a key instrument in God's hands not only for raising up laborers for the harvest but also for revitalizing the Church with a world vision at home. For example in 1894 the SVM had 30 groups with 3,000 students for regular study on missions and prayer. By 1920, there were 3,000 *groups* with 47,666 students. Nine-tenths of these had never signed the SVM pledge, but were still earnestly exploring the SVM vision for the world. This movement of awakened students in prayer for world evangelization helped revitalize thousands of business-men who banded together as the Layman's Missionary Movement, in regular city-wide meetings for information and prayer. And the Layman's Missionary Movement was officially birthed during a conference held at Williams College in August of 1906, a hundred years after the Haystack Prayer Meeting.

So, beginning at Williams College with five students in prayer, we can trace the "Williams College Connection" for a century or more. In doing so we verify one principle theme: When God brings revival in the life of His Church it restores vision for the forward advancement of His purposes to the ends of the earth. Further, He frequently places His hands on young men and women to become the pacesetters who capture the fire of that vision, to lift the banner high before the whole Church, and by prayer and outreach become the first wave of those who take the gospel into the unoccupied areas of the world.

What if it happened again? Could it happen again? Is it happening again?

A few years ago, Arthur Glasser, professor at the Fuller School of World Mission, wrote in *Missiology* his observations on the mood among Christian students at this very hour:

> Actually, 1980 was by far, the busiest year in the total history of the Church in terms of the training and sending of youth to bring the gospel to those who have yet to hear it. Although all their activities are highly diffused and decentralized, the sheer numbers involved quite overshadow the Student Volunteer Movement, even in its best years. Best of all, a new slogan is beginning to grip the hearts and beginning to send soaring the imaginations of these youths. It is far more demanding of personal faith and far more measurable a goal to be achieved than the one Arthur T. Pierson gave the SVM. Not "the evangelization of the world in this generation," but "A Church For Every People by the Year 2000." When one realizes at this late hour there remains over 16,750 separate people groups without a distinctly Christian presence in their midst, we can conclude that this slogan will almost certainly shape church and mission strategy during the closing years of this century. So then, let us brace ourselves! Our Soci-

ety (of missiologists) will have far more tasks to perform and far more problems to explore in the days ahead than it has had in the past. And why? Largely because of the resurgence of missionary concern among all peoples all over the world. In this respect, 1980 was truly significant.[5]

Certainly the "seismologists" of revival who met at Oxford suggest we may be on the verge of an unprecedented worldwide awakening. One of the dramatic indications of this is what God is doing with students right now—the heart He is giving them for world missions and the way He is mobilizing them for prayer. If students are the pacesetters who take the sunrise of awakening seriously and move out with the fruits of awakening to the ends of the earth, and if God is laying His hands on students worldwide to give them unparalleled responsiveness to Christ's global cause, then can that awakening be far behind?

Biblically and historically speaking, there appears to be a pattern of "little awakenings" (or tremors) before a "great" awakening occurs. In these preparatory revivals God deals with potential leaders—often young people—who a few years later are the ones He calls on to help channel the full impact of a general revival toward the fulfillment of the Great Commission. Whitefield, Carey, Mills, and Wishard are only a few examples.

Speaking of North America alone, there are seventeen thousand mostly young people, in short-term missionary work right now. That's up from five thousand in 1976. What does it all mean? What is God preparing for?

Look at IVCF's recent Urbana Student Missions Convention. Eight thousand students signed missions decision cards that required them to check one, two, or three of ten options for immediate practical follow-through on their commitment to world evangelization.

Many of those cards were returned not in the moment of an emotional appeal at the conference but days later through the mail. During the following February those students attended Urbana Onward training workshops nationwide. Towards the end of the spring term, in order to measure where people were in their decision, we sent out a survey to the eight thousand card signers. It forced them to evaluate their December decision, their February follow-through, and their needs for more help. It took about fifteen minutes to fill it out. Many of them received this questionnaire right on top of exam week. Then, to top it off, they had to buy their own stamp to send the survey back to us. How many of those eight thousand would you expect to get back? We were amazed: two thousand! Students are serious about God's new direction in their lives. And what do you think was the most frequently checked option, most practical option, most desired option, on the card? To move on world evangelization through a ministry of prayer.

Or, study the portfolio on evangelical student ministries like Campus Crusade, working in 150 countries; Navigators in 35; and the International Fellowship of Evangelical Students (of which Inter-Varsity is a part), working in over 60. Consider also the ministry of International Students Inc., working in our own country with hundreds of foreign students from many nations. Together these organizations form a massive mobilization of young people with a vision for world evangelization. Recently these four movements jointly produced a book called *Operation Prayer: An International Prayer Diary*. It contains solid prayer briefings for every day of the year, eventually covering every nation of the world. It pinpoints the victories and the challenges in God's work among the nations. Thousands of students are now united by this tool to intercede daily for revival and world missions, agreeing across organizational lines on specific requests.

Beyond North America, note the congresses held in Europe by the European Missionary Association (TEMA), an "Urbana" counterpart in Europe. Over seven thousand have attended each congress. And in between these quadrennial conferences, TEMA has mobilized a twenty-four hour prayer chain among European students in thirty nations of that continent.

Awakenings, missions, and students in prayer are converging in Norway as well. Just a few months ago I was talking to some of the leaders of the churches' revival movement there. I asked them, "What is your great concern right now?" They replied, "To see this spiritual ferment of prayer turned outward, with students leading in a new commitment to world evangelization on the part of the Norwegian church."

Take Korea, as well, where revival and prayer are a way of life. At a recent World Evangelization Crusade Conference, organized to challenge Koreans with the vision for the Great Commission, a million people turned out every night to pray and to listen. On the last night when the opportunity was given to signify willingness to go anywhere to serve Christ's global cause, literally thousands of young people stood to say this was the desire of their hearts, and thousands of parents stood to say they were willing to release them.

Just about a year ago at another so-called "Urbana" held in the Philippines, there were six hundred Asian students, many of them traveling great distances at a tremendous sacrifice to be there. Three hundred of them stood the last night to commit themselves to go anywhere to serve the cause of Christ.

Let me share with you one last illustration of what I'm seeing. In Edinburgh, Scotland in 1980, there were 170 students and student workers from 26 nations who gathered together to pray and think about how to mobilize the churches in our various nations with a vision for the unreached peoples of our world—how to do that as students and as student movements. The very fact itself that an international body met with similar vision and concern for total world evangelization indicates that the Spirit of God is preparing this student generation for something beyond what we have yet seen. Out of many hours of discussion and even longer hours of prayer, the Student Consultation on Frontier Missions composed a "Declaration of Intent" that was unanimously embraced. It reads:

> By the grace of God and for His glory, I commit my entire life to obeying His Commission of Matthew 28:18-20, wherever and however God leads me, giving priority to those peoples currently beyond the reach of the gospel (Rom. 15:20-21). I will also endeavor to share this vision with others.

That vision has been carried back by these students to their various countries, and has been useful as a new prod for mobilizing movements of prayer.

How will you respond to the coming awakening? Will you be a pacesetter of its worldwide impact? The Williams College students praying under the haystack formulated their own slogan: "We can do it, if we will." It's a great statement. I hope all of us have a similar growing boldness for the cause of Christ. But it's only as we labor in a spirit of dependent prayer under the leadership of the Holy Spirit, with a growing passion for the glory of the Lord Jesus Christ, that such determination will avoid becoming a work of the flesh—that it will remain in truth, a work of God. We can do it, if *He* will!

Our first response might well be, therefore, to examine our zeal for missions and be sure that it is anchored in the work of *God* in our lives and in His Church. How do we do that? Here are some suggestions.

First, *rejoice* . . . rejoice in hope. "May the God of hope fill you with all joy and peace as you trust in him, so that you may overflow with hope by the power of the

Holy Spirit" (Rom. 15:13). May this be the hour when we all sense what God has done and is able to do through His people, through us individually, and through His people together in this generation. Then may we rejoice, abounding in hope before the prospects ahead for the global cause of Jesus Christ.

Secondly, *repent.* What areas of our lives are preventing us from abandoning ourselves fully to Christ and His global cause? What areas of relationships, lifestyle, or priorities need to be purged from our hearts because they keep us from seeing Christ clearly and from loving His world the way He does? Where do we need to be converted out of the world to Christ, and where do we need to be converted with Christ back into a caring involvement for His world?

Thirdly, *grasp the gospel.* Be sure we each know the gospel for our own life. Where do we not grasp the gospel as clearly as we ought, our zeal for the Lord will not be as "on target" as it should be. In all of our thinking about where and how to go, and the important issues of getting from here to there, we must take time to think about the gospel of the grace of God: what Christ has done for us, in us, and through us. Awakening and missions are about the gospel.

Fourth, *prepare to be a pacesetter;* maybe as a cross-cultural missionary, maybe as a mission mobilizer in a local church or among students on campus— but prepare! Prepare yourself to be instrumental in all God wants to happen to bring about an outpouring of His Spirit in our generation. Prepare to be in the vanguard that channels blessings of that awakening to the ends of the earth.

Above all, *launch out in prayer.* Every great awakening has been initiated and sustained by a movement of prayer, often by using students in prayer. Often it was spontaneous. People individually burdened for the work of God—for the reviving of His Church and the expansion of His Kingdom—found one another and said, "We must pray together until God does a new work in our midst."

As I travel the campuses and churches of this country, one of the basic ways I measure whether a biblical zeal for world missions exists in any given place is to look for evidence of a movement of prayer. Often I have found that there are two different small groups meeting for prayer, and they may be totally unaware of each other on their campus or in their church. One group is praying for particular concerns in world missions: the other for the revival of their Christian fellowship. I have encouraged those two groups to find one another, band together, and allow their individual prayer agendas to be integrated with one another so that they can take on the *full* scope of God's concerns. Such balanced praying has always undergirded global awakening and world evangelization. Mixing these two prayer groups can be quite explosive!

At a student-sponsored missions conference in California two years ago, we spent a whole weekend in intensive training. Some of us decided to gather on Sunday evening for prayer. We announced the meeting about four o'clock on Sunday afternoon. Then it started to rain. It poured! When it pours in California, almost everything shuts down. For a Californian, heavy rain can feel like a blizzard feels to a Midwesterner. So the IVCF staff worker at whose house we were to have the prayer meeting said, "You know, I'd be very surprised if anybody shows up at all. What with the rain, the lateness of the hour, the unfinished homework to do for Monday, I'm not too hopeful." And then they started to come . . . and they came . . . and came. There were about fifty students, wet and warm, and crammed together in that staff worker's living room. They had come to pray. Suddenly, I knew beyond a doubt that God had deeply met us in our conference on world missions. The evidence? An aroused heart in so many to pray together for revival and world evangelization.

More than ever before, the Church today needs similar pacesetters who have a vision for the unreached peoples of the world, who see the deep-seated spiritual needs in the life of the Church, and are willing to step out, not first of all in a geographic or cultural way, but to be pioneers of *faith*. As pioneers, and pacesetters, they will express their commitment preeminently by banding together to pray. Such a movement of prayer for global awakening and world evangelization will be God's tool for activating the Church at large to reach to the ends of the earth in powerful, new, God-given ways before the end of this century.

Of course, looking for awakenings and new outpourings of the Spirit is not an excuse to back off in casual inaction until we get some new "experience" from heaven. Rather, we must be faithful to the directions God has already set before us; be faithful to all God has already done in us, even as we search out new dimensions in our walk with Christ. We must keep moving even as we seek God and cry to Him to do something even *more* glorious in us, in His Church, and in His mission to the world. In fact, commitment to an intercessory ministry is *strong* action and a *very* responsible approach to the Great Commission.

In Southern California two years ago they honored the Student Volunteer Movement by gathering a hundred former Student Volunteers, most of them in their eighties and nineties. During the ceremony at the U.S. Center for World Mission a group of present-day students joined with these former SVMers, most of them former missionaries, and called the evening "The Passing of the Torch." It was an evening to celebrate the vision of the SVM and also to say to a new student generation, "Now, it's your torch to pick up and carry on."

There *is* a torch. It is God's torch and the fire is the Holy Spirit. The challenge before every one of us in this hour, especially in light of history, is to look back to see how God has worked, to rejoice and praise Him for it, to look forward to the unfinished task, and then to take that torch from the hand of Christ and to move with Him together, for His glory, through His Church, to the ends of the earth. That movement will be first of all a movement of prayer.

May God help us. We can if *He* will.

Notes
1. J. Edwin Orr, *The Eager Feet* (Chicago: Moody Press, 1975), p. 95.
2. J. Edwin Orr, *The Fervent Prayer* (Chicago: Moody Press, 1974), p. 193.
3. J. Edwin Orr, *Campus Aflame* (Ventura, CA: Regal Books, 1971), p. 120.
4. David Howard, *Student Power in World Missions* (Downers Grove, IL: Inter-Varsity Press, 1979), p. 85.
5. Arthur Glasser, "1980—Where Were the Students?" *Missiology*, January, 1981, p. 13.

15

THE UNFINISHED TASK
Warren W. Webster

In this book we have reviewed our spiritual roots as Americans concerned for world evangelization. We have been stirred, refreshed, and challenged by pioneer missionaries such as Elizabeth Cridland and Elisabeth Elliott.

Following is a little quotation from another pioneer missionary. This lady served for forty years with her husband, a medical doctor, among lepers in Africa.

At 81 years of age I am taking a post-graduate course in the University of Life. It is different from any school that I have ever known before. There is no catalogue of classes and no timetable. The studies are continuous all day and sometimes into the night. We have no textbooks, save one, and no teacher but the Holy Spirit. Each student makes his own choice. There are no languages to study, no geography, no history, no science, but there are many elective courses, and I am taking them all. Courses on faith, on wisdom, prayer, patience, love, and joy. You see, I am working for a graduate degree to be conferred upon me by the Master Teacher on the day of my final graduation. I am working hard to keep on the dean's list so I won't miss the most important of all degrees—far greater than all the B.A.s, M.A.s, Ph.D.s, L.L.D.s and the X.Y.Z.s in this world. It is the degree of A.U.G., "Approved Unto God."[1]

The Apostle Paul said, "Study to show yourself *approved unto God,* a workman that need not to be ashamed, rightly dividing the word of truth" (2 Tim. 2:15, *KJV,* italics added). At whatever stage you are in training, whatever degree you possess or are working for, I commend to you the higher degree of A.U.G., "Approved Unto God."

ASSESSING THE UNFINISHED TASK

A great hymn of the church, "Jesus Shall Reign Where'er the Sun," was written by Isaac Watts, an Englishman, more than 250 years ago in 1718. That was 70 years before William Carey went from England to India to launch the English speaking world into modern missions. It was some 90 years before the British and Foreign Bible Society was founded. And yet there was a man of faith and vision who wrote of a day when Jesus would reign wherever the sun makes its successive journeys.

Today, if you have the money, you can buy a ticket on an intercontinental jet and follow the sun in its figurative journey around the earth, and you will scarcely find a land where there are no Christians. This is one measure of the extent to which the task of world evangelization is in process. God is at work calling out a people for His name from all nations and the Lord is building His church on a global scale.

We know of only a few nations where there are no indigenous Christians. One of these is the Muslim country of Mauritania in West Africa where Christian witness, for the most part, has been forbidden. Much the same could be said of Libya and Saudi Arabia, also

Muslim states. Mongolia is another land where, as far as we know, there are no indigenous believers. There are a few Christians in Mongolia, mostly Russians and Chinese. We know of some Mongolian Christians but they are in exile in places like Korea and Taiwan. Some of them are broadcasting the gospel back into Mongolia looking to a day when the church will be established among their own people.

There are a number of other lands where the church has taken root but where Christians are still a tiny minority. We think of places like Afghanistan and Tibet, now part of China. But Dr. Samuel Moffett, former missionary to Korea, reminds us that:

> Even where there are no organized churches, even where missionaries are turned away with guns and Christianity is a forbidden faith, you will find Christians. Perhaps only one, two, a handful, perhaps only foreigners, but they are there and they belong to the oldest and strongest world-wide fellowship the world has ever known, the people of God, the church of Jesus Christ.[2]

We live in a world where the sun never sets upon the church of Jesus Christ. The seed of the gospel is more broadly planted and more deeply rooted among more peoples than ever before. In the last two hundred years since the rediscovery of mission on the part of evangelical protestants the Christian faith has literally exploded around the globe. Missionaries have reached out to virtually every country to make Christianity the largest, and the first truly worldwide, religious faith.

But the day of missions is not over. While we are encouraged by the heritage of the past and the progress of the present, we know that a great unfinished task remains. We have focused in this book on the vast mosaic of people groups which make up the world scene with its diversity of languages, religions, tribes, clans, castes, occupational groupings, and various combinations of these. While we can find some Christians in every political nation on the face of the earth, we estimate that nearly half of the world's population lives within people groups where they have no near Christian neighbors to share the gospel with them.

In India, for example, a Christian community of some 25 million people has developed over the years. Many of them are rather nominal Christians just as many professing Christians in America are very nominal. One major concern is that most of the 25 million Christians in India come from less than 100 of 3000 or more Hindu castes. When you think about neglected and unreached people groups the castes of India provide a classic example. While there are millions of Christians in India there are many great segments of Indian society yet to be claimed for the glory of God and the cause of Jesus Christ. It isn't enough to say the Church has taken root in India. We thank God that the Church is there, but what about all the ethnic, linguistic, and social groupings in which there is no Christian witness? This is part of the unfinished task.

Not everyone thinks of Europe as a mission field. It is hardly an unreached area, for Christianity in some form has been there for centuries. Nevertheless, much of Europe remains unevangelized. From an evangelical perspective southern Europe ranks next to the Muslim world as one of the least evangelized parts of the globe. In contrast to glowing reports of growing churches in Africa, Asia, and Latin America, the once great churches and cathedrals of Europe are, for the most part, strangely empty and silent. We are told that France now has more Muslims than evangelical protestants. In the former French colonies of Africa it is far easier to hear the gospel than it is in France. One will sooner run across a believer in the former Belgian Congo, now called Zaire, than in Belgium itself. There are reportedly more Bible teaching, Bible preaching churches in Brazil than in all of Belgium, France, Spain, Portugal, Austria and Italy combined. Ground lost in the West to secularism, materialism and communism needs to be reclaimed for the cause of Jesus Christ.

How do we know when the task of world evangelization is finished? Our Lord, speaking to His disciples toward the end of His ministry but before His crucifixion, promised: "This gospel of the kingdom will be preached in the whole world as a testimony to all nations, and then the end will come" (Matt. 24:14). He said much the same thing after His crucifixion and resurrection, as recorded in Luke 24:47. He reminded His disciples that the gospel of repentance and forgiveness of sins in His name must go out from Jerusalem to all nations.

The task will not be finished until the gospel has been preached as a testimony to all nations. This does not mean simply all political nation states. Those borders have already been crossed. When Jesus commanded His followers to make disciples of all "nations" he used the Greek word *ta ethne* from which we derive our word "ethnic." The word Jesus used for "nations" can refer not only to nations as political units but to peoples, cultures, and tribes, each having a distinct ethnic, linguistic, or religious background. They are the "nations" to be evangelized and discipled. If you want to know why our Lord did not return in the year A.D. 1000 or 1500 or 1900 or 1980, part of the answer is that the gospel had not yet been preached to all biblical "nations." The end of the age awaits the completed proclamation to the ends of the earth.

When I was a university student active in Inter-Varsity following World War II, we could count half a dozen or more countries which had no Christians, no missionaries, no churches, and didn't want any. These included Saudi Arabia, Afghanistan, Tibet, Nepal, Bhutan, Sikkim and Mongolia. I have watched with interest over the intervening years and have seen the gospel take root in nearly all of those lands. Now the next phase of our task focuses on reaching the people groups that have been bypassed, as well as the millions of unevangelized individuals in cultures that have already been penetrated by the gospel.

RESOURCES FOR THE UNFINISHED TASK

We have more resources to deploy in world evangelization than ever before.

The Word of God. We sing a hymn written by Charles Wesley back in 1732, "O For a Thousand Tongues to Sing My Great Redeemer's Praise." At the time Wesley wrote that hymn the Bible did not speak a thousand tongues. By 1732 the Scriptures had only been translated into sixty-six languages. Today the Bible Societies report that some portion of the Word of God, at least one book, is available in more than seventeen hundred languages which are spoken by some 97 percent of the world's people.

This is unquestionably the greatest accomplishment in language communication which the world has ever seen. Neither the Communists on the one hand nor the United Nations on the other have come anywhere close to the record of Christians in getting their message out in so many languages spoken by so many people. But the task is still not finished. Bible translators estimate there are six to seven thousand languages and dialects spoken in the world today. Because of mutually intelligible dialects not all of them require separate translations, but it is estimated that some Scripture translation is desirable in at least three thousand additional languages. There are currently more than three thousand Bible translators at work on new translations or revisions in one thousand languages, but many more are needed. This, too, is one dimension of the unfinished task that calls for men and women to shoulder the burden of responsibility. How would you like to live in a culture where you didn't even have John 3:16 in your own language? What can you do about it?

The Word of God in the languages of men is one of our prime resources for completing the unfinished task. We have more Scriptures available in more languages than ever before, but a great deal remains to be done.

The People of God. Committed Christians are a necessary ingredient in world evangelization. A survey taken at four-year intervals indicates that from 1975-1979 the number of North American Christians in missionary service overseas on an annual basis increased from about thirty-six thousand to fifty-three thousand. Admittedly, a large part of the increase was in short-term workers but there was a significant increase of five to six thousand in career personnel. I see this interest being fanned by Urbana student mission conferences. I see it in the upward curve of more people volunteering for missionary service. I see it in the rapidly increasing number of missionaries and mission societies emerging from Third-World churches. To me it says that God the Holy Spirit, who knows what He wants to do in the end of the age, is providing the resources of personnel to finish the remaining task of getting the gospel to totally unreached people groups as well as to the multitudes of unevangelized individuals within cultures where the gospel has already taken root.

Material Resources. Despite inflation and its inroads, we here in America continue to be blessed with relatively abundant resources for contributing to world evangelization. A study of contributions to 714 Christian missionary organizations in North America showed that total giving increased over the previous three or four years at a rate in excess of inflation. When corrected for inflation it showed a real increase in giving for evangelism and development ministries on the part of God's people, for which we are grateful.

Spiritual Resources. The fourth category of resources has been underscored repeatedly in this book by Christy Wilson, David Bryant, and others. It is the resource of prayer and the work of the Holy Spirit in empowering the church for world evangelization. I trust that all of us have been firmly impressed by the example of Samuel Mills and his companions in that first Haystack Prayer Meeting. We need to be praying Christians ourselves at a new level of commitment and seek to multiply world Christian prayer groups wherever we go.

That, too, is part of the unfinished task.

COMPLETING THE UNFINISHED TASK

We began by briefly assessing the nature and scope of the unfinished task of world evangelization. Next we looked at our basic resources for the task. Now I want to set before you what I believe is the biblical context for completing the task.

You remember that when our Lord was here on earth He did things called "miracles" and He said things called "parables." In miracles He took the truth and acted it out. They were visual aids in a day when people didn't have television and moving pictures. In parables He took the truth and spoke it out in graphic language that was easily remembered if not always easily understood. Seven of those parables we find recorded in Matthew 13. Four of them deal with the growth of the Kingdom. I call your attention simply to one of them—the parable of the wheat and the weeds. Jesus said: "The kingdom of heaven is like a man who sowed good seed in his field. But while everyone was sleeping, his enemy came and sowed weeds among the wheat, and went away. When the wheat sprouted and formed heads, then the weeds also appeared. The owner's servants came to him and said, 'Sir, didn't you sow good seed in your field? Where then did the weeds come from?' 'An enemy did this,' he replied. The servants asked him, 'Do you want us to go and pull them up?' 'No,' he answered, 'because while you are pulling the weeds, you may root up the wheat with them. Let both grow together until the harvest. At that time I will tell the harvesters: First collect the weeds and tie them in bundles to be burned, then gather the wheat and bring it into my barn'" (Matt. 13:24-30).

Next we read another parable He put before them. And then another. Jesus' disciples were perplexed. The word pictures He drew were very graphic but their spiritual meaning was not fully apparent.

Later that day they came to the Master privately and said, "Explain to us the parable of the weeds in the field"

(v. 36). What follows is one of the clearest explanations of all His parables. He told them that the one who sows the good seed is the Son of Man. The same one who said, "I will build my church" is also the prime seed planter in the field. Christ as Lord of the harvest bears the burden of responsibility for supplying resources of personnel and material to complete the task.

The field represents the world, and it is here we find the phrase that is emblazoned on the Haystack Monument: "The field is the world"—not just regions beyond; not just frontier peoples; but people everywhere. Let's not commit the fallacy of focusing so much upon distant peoples that we cease to recognize the field is also the world around us—our campuses, our neighborhoods, our home situations, the inner cities of our great deteriorating urban centers. Too many people dream about the great things they are going to do for God when they get "over there." This is a mistake. Focus rather on what God would have you do where you are now. One of the best things you can do in preparation for being a cross-cultural missionary is simply to witness to as many people as you can in as many different situations as possible right where you are. The field is the world—including the square yard of territory you are occupying right now. But it also extends to the ends of the earth!

What does the good seed stand for in this parable? In the first parable of Matthew 13, the parable of the soils, the seed represented the Word of God. But not in this parable. Here Jesus says, "The good seed stands for the sons of the kingdom" (v. 38). Who are the sons of the kingdom? Those who are submissive to the reign and rule of God as revealed in the Scriptures. We might say in today's idiom that the good seed stands for born-again believers. Committed Christians as sons of the kingdom are to be sown as living seeds in the furrows of the world to multiply and bring forth fruit.

There is a logical connection between the seed which is the Word of God and the sons of the kingdom as good seed God uses to carry out His purposes. For it is only through the Word of God that people become the children of God, as Peter says: "You have been born again, not of perishable seed, but of imperishable, through the living and enduring word of God" (1 Pet. 1:23).

The weeds represent the sons of the evil one—those who by virtue of either ignorance or rejection of God's revelation in Christ are followers of the prince of this world. The enemy, of course, is the devil. Now note what the harvest represents. The harvest stands for "the end of the age," and the reapers are the angels (Matt. 13:39).

If we take these elements of the parable, like pieces of a puzzle, and fit them in to verse 30 they describe for us the context of world mission today. They picture the setting in which you and I are called upon to complete the task of world evangelization.

Jesus said, "Let both grow together" (v. 30). Both what? Both the wheat and the weeds. Both the good seed and the bad seed. Both believers and unbelievers. This describes precisely what we find in the world today—on every continent, in every country. The weeds are there! They are growing profusely in some places. The weeds of immorality—permissiveness, promiscuity, pornography. We are reminded of the words of Paul to Timothy that in the last days "evil men and imposters will go from bad to worse" (2 Tim. 3:13). The weeds of immorality are growing.

The weeds of atheism, secularism, humanism and materialism are also growing in some places. In the Far East we see the weeds of Hinduism and Buddhism continuing to thrive in their own setting. From the Middle East the weeds of Islam are spreading. Elsewhere the weeds of animism and fetishism continue to crop up. The weeds are there. We would be foolish to deny it.

But I would counsel you not to focus so exclusively on the growth of the weeds that you fail to see, and participate in, the growth of the wheat. Jesus taught that the good seed of the wheat will grow right up to the harvest which is "the end of the age." Here we have clear teaching on the authority of our Lord Himself that we can expect the possibility of seed planting, watering, and harvesting right up to the end of the age.

Some soil may be better than others. We should not necessarily expect the same level of harvest in all parts of the field. Jesus' parable about the different soils made that quite clear. There is greater receptivity in some soils than in others, but unresponsive soils have been known to turn responsive with careful cultivation. About the only places in the world where nothing is happening spiritually are those places where Christians are so paralyzed by pessimism or limited by restrictions that they are not out sowing the seed. Other Christians who don't know any better than to have prayer meetings, knock on doors, pass out literature, meet human needs, and make strategies for reaching the unreached are seeing things happen even in resistant areas. The wheat is growing—right in the midst of the devil's weed patch!

Every Sunday we estimate that in various towns, cities, and hamlets across the globe some two hundred new churches are started, but not just on Sunday. We expect two hundred more new churches on Monday, another two hundred churches on Tuesday and so on throughout the week and on into the future. This is simply the average rate at which the Lord is building His Church. Studies indicate that every week of the year fifteen to sixteen hundred new churches are started around the world to the glory of God.

The wheat is springing up among the weeds of fetishism and animism in Africa. In the year 1900 fewer than 10 million Africans claimed to follow the Christian faith. Now there are more than 200 million professing Christians in that continent. Reportedly more than 6 million Africans are joining Christian churches each year at an astonishing rate of some sixteen thousand per day. Approximately one-fourth of these are coming from non-Christian backgrounds.

The wheat is also sprouting in the deserts of Islam. Next to the Christian faith there are more professing Muslims than any other religious group. Yet there are more Christian missionaries working in the state of

Alaska than there are in the entire Muslim world of 800 million people. This tremendous imbalance is due not so much to neglect as to the opposition and closed doors of Islam. While we know of no indigenous Christians in Saudi Arabia there are more Christians living and working there in the homeland of Islam than at any previous time in history. Christian construction laborers are there from Korea. Christian technicians and diplomats have come from Europe and America. From India and Pakistan there are Christian doctors, nurses, and laborers who represent the Body of Christ.

Recently a group of Jordanian Arab believers returned from Saudi Arabia with a report of a Pakistani Christian laborer who had been bold enough to share the Christian message openly among Muslims in Arabia, which isn't supposed to be done. As a result he was called in by the local police official who gave him a warning. "You are forbidden to preach Christianity in Saudi Arabia," said the official. "You can live and work here as a Christian but you may not preach this message."

The Pakistani Christian laborer replied, "I have to preach. The Lord Jesus Christ commanded His disciples to go into all the world and preach the gospel and I have no alternative."

The Muslim official trying to pacify the Pakistani Christian reminded him, "It is not necessary to preach the message of Jesus. We Muslims already believe in him as a prophet from God."

"Yes," said the Pakistani, "but we believe that Jesus Christ is more than a prophet and that He is coming back to earth some day."

"Oh," said the Muslim, "we believe that Jesus is coming again too."

"Well, when Jesus does come back to earth," said the Pakistani evangelist, "I am going to go straight to Him and tell Him you wouldn't let me preach the gospel here."

"Oh, no, don't do that!"

As far as we know that ended the matter and the Pakistani Christian is still there sharing his faith whenever he can. This is just one more evidence that the wheat is there even in the midst of the weeds of Islam.

The wheat is also springing up in the midst of Roman Catholicism in Latin America where many people are Catholics by day and Spiritists by night. In the last few decades of the twentieth century a massive response to evangelistic efforts has taken place in South America. In 1900 there were fewer than fifty thousand evangelical Protestants in that entire continent. By 1945 they numbered around two million. Today there are over thirty million evangelical Christians in Latin America. Apart from the United States, Brazil now has the largest evangelical population of any country in the world. We have rejoiced since Vatican II as Roman Catholics in growing numbers have turned to the written Word of God in which they are personally discovering Jesus Christ, the Living Word.

The wheat is also springing up amidst the weeds of Communism in Europe and parts of Asia. Today, in Romania, warehouse churches are packed out by believers who don't have permission to build lovely new buildings but who are growing in their Christian faith. In Poland and in several other East European countries evangelical witness is growing. In Russia itself there may be as many as fifty million members of Russian Orthodox churches, and at least one in every eighty Russians is reported to be an evangelical Christian.

Reports of the growth of the wheat in China during the past thirty years have reached us with indications of a massive harvest that has been quietly going on in spite of Communist oppression. When I was in China recently, I attended a worship service in one of the Three Self Patriotic Movement churches. These churches are officially recognized and controlled by the government. In the past few years several hundred such churches have been officially reopened. But what are a few hundred churches among more than one billion people? In the missionary era prior to 1949–1950 we are told there were some nineteen thousand churches and chapels in China. Though only a few hundred churches are now officially open we need to remember there may be forty to fifty thousand house churches functioning in China as well. Recently word came via Hong Kong telling of a house church in China of some two thousand members which meets outside under a crude shelter with apparent freedom. Other reports tell of communes where half or more of the total commune membership have become Christians.

Students will be interested to know that when the Communists took over China they not only closed churches and expelled missionaries but they closed Bible schools and Christian colleges. There were hundreds of Christian students whose lives and education were seriously affected by the closing of these schools. Many of them were sent out to the far corners of China into remote provinces as agricultural workers, barefoot doctors, and common laborers. They often were sent far away from their families and in many cases even husbands and wives were separated. Perhaps the Communists thought that by dispersing the Christians they would put an end to the Christian faith. They didn't realize the followers of Jesus are like seeds. So they simply scattered Christian seed all over China. Only now are we beginning to realize that wherever those Christian seeds were scattered the Christian witness took root and in place after place little house churches sprang up in the local soil. Today it is no wonder there are more Christians in more places in China than there have ever been before. Estimates run as high as thirty to fifty million Christians in China today. That would mean nearly 5 percent of the population. Praise God, the wheat is growing in the midst of China.

The wheat is growing in other parts of Asia as well. Reports from Indonesia, the Philippines, and Korea tell of abundant harvests. A hundred years ago there was not a single Christian church in Korea. Forty years ago in the capital city of Seoul there were only seventeen churches and fewer than 1 percent of the Korean people were professing Christians. Now there are six thousand churches in Seoul alone and more than 20 percent of the total population claim to be Christians. The largest Presbyterian church and the largest Full Gospel church in the world are both found in Korea. Korea has also seen the largest public evangelistic gathering in history with as many as 2.7 million people present in some of the great outdoor meetings. Korean churches are known for their early morning prayer meetings and their home cell groups that meet during the week. They are also playing an increasingly important role in sending missionaries to other people. The wheat is growing amidst the weeds in Korea and elsewhere in Asia.

When we see what the Lord is doing to build His Church on a global scale we should be encouraged to finish the task. We are on the right track. God is at work according to His timetable and things are moving according to His plan. As a world Christian your response should be to take the Great Commission seriously and plan strategically for your involvement in world evangelization. You should do this whether God leads you to live and work in America or to take the gospel to people of another land and culture.

We have been thinking about the importance of seeding, sowing, and harvesting in completing the unfinished task. This final illustration comes from a Church Growth Conference I attended in Korea.

One of the pastors told about a dream he had one night. In his dream he found himself walking down the street of his hometown. He recognized people and stores. On reaching the corner he saw a new shop that hand't been there before. From the outside he couldn't tell what kind of a shop it was. In his dream he walked across the street and looked in the window. Then he timidly opened the door and looked in. There was just one person behind the counter who looked rather like an angel. He approached a bit nervously and said, "Excuse me, but what do you sell here?"

"Oh," said the angel, "we sell everything your heart desires."

"In that case," said the minister, "I want peace on

earth, an end to sorrow, famine and disease, racial hatred and prejudice. I want goodness to prevail . . . "

"Just one moment," smiled the angel, "you haven't quite understood. We don't sell fruits here, only seeds."

When I heard that story I was reminded that it is not our task as American Christians to distribute the cut flowers of Western civilization which quickly wither and die. It is not even our primary calling to distribute the fruits of the gospel though we do what we can to minister to the whole man through ministries of compassion in the name of Christ. Our primary task is to sow the seed of the gospel in the soul of a people where it will spring up to bear its own fruit. From those gospel seeds all good fruits ultimately come. So let us keep on planting the seed which is the Word, in the field which is the world, watering that seed with our prayers and, if need be, with our tears, looking to God to give the increase until Jesus comes.

Notes
1. Prayer letter written by Julia Lake Kellersberger.
2. Samuel H. Moffett, *Where'er the Sun* (New York: Friendship Press, 1953), pp. 4-5.

16

PRAYER FOR THE NATIONS

Ralph D. Winter

(Note: This unrevised tape of my prayer out by the haystack monument that day reflects the fact that I had just seen—for the first time—the stone globe marking the spot. No doubt used as a target by rock-throwing students across the years, its pitted surface engraved itself on my heart. I prayed in dismay and anger, humbled and almost undone. R.D.W.)

Lord as we bow in your presence, we think of Jesus who looked on the nation of Israel from a mountaintop and wept. He looked upon a people who had opportunity but who refused it. As we pray for the nations, Father, first of all we reflect upon our own. Oh, Lord, they are our people, your people, precious in your sight. Nevertheless, many of us are wayward people, rebellious children; we have not obeyed with a beautiful, filial love. Heavenly Father, will you forgive us for the coldness of our hearts, for the busyness of our lives as we have bustled about even attempting to do your work, without being with *you* in that work!

And as we look upon our nation, Father, which has been more preoccupied about preserving the blessings you have given to us than sharing those blessings, it makes us fearful. As Jesus looked upon Jerusalem, He noted that the nations had only reluctantly and partially yielded up blessings. And He predicted that those nations would sometime soon surround Jerusalem and destroy it—utterly, utterly destroy it. His tears came, Father, because He knew what good you had intended, what blessings could have been poured upon your people if only they had properly realized the blessings they had received. Oh, God, in a country where 80 percent of all the world's trained Christians live, Father, help us not just to gather to seek the salvation and cleansing of this country, but seek to share what we've received from you.

And so, Father, we seek to be close to you in this very place where five boys, fearful of disturbance amidst their own people, sought the shelter of nature itself. We, too, gather in this glade, in this haven place, to draw apart from this town and from our country.

We are mindful of the fact that most of our people are heedless and hopeless. Lord God, help us. We believe, help thou our unbelief. Help us now, Lord, to reconsecrate ourselves with the nations of the world in view.

What a challenge Warren Webster has given us in this review. It has thrilled us, chilled us, and opened our hearts, as well as torn away the veil of our minds. We've gazed across the world to see Nigeria and Pakistan, almost in the sense that Jesus looked upon His nation. And Father, we pray that we might be more useful than we've been, as we seek to serve and to do your will. We're glad, Lord, that we're not going backwards; we're glad that there are more people in the world now but fewer nations to be penetrated. We're glad, Lord, that the rate of population growth is not exceeding the rate of growth of the Christian movement.

We sing and pray that Jesus shall reign in all of these nations, that peoples and realms of every tongue might dwell on your love with sweetest song. And, Lord, you know the world is mostly children and that those infant voices long to proclaim their early blessings on your name.

And so, Father, reign, reign in our own hearts today as never before. Oh, God, reign in our nation. We pray thy will shall be done on earth as it is in heaven. Oh, God, may that become an exciting, powerful reality in a new revival of prayer, of deepening love, of outreach in our own nation and around the world. Father, we want to be as Jesus was. He didn't constantly talk about missions, but demonstrated His love for little children, for blind people, for people with withered hands whom others would shun and turn from. Oh, God, may our evangelical people in this country become known as those who are sensitive to those whom they can see—lest it be a farce that they claim to love those whom they have not seen.

Father, we really await your voice. Our prayers, Lord, must be listening prayers. So much has been given to us. It seems as though we have many, many people but are not organized as teams. Thousands of people are mired and ensnared by many trivial and secondary concerns, available only theoretically for your highest. Oh, God, we thank you for the challenge to give our utmost for your highest.

We pray for these nations, nations which have never been closer to us or better understood by us or more accessible to us. Never before have there been so many eager, bright-eyed believers in every nation to join with us in this outreach. Oh, God, do not let us turn away in pessimism, in dismay, or in distraction. Do not let us be overwhelmed by the preoccupations of our own people or our secular world with its gross pursuit of distractions.

Forgive us that our evangelical world continues to compile books about fulfillment of ourselves. Yet not a bookstore in our country carries a book that tells us about the hidden peoples and portrays them with *National Geographic* color. Lord, our films, our instructional Sunday School materials are virtually devoid of any reference to the nations of the world. Our hymnbooks, Lord, have a few pages crowded in the back that talk about how we should share the blessings. But all the rest of the book is devoted to the blessings, the blessings, the blessings. Oh, God, convict us of how hasty, how careless we are. We are absorbed in ourselves and in those things which make for our security. Forgive us for our faintheartedness that is overpowered by insecurity. Forgive us for insecurity that seeks constantly for a security which is found only by giving over to you all that we are.

And, Father, I pray most of all that as we go from this place we might have a firmer grasp on your task of world evangelization and its role in our lives. Give us collaborative energy which alone will make up for the retirement of missionaries which we think of in pure statistics. Pure statistics like 60,000 missionaries of whom a third will retire in the next 10 years. Oh, God, help us to be free from the secondary good things that would so easily replace the best.

Father, if somehow we could pledge ourselves anew to a daily regeneration of vision for your highest, help us to know how to do that. Gracious Father, we just want to thank you and praise you for your faithfulness across the generations. As we gather here, there is no doubt in our minds that you are as able today as in 1806. Oh, Father, give us renewed courage, not for our own benefit, not for our careers' sake, not for our program's sake, but only for your glory. May your will be done on earth as it is in heaven. We pray this in Jesus' blessed name. Amen.